A30116003839329B

Investigation into the Clapham Junction Railway Accident

Presented to Parliament by the Secretary of State for Transport
by Command of Her Majesty November 1989

THE DEPARTMENT
OF TRANSPORT

LONDON: HMSO

Cm 820   £18.50 net

Frontispiece

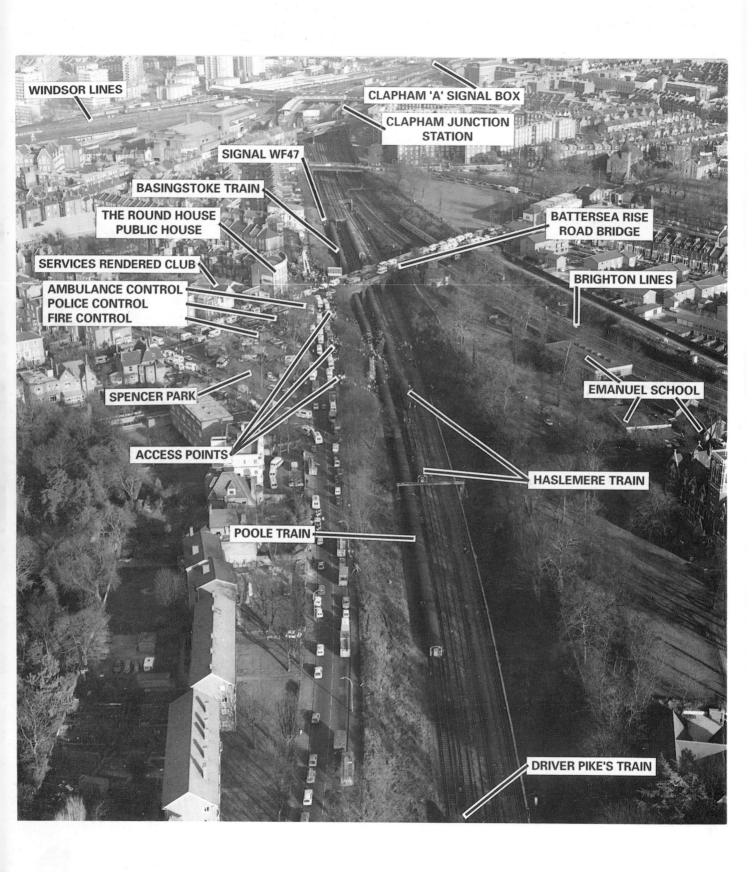

WINDSOR LINES

CLAPHAM 'A' SIGNAL BOX

CLAPHAM JUNCTION STATION

SIGNAL WF47

BASINGSTOKE TRAIN

THE ROUND HOUSE PUBLIC HOUSE

BATTERSEA RISE ROAD BRIDGE

SERVICES RENDERED CLUB

BRIGHTON LINES

AMBULANCE CONTROL
POLICE CONTROL
FIRE CONTROL

EMANUEL SCHOOL

SPENCER PARK

ACCESS POINTS

HASLEMERE TRAIN

POOLE TRAIN

DRIVER PIKE'S TRAIN

Inspector:
Mr Anthony Hidden QC

Investigation into the Clapham Junction Railway Accident

Room S5/03
2 Marsham Street
London SW1P 3EB

Fax. No. 01-276 6364
Direct line 01-276 0838/5420/5433/5959/6539
Switchboard 01-276 3000

27 September 1989

The Rt. Hon. Cecil Parkinson M.P.
Secretary of State for Transport
Department of Transport
2 Marsham Street
London SW1P 3EB

Dear Secretary of State,

CLAPHAM JUNCTION RAILWAY ACCIDENT INVESTIGATION

On 13 December 1988 your predecessor as Secretary of State invited me to hold a formal Investigation into the causes of and circumstances attending the Clapham Junction railway accident. I have now completed that Investigation and enclose my Report.

Yours sincerely
Anthony Hidden

ANTHONY HIDDEN Q.C.

STRUCTURE OF THE REPORT

STRUCTURE OF THE REPORT *(contd.)*

THE RECOMMENDATIONS

APPENDICES

APPENDICES *(contd.)*

LIST OF PHOTOGRAPHS

Figures 1 & 2:

Aerial views of the accident site.

Figure 3:

Driver Pike's train stationary approximately 60 yards from the rear of the Poole train.

Figure 4:

An interior view of a driver's cab showing the controls.

Figure 5:

An interior view of the type of buffet car on the Poole train, showing the non-fixed seating, facing forward in the direction of travel.

Figure 6:

A further interior view of the type of buffet car again facing forwards, showing the closed shutters on the left, behind which are the kitchen and serving areas, and the passenger space on the right.

Figure 7:

A view of the buffet car of the Poole train taken on the evening of Monday, 12 December, showing the destruction of the kitchen and serving areas on the left (nearside) of the coach, and the damaged loose seating.

Figure 8:

An interior view of Mark I rolling stock similar to some carriages of the Poole train, showing lateral luggage racks.

Figure 9:

An interior view of a carriage of the Basingstoke train, showing damaged transverse luggage racks.

Figure 10:

A view of Clapham Junction "A" signal box with the relay room at the extreme right above the first third of the leading coach of the passing train.

Figure 11:

A view of the relay room looking towards the entrance, showing the relay racks; and the trees of the wiring. Relays TRR DM and TRR DN are on the bottom shelf on the right in the last section towards the door.

Figure 12:

Relays in Clapham Junction "A" relay room, showing track relay "DN" adjacent to track repeater relay "DM".

Figure 13:

Relay TRR DM, taken on 12 December 1988, at approximately 14.00 hours.

Figure 14:

Fuse racks. Row 12-f107, taken on 13 December 1988.

Figure 15:

Extract from the working model demonstrating Job Nos. 104 and 201 and the wiring errors made. The black wire along the top of the diagram connected at DM TRR and Row 12-f107 should have been disconnected at both ends but was wrongly left connected at the fuse end of Row 12-f107. Although disconnected at the relay end the wire was left loose and made metal-to-metal contact at DM TRR, a false feed of current to by-pass DL TRR. Hence the occupation of track circuit DL by a train had no effect on signal WF138 and it did not turn back to red as it should have done.

Figure 16:

Working model of the relevant signalling circuit, showing wiring errors, and topographical model of the crash site.

ACKNOWLEDGEMENTS

Figures reproduced by courtesy of:

British Transport Police:
Figures 3, 4, 5, 6, 8, 11, 12, 13 and 14

British Railways Board:
Figure 9

Central Office of Information:
Figures 15 and 16

London Fire and Civil Defence Authority:
Figure 7

Metropolitan Police:
Cover picture, Frontispiece and figures 1 and 2

The Guardian:
Figure 10

Regulation of Railways Act 1871

In the matter of a collision near Clapham Junction Station on 12 December 1988

Whereas:

(1)   a collision occurred between the 07:18 Basingstoke to Waterloo train, the 06:14 Poole to Waterloo train and a train of empty coaches south west of Clapham Junction Station at about 08:10 on 12 December 1988 (hereinafter called "the accident") which was an accident of which notice is for the time being required by or in pursuance of the Regulation of Railways Act 1871 to be sent to the Secretary of State for Transport (hereinafter referred to as "the Secretary of State"), and

(2)   it appears to the Secretary of State that a formal investigation of the accident is expedient

NOW THEREFORE the Secretary of State, in exercise of the powers conferred by section 7 of the Regulation of Railways Act 1871 and now vested in him hereby makes the following Order –

The Secretary of State directs that a formal investigation of the accident and the causes thereof and of the circumstances attending the same be held and he hereby appoints Anthony Brian Hidden QC to hold the same with the assistance of Major Christopher Basil Holden, an Inspecting Officer of Railways, Dr Thomas Bryce McCrirrick, CBE and Dr Alan Arthur Wells, OBE as assessors.

Signed by authority of the
Secretary of State

6 January 1989

J R COATES

An Under Secretary in
the Department of
Transport

PROCEDURAL HISTORY

1.   At 8:10 a.m. on the morning of Monday, 12 December 1988, a crowded commuter train ran head-on into the rear of another which was stationary in a cutting just south of Clapham Junction station. After that impact the first train veered to its right and struck a third oncoming train. As a result of the accident 35 people died and nearly 500 were injured, 69 of them seriously. The names of those who died are set out at Appendix A. They were all travelling in the front two coaches of the first train.

2.   On the following morning your predecessor as Secretary of State for Transport invited me to hold a formal Investigation into the causes and all the circumstances attending the accident under section 7 of the Regulation of Railways Act 1871.

3.   The Order making the appointment is reproduced opposite.

4.   On 6 January 1989, three Assessors, technical experts of the highest reputation in their fields, were appointed to assist me. They were:

Major Christopher Holden, B.Sc.(Eng), F.I.R.S.E.
– an Inspecting Officer of Railways

Dr Bryce McCrirrick, C.B.E., F.Eng, F.I.E.E.
– President of the Institution of Electrical Engineers

Dr Alan Wells, O.B.E., F.R.S., F.Eng, M.I.Mech.E, F.Weld.I.
– former Director General of the Welding Institute

5.   I owe each of them a debt of gratitude for the wisdom, judgement and dedication which they have brought to their tasks, and for the spirit of helpful cooperation which has existed in all the work we have done together. The assistance they have given me has been enormous. The conclusions expressed in this Report are, of course, my own; if these are flawed then the flaws must be laid at my door and not at that of the Assessors.

6.   The Investigation was opened at a preliminary hearing in London on 10 January 1989. A number of applications for leave to appear at the Investigation were made and all applications save one were granted. The solicitors for the bereaved and injured formed a consortium and applied for joint representation, which was granted. As the Investigation progressed I granted representation to further individual parties. A list of represented parties is set out in Appendix B.

7.   That list includes the name of ML Holdings plc. At the preliminary hearing leave to appear was sought by and granted to that Company who had supplied certain new signalling equipment for the Clapham Junction area to British Rail. It became clear to me before the first day of the formal hearings that there could be no question of that equipment having any responsibility for the accident, and accordingly, when those hearings opened, the Company was released from further attendance.

8.   There were appointed as Counsel to the Investigation, Mr David Latham, Q.C., Mr Philip Havers and Mr John Gimlette, who were instructed by the Treasury Solicitor. I wish to express my deep appreciation and admiration for the way in which they discharged their duties and the assistance they gave to the Court. The courteous, calm and purposeful way in which they set about those duties was reflected in the creation of what I believe to have been the right atmosphere for an Investigation such as this. To them and to all, without exception, who appeared for the Represented Parties, I express my gratitude.

9. Throughout the Investigation I sought to follow the procedures recommended in the Report of the Royal Commission on Tribunals of Inquiry under the Rt. Hon. Lord Justice Salmon (Cmnd.3121). After the opening of the Investigation sufficient time was given for parties to prepare for the formal hearings which began on 20 February 1989. All individuals originally considered as potentially susceptible to criticism during the course of the Investigation had been sent a letter setting out those potential criticisms. These letters gave them the opportunity to obtain legal representation and to seek leave to appear before the Investigation. Later, and as the evidence progressed, it appeared possible that other people might also be the subject of criticism: they, too, received similar letters and were similarly able to seek legal representation and leave to appear.

10. The Court heard evidence from 122 witnesses over a period of 56 days, which concluded on 24 May 1989. The hearing was then adjourned in order to give represented parties time to prepare written final submissions. A further day had been set aside by the Court so that parties could, if they wished, make oral submissions to augment those written submissions. Those oral submissions were heard and the public hearings were finally concluded on 6 June 1989.

11. In total the Court considered over thirteen thousand pages of documents. Considerable use was made throughout the hearings of a video camera with multiple monitors, in order that members of the public attending the Court would better be able to follow and assimilate the mass of documentation. Video films and topographical and diagrammatic models were also used to assist in the presentation of the evidence.

12. Both before the hearings, as well as throughout their entire course, and at every stage thereafter, I have had enormous support and assistance from every member of the Secretariat who have given unstintingly of their time and effort. The leadership shown by Jenny McCusker, the Secretary to the Investigation, could not have been bettered. I have the highest regard for her ability, integrity and dedication. I would also wish to express my sincere and warm thanks for the loyalty and good spirits of Alexandra Turnball, Robin Toase and Louise Wright in all they did. The fifth and final member of the Secretariat was Joyce Fallconi, my personal secretary, who also singlehandedly achieved what seemed impossible in the typing of the entire Report and all the manifold drafts which had gone before it. The heavy workload never for a moment affected the good humour, skill and toleration for which I must express deep personal gratitude.

13. During the Investigation, many letters were received by my Secretariat from members of the public, public bodies and other organisations. As was to be expected, a great majority of the letters expressed concern about safety generally, and more specifically, in relation to wiring, signalling and lighting. Many writers suggested the use of radios, radar, videos and computers as possible means of prevention of further accidents. Plans were submitted with some of the correspondence. I have read and considered every letter and I am grateful to everyone who took the trouble to write and for all the comments and suggestions that have been made.

14. In tragic circumstances on Saturday, 4 March 1989, after only two weeks of the hearing of evidence, a fatal rail accident occurred just north of Purley station in Surrey. That is the subject of a separate investigation under the auspices of the Railway Inspectorate. However, your predecessor asked that if there were any issues common to both investigations, I should take those issues into account. I have been provided with copies and have read all the transcripts of the public hearings of the investigation into the Purley accident and I make reference to them, where relevant, in a number of chapters of this Report. That inquiry, however, went into camera at one stage of the evidence and I am unable to take into account that part of the proceedings.

15. If that were not enough, only two days after the Purley accident, on Monday, 6 March 1989, a further fatal accident occurred at Bellgrove in Glasgow. The next morning on Tuesday, 7 March 1989, Dr Wells (who had travelled at my request on Sunday, 5 March 1989, to Purley to examine the wreckage of the two trains which had collided) now flew to Glasgow for a similar purpose. His task in each case was to see whether there were any structural lessons to be learned from examination of the rolling stock involved in those accidents. The analysis he was

able to make of the structural integrity of the stock involved in all three accidents and of the performance of the internal fittings is at Appendix G. I have read and considered the transcripts of the Railway Inspectorate Investigation into the Bellgrove accident, all of which have been kindly supplied to me by the Chief Inspecting Officer of Railways.

16. I have reviewed the whole of the evidence which was put before the Court and have concluded that certain issues canvassed during the Investigation do not fall to be considered in detail in this Report in that they have, at best, only a very limited relevance to the causes and circumstances of this accident. In my review I have attempted at all times to remind myself of the dangers of using the powerful beam of hindsight to illuminate the situations revealed in the evidence. The power of that beam has its disadvantages. Hindsight also possesses a lens which can distort and can therefore present a misleading picture: it has to be avoided if fairness and accuracy of judgement is to be sought.

17. Both before the hearings began and after the close of evidence, I made a number of visits in order to gain first-hand knowledge to assist me in relation to a number of issues, on most of which I was accompanied by my Assessors and the Secretary to the Investigation.

18. First, on Wednesday, 14 December 1988, between 08:00 and 08:30, I visited the scene of the accident on my own to familiarise myself with the terrain of the cutting and the state of traffic at that time of day. On 9 January 1989, the Secretary and I visited the British Transport Police Incident Room at Waterloo Station.

19. Before the formal hearings began on 20 February 1989, the Assessors, the Secretary and I had twice travelled along the line in an observation car to familiarise ourselves with the track and the signalling equipment on the route. We had all by then visited the scene of the accident. We had all visited the Clapham Junction "A" signal box and relay room on a number of occasions. We had inspected all the rolling stock involved in the accident and had taken particular note of the most damaged vehicles. Dr Wells had made and continued to make a detailed series of inspections which were particularly helpful in establishing the exact reasons for the severity of the damage to some of the rolling stock.

20. After the hearings were concluded we visited the communications centres for the London Ambulance Service, the London Fire Brigade and the Metropolitan Police. On 18 July 1989, a day when no trains were running, I walked the track from the country side of Earlsfield station to Clapham Junction itself.

21. I am extremely grateful to those in all the organisations involved who made those visits possible. Each of those visits was extremely useful and helped to improve our understanding of the evidence given to the Investigation.

22. Two technical sub-committees were formed to explore possible areas of agreement on technical issues which might exist between the Assessors, BR and the consultants advising Counsel to the Court, Kennedy Henderson Ltd. I should like to express the gratitude of the Assessors and of myself for the staunch assistance to the Court which the consultants provided, and in particular for the help of Mr Neil Harris. The first committee met on three occasions to consider the structural integrity of the coaches involved in the collision: it was chaired by Dr Wells. The second met twice under the chairmanship of Dr McCrirrick and Major Holden to discuss systems of automatic train protection.

23. The purpose of this Investigation was not to look for one simple, single solution to account for the tragedy but to seek to establish both the immediate and the underlying causes of the accident and all the circumstances attending it. That target sought to ensure that every conceivable lesson of the tragedy was learned and that the risk of such an accident happening again was reduced as near to zero as was humanly possible. That was and is the aim of this Investigation.

Purley 4/3/89
Bellgrove Glasgow 6/89 - structural integrity

3

INTRODUCTION

1.   On the railway lines between Waterloo and Wimbledon four tracks run through a cutting a mile or so to the country side of Clapham Junction railway station. The nearest track to the steep embankment running alongside a road called Spencer Park is the Up Main line. Peak hour trains pass through that cutting on a normal working morning at intervals of less than two minutes. The signalling system upon which the running of the railway depends is designed to ensure that these intervals can be maintained with complete safety. There is nothing abnormal or intrinsically dangerous in that degree of headway or gap between trains.

2.   Equally, there is nothing abnormal or dangerous about the physical state of the line as it runs the last mile before Clapham Junction, first along a straight, then descending in a gentle left-hand curve through the cutting. The accident happened between the last two signals before the station which are first WF138 and then WF47. WF47 is the signal before the points that lead into the station platforms. There should have been nothing in any way unsafe about a two-minute headway between trains over such a track. There should have been nothing unsafe about the signals and, in particular, about signal WF138.

3.   Just after 08:00 a.m. on Monday, 12 December 1988 three specific trains were running towards that cutting on their normal timetables. Two passenger trains were heading into Waterloo along that line, one, the 07:18 from Basingstoke, the other, running behind it from the South Coast, the 06:14 "Poole" train. The third train, the 08:03 Waterloo to Haslemere, was running without passengers out of London on the adjoining and opposite Down Main line.

4.   At about 08:10 that morning the driver of the "Poole" train, Driver John Rolls, having come into the cutting on his way into Waterloo from Wimbledon and having passed signals in his favour at all stages, cleared the visual obstruction of the steep bank on the left-hand curve. At that moment he must have come upon what was, in signalling and therefore in driving terms, unthinkable and impossible: immediately ahead of him was the Basingstoke train on the same line, stationary and within a distance in which the "Poole" train could not possibly be stopped.

5.   Despite full emergency braking of the "Poole" train, its leading coach collided head-on with the rear of the Basingstoke train. That collision forced it out to its off-side where it struck the third "empty" train going in the opposite direction towards Haslemere. This second impact was more of a glancing blow, which, while it derailed part of the Haslemere train, probably kept the "Poole" train from moving further to its off-side across the other tracks.

6.   An appalling accident had happened. This was at once apparent to people nearby who heard the noise of the impact or saw the dust rise from the cutting. Their telephone calls triggered from the emergency services a response which was totally admirable in its speed and efficiency. The scene of the accident, the position of the emergency services control vehicles and the access points to the track are illustrated in the Frontispiece. The emergency services worked together at the site in an exemplary manner to carry out the rescue operation. The sole cause for concern was the delay in communication of certain vital information to hospitals which I shall analyse in Chapter 5.

7.   Local police units were arriving by 08:17 when the first fire engine drew up in Spencer Park alongside the cutting. It was followed shortly after by the first ambulance at 08:21. There then began an intensive rescue operation to locate and evacuate the injured, the dead, the shocked and the fortunate remainder of the crews and passengers on the three trains who had escaped, at that time, unscathed.

8.   The 35 people, train crew and passengers, who died as a result of the accident had all been carried in the first two coaches of the "Poole" train, which were ripped open on their left-hand sides. The first third of the leading coach of the "Poole" train suffered total disintegration. The second coach was a Trailer Buffet car in which there were tables and chairs at the rear end, with the food preparation and serving space ahead on the left-hand side and the passenger space on the right. The buffet was not open that day and its shutters were closed. The most seriously injured of the casualties were to be found in the first three carriages of that train.

9. The rear coach of the Basingstoke train was lifted bodily by the impact and ended up lying on its left side on the bank above the cutting wall. Its rear bogie pierced the roof of the third coach of the "Poole" train at the front over the luggage compartment. The next to rear coach of the Basingstoke train was derailed and came to rest leaning against the embankment. Figures 1 and 2 give an aerial view of the scene showing where the carriages came to rest.

10. The rescue operation was both helped and hindered by the geography of the accident site. Road access was good to and from the large triangular grass area of Spencer Park where the rescue vehicles congregated and their Control Units were parked. However, the steep slope down from Spencer Park to the 10 feet high concrete walls of the cutting above the tracks made difficulties for the rescuers. For a time, too, there was uncertainty as to whether or not the traction current was still on and thus whether the lines were still live. In fact the crash itself had cut out the traction current.

11. The rescue work was long and difficult and involved delicate manoeuvring, lifting and cutting of wreckage in order to extricate those who were trapped. It was only at 13:04 that the last casualty was evacuated to hospital and it was 15:45 before the last body was taken from the accident site.

12. That day 33 people died as a result of the accident: two others had died from their injuries before the opening of the formal hearing more than a month later. Of the 69 people who were seriously injured, one is at the time of writing this Report still being treated in hospital where he is likely to remain for some time. Many of the seriously injured have suffered permanent disablement. There were 415 people who received minor injuries. In addition many who were not physically injured still suffer the emotional scars which they have inherited from the accident. They are not only those who were travelling on the trains involved in the crash, but also those who came to the rescue.

13. Such an appalling toll of human life and injury demands the investigation of what it was that could possibly have gone wrong, by the asking of obvious questions:

    (i) The first question must be:

    How had the accident happened?
    Since the signalling system is designed to ensure that such a terrible accident could never happen there is therefore a simple answer to that first question:

    The signalling system had failed.

    (ii) That first answer at once raises an equally obvious second question:

    How had the signalling system failed?

    To that second question it is possible at this stage to give a relatively brief answer:

    During alterations to the signalling system a wire should have been removed. In error it was not. It was still in the system and was making an electrical contact with its old circuit. It was therefore able to feed current into the new circuit when the circuit should have been dead. That current prevented the signal from turning to red.

    (iii) The answer to the second question immediately raises a third question which is central to this Investigation:

    How had that situation been allowed to happen?

    It is to find an answer to that third question that the body of this Report must be directed. It is to the body of the Report itself that the examination of detailed factual and technical evidence must be left.

PART ONE: THE ACCIDENT

Chapter 1: How the new signal went wrong

The new signals
1.1 The Weekly Operating Notice which the Southern Region of British Railways (BR) issue to train crews to keep them up-to-date had an entry in the issue for Saturday, 10 December 1988 which read:

"Signal WA25 has been abolished and a new 4-aspect automatic signal WF138 has been provided,...."

It was that new signal WF138 which two days later in the morning rush hour of Monday, 12 December failed to prevent a second train from occupying the same track as an earlier one and failed to stop the front of the second from running into the back of the first.

1.2 It is the essential function of a signal to act as a sentry. It guards the next section of track on which a train is about to travel, it permits that train to enter the section and then forbids entry to any other train. Signal WF138 failed to discharge that function that morning. To understand how it failed we must look at the physical location of the signal, at the principles upon which the railway signalling system is based, at the relay room and the relays, and at the way in which signal WF138 was brought into commission.

The physical location: the track and the signals
1.3 A hundred or so yards on the London side of the various platforms that make up the sprawl of Clapham Junction Station, and actually positioned above the Windsor Line tracks, there sits Clapham Junction "A" Signal Box. It is the nerve centre for all the signalling on either side of the station, save for that of the Brighton line. It houses, in addition to various ancillary rooms, the signalling floor ("the Box"). Next door to, and at the far end of, the Box there is a room known as the relay room. Running to and from this relay room is the electrical wiring which operates each of the signals within the Clapham Junction area. In the Box itself work the signalmen who preside over the signal levers in the frame, the train describers which identify the trains about to come through Clapham Junction, the signalling diagrams, the telephone systems and all the apparatus of the signalling function.

1.4 On the Up Main line into Waterloo the Clapham Junction signal furthest away in the country direction and within the Clapham Junction area is WF152, which stands almost exactly two miles away from the relay room. Its position and its relation to other signals is shown in Appendix K.2. It is about 300 yards to the country side of Earlsfield station. Earlsfield is the only station on the way into Waterloo between Wimbledon and Clapham Junction. The signals before WF152 are operated from the Wimbledon "A" Signal Box. They have numbers which are prefixed by the letter "WH", rather than the Clapham Junction prefix of "WF". (The "Wimbledon" signal identified on Appendix K.2 as WH165 on the Down Main line is included merely to identify the position of its signal post telephone).

1.5 As can be seen in Appendix K.2 there are only 4 signals which a train must pass on the Up Main line from Earlsfield before coming into Clapham Junction station. Their WF (Clapham Junction) numbers decrease the nearer towards London they are sited:

- The furthest out of these, WF148, is sited at the London end of Earlsfield station.

- The next signal WF142 is in a straight line with WF148, but is about 700 yards closer to London.

- After WF142 comes WF138, which is round a left-hand bend another 700 yards up the line. WF138, the last but one signal before the station itself, is just under a mile from Clapham Junction "A" Signal Box and relay room. That mile or so is therefore the distance that the wiring has to run to and from the relay room.

- After WF138 the track runs through the cutting with concrete walls rising on either side until just before the points at the entry to platforms 7 and 8 at Clapham Junction is signal WF47.

1.6   In considering the Clapham Junction accident it will be necessary to look in particular at:

(i) the stretch of track 776 yards long between signals WF138 and WF47; and

(ii) the electrical circuits involving both the relay room and signal WF138.

Basic principles of Railway Signalling

1.7   It is the prime object of railway signalling to prevent two trains occupying the same stretch of track by putting a block on that stretch of track. To achieve this object, the track is divided into sections and a signal is sited at the beginning of each "block" section. The duty of the signal is to prohibit entry on to the section to any following train until the preceding train has cleared not only the block section itself but also a further distance known as the "overlap". It prohibits that entry by showing to the oncoming driver a red aspect.

1.8   Under the provisions of the BR Rule Book, a driver is compelled to stop at a red signal. As can be seen in Appendix K.12 on a four aspect signal such as WF138 the aspects run from top to bottom in the order:

- yellow

- green

- yellow

- red.

For a single yellow aspect, only the lower yellow lamp is lit.

1.9   A single aspect indicates "caution", a double yellow indicates "preliminary caution, and a green indicates "clear". These three aspects are known as "proceed aspects", so that a driver may literally "proceed" past them. He must, however, stop before a signal if it is showing a red (danger) aspect.

1.10   A simple example of the way in which the system works may be helpful. As a driver proceeds up the track, if there were a train ahead of him stationary at the fifth signal from him, the driver of the moving train would pass the first signal at green, the second signal at double yellow and the third signal at yellow. These sequential indications would tell him to expect that the fourth signal he was to see would be showing a red aspect and therefore that he must be able to stop his train before that red signal. The reason why he would be given that instruction to stop would be the presence of the stationary train ahead of him at the fifth signal. (This sequence is illustrated in diagrammatic form at Appendix K.13).

1.11 As that driver's train passed a signal showing a "proceed" aspect, that signal would automatically revert to red (for danger) until the train had passed clear, not only of the section itself, but of the overlap distance of the next signal ahead. The signal would revert to red because it had detected the presence of the train on its track by reason of the train's effect on an electrical circuit carried in the track.

1.12 There is in the circuit an electrical relay. The wheels of the train short out the track circuit which accordingly goes dead. As a result the relay "switches" the current off in the "intelligence" circuit to the signal. This automatically makes the signal revert to red.

1.13 It is in this way that a signal "sees" the train on its own section of track and accordingly turns immediately to red to protect that train. For any signal to be able to do this it must be sent the correct message. For WF138 to "see" a train on its track the correct message had to come from a relay nearly a mile away in the relay room.

1.14 It is important at this stage to emphasise the distinction between the two basic types of signal, the controlled and the automatic:

(i) the controlled signal, whose aspects are dictated by the signalman's actions in moving the levers in the frame in the Box; and

(ii) the automatic signal, whose aspects are dictated automatically and without the intervention of the signalman by the movement of a train upon the tracks.

Additionally, since all signals react to a change of aspect of a signal immediately ahead, both a controlled and an automatic signal can react to each other in such circumstances.

1.15 It should be explained that shortly before each signal a driver is given an audible warning in his cab as to whether the next signal will be showing green or some other colour. The Automatic Warning System (AWS) which does this consists of equipment on the track between the lines which reacts when the train passes over it and gives the driver an audible warning as to the aspect the next signal is showing. If it is a green light the driver will hear a bell, but if it is double or single yellow, or red he will hear a horn. On receiving that warning indicator by the horn, the driver must cancel the indication. That cancellation will have three consequences:

(i) the horn will stop;

(ii) it will prevent or cancel the application of the brake which would otherwise happen automatically; and

(iii) it will cause a visual indicator which normally shows a black disc to display instead yellow spokes (called in railway jargon "the sunflower". This can be clearly seen in Figure 4):

The equipment consists of a permanent magnet and an electro-magnet fixed between the rails usually about 200 yards on the approach side of the signal.

The Relay Room and the Relays

1.16 The relay room at the end of Clapham Junction "A" signal box is only a few yards wide throughout its length (see Figure 11). Whereas the next door Signal Box has good natural light through windows on either side, there is no natural light in the relay room, which is lit by fluorescent lighting from the ceiling. This, while giving enough light for visual observation of the relays and the fuses, presents a rather gloomy appearance and requires additional light for detailed electrical work.

9

poor light
&
cramped -

person cannot work/check
relays adequately

1.17 Inside the door there is a passageway on either side of which are four tiers of wooden racks which carry the many relays upon which the system depends (see Figures 11 and 12). There are six bays of racking on the way to the far end of the relay room and on each shelf in each bay there is room for four relays. These relays are a little larger and heavier than an average car battery and have glass sides so that their physical operation can be visually checked.

1.18 Their function is rather like that of a switch to make (or break) an electrical contact and thus to permit or prohibit the flow of electrical current. There are contacts within the relay which are clearly visible through the glass. When a current flows through the circuit the front contacts close together. This is the electro-magnetic aspect of their function. Thus, if the flow of current ceases then the relay becomes de-energised and the contacts physically drop away, bringing the front contacts into a different position. When current flows again in the circuit that current in the relay coil causes the front contacts to close again. The presence or absence of electricity therefore combines with magnetic force to determine the physical position of the contacts.

1.19 The proper title of such a relay is a Single Element Vane Relay. Despite the age of the design, which is almost as old as the century, such relays have an enviable reputation for reliability. Almost the sole advantage of more modern counterparts is the marked decrease in size which miniaturization makes possible. Certainly it is abundantly clear that the design and the age of these relays had nothing whatever to do with the Clapham Junction accident.

1.20 If the signal which is being operated by the relay is sufficiently close to the signal box, then there will only be the need for one track relay (TR) in the track circuit, controlling that signal. If, however, the signal is further away there may be a need for a track repeater relay (TRR) to carry out the necessary function.

The relays for signal WF138

1.21 Thus, nearest to the door and on the bottom shelf the third relay is TR DN (the track relay for track circuit DN) and the fourth relay is TRR DM (the track repeater relay for track circuit DM). Next, separated only by an upright of the shelving, is TRR DL (the track repeater relay for track circuit DL). Both track circuits, first DL and then DM, control the aspect shown by signal WF138.

1.22 It is this last relay, TRR DL, which continues the circuit that runs out to and back from signal WF138. That circuit, when energised, enables signal WF138 to show a proceed aspect. When, however, the track circuit is shorted out by the wheels of a train going past WF138 and first entering the track circuit DL, the relay does not receive any current and has its front contacts drop open. This prevents signal WF138 from showing any aspect other than a red.

1.23 Save for one circumstance, the track circuit DL running between Clapham Junction "A" relay room and signal WF138 should have current running permanently through it. That circumstance arises when the wheels of a train have just passed signal WF138 and have therefore moved on to the stretch of rail through which runs track circuit DL. When those train wheels reach that section of track the current is shorted out, the relay TRR DL loses its energy, its contacts open, and the signal changes to red. Signal WF138 is similarly affected by the movement of a train onto track circuit DM.

1.24 That is the way the entire signalling system was designed to work in relation to all signals and therefore in relation particularly to WF138. It is the way the system should have worked. However, the relay TRR DL could only perform its function as a switch cutting off the current provided that it was not by-passed and therefore rendered inoperative by any false connection of wires, any "false feed" of electricity.

1.25 Everything else involved in the track circuit might be working perfectly correctly, but if the contacts of relay TRR DL were by-passed, then, when a train entered track circuit DL, signal WF138 would fail to turn to red and would instead show a proceed aspect. Thus, a driver would be given a totally false indication that it was safe to proceed.

1.26 An unintended flow of current, technically described as a "false feed" of current, would remove from the signal the ability to "see" the train on the track that it was guarding. That train would therefore have become invisible to the signalling system. The signal, not knowing the train was there, would not turn to red to protect it. It would continue to show a proceed aspect. It would have failed in its duty as a sentry in that it would be doing nothing to stop the entry onto that section of the track of another train. It would, in fact, be inviting that second train onto the track by showing a proceed aspect.

1.27 Such a failure, such an invitation to proceed, would be a contradiction of the whole philosophy of "fail safe" operation of signalling systems, and would be utter anathema to the railway signalling engineer. His philosophy requires that, if there be a failure, that failure falls on the right side of safety: a "right-side failure", as it is called in railway jargon. A failure such as is described in paragraph 1.25, however, would not fall into this category. It would be a very different matter. It would be a failure which falls on the wrong side of safety.

1.28 A "wrong-side failure" can cover many situations which vary in all their circumstances from the relatively trivial to the extremely serious. An example of a wrong-side failure with potentially disastrous consequences would be a false feed to a track circuit which caused it to be energised when it should be dead, thus causing a signal to show a proceed aspect when it should show red.

The creation of signal WF138

1.29 The four-aspect colour-light signalling system was first used at the end of the 1920s. Since then it has been progressively applied to all intensively used lines on British mainline railways and is still the standard for new schemes on such lines. There was therefore nothing new about the type of signal WF138 which was to replace WA25 according to the information in the Weekly Operating Notice for that week: it was just a new signal in a slightly different place. Since there is nothing new in concept or installation, it should have presented no problems to the installers or to the testers of the work involved.

1.30 The final work necessary to replace the old signal WA25 and bring into operation the new signal WF138 was carried out on Sunday, 27 November 1988. It involved two wiring jobs known as job No.104 and job No.201 which were part of Stage 7B of the Waterloo Area Resignalling Scheme (hereafter called WARS). The physical preparation of those two jobs had to be done during the working week before Sunday, 27 November 1988, and the actual completion of the work had to be done on that Sunday by connecting the wires. The conceptual preparation had been done much earlier in that the Design Office had prepared and issued the wiring diagrams for those job numbers.

1.31 The whole massive resignalling operation which WARS involved had taken many years to plan initially and many years in the obtaining of financial approval. The operation became not only necessary but vital as a result of the deteriorating condition of the existing signalling equipment in the Waterloo area. Most of this had been installed in or about 1936. It had become essential to create a plan to rationalise and resignal the whole Waterloo area.

1.32 It will be important to look later in Chapter 12 at the disturbing length of time which the WARS project took from its first seeds in an early Project Development Paper in the year 1978 to its imminent completion, still in the (albeit very near) future. Even as this Report is written the Final Commissioning of the new system and the de-commissioning of Clapham Junction "A" Signal Box still lies in the future.

1.33 The work necessary in the relay room on the weekend of 26/27 November 1988 in order to take signal WA25 out of service and replace it with the new signal WF138 was not difficult and should have taken only a few hours. That work was to be done on Sunday, 27 November 1988 by a senior technician, Mr Brian Hemingway, who had been allocated the assistance of a technician, Mr Patrick Dowd. The supervisor in charge of the work that day was Mr Derek Bumstead. Once the work had been completed and the line was ready to be put back into service, it had first to be tested by the testing and commissioning engineer, Mr Peter Dray.

The work goes wrong

1.34 The detailed nature of the weekend work, its design and execution, together with the supervision, monitoring and testing of that work once it had been done, will be considered in later chapters. It is illustrated in a diagrammatic form at Appendix K.3 which is in fact an extract from the wiring diagram used by Mr Hemingway and in Figure 15, a photograph of a working model constructed for the Investigation. That diagram will be considered in greater detail in Chapter 7. For the moment, suffice it to say that under the previous wiring system an old wire ran from a relay to a fuse. That relay was called TRR DM because it was the track repeater relay for track circuit DM.

1.35 Under the new system for the new signal WF138, the circuit was to go from TRR DM relay to the fuse by a different route, which was to include a further relay, TRR DL, the track repeater relay for track circuit DL. New wires had been prepared during the week to run from the relay TRR DM to TRR DL and then on from TRR DL to the fuse. Mr Hemingway's task at the weekend was to connect those new wires and disconnect the old wire. That disconnection had to be made at both ends of the old wire, both at the relay end, at TRR DM, and at the fuse end.

1.36 In fact no disconnection was made at the fuse end and, although at the other relay end the old wire was disconnected, it was not cut back as it should have been, nor was it secured out of the way of its previous contact. Although it was pushed away to one side, the wire was accordingly left long enough and close enough to its previous contact for it to be physically possible for it to return to its old position if the wrong circumstances arose.

The eve of the accident

1.37 Those circumstances did arise. Two weeks later on the day before the accident, Sunday, 11 December 1988, Mr Hemingway was again doing work in the relay room, but with a different assistant. The work was not related to the earlier work. It involved the changing over of a relay. That relay, TR DN, happened to be immediately to the left of relay TRR DM on the racking. In the course of the physical effort involved in the changeover of the new TR DN for the old, the positions of the wires to TRR DM were disturbed and particularly that of the old wire between the fuse and the relay TRR DM. Those consequences were not only unintended, they were disastrous.

1.38 During the work two weeks before, not only had the old wire not been disconnected from the fuse, but it had not been cut back, nor secured away from its old contact. Now that its position had been disturbed by this Sunday's work it was able to move back into its old position. Once there, it was able to make metal-to-metal contact with its old terminal and permit current to flow direct from the relay TRR DM to the fuse.

1.39 Just as the original wiring errors two weeks before had not been detected, so the new situation also remained undetected. The old wire could now take up its previous position and could send out a false feed of current from the relay TRR DM to the fuse, and hence to signal WF138. The potential for disaster now existed. Thus, even when the wheels of a train should have shorted out the

12

[Handwritten margin notes:]

Wiring job not done properly or safely
- time was an issue
- under pressure
- the technician but was supposed to do the best
** not conundrum*
didn't check it was...

- why change assisstants?
- why make bigger mistakes than before?
- 'not satisfied' or motivated in their job
→ led to disaster

why where the new wiring job nor double checked by inspectors?
- why was safety implications nor checked?

track circuit, DL, and turned WF138 to red, no change would happen: WF138 would continue to show a proceed aspect. The old wire, still connected at the fuse end and with its other bare metal end in contact with the terminal that had been its old home, was now a "rogue" wire.

1.40 There was to be no disaster that night, or early the following morning: the track was not put back into commission until between 4:00 a.m. and 5:00 a.m. the next day. Once trains began to run on that Monday morning there would still be no disaster at first. There would be no disaster as long as trains kept running through the cutting with a good enough gap between one train and the train ahead of it.

1.41 However, when Driver McClymont stopped the 07:18 Basingstoke to Waterloo train at signal WF47 to telephone the signalman, in the utter faith of a railwayman that the signal behind him, WF138, had to be at red, it was not. It had given up its sentry duty. It had not "seen" the arrival on its tracks of Driver McClymont's train. WF138 was not forbidding any other train to enter upon its tracks. It was inviting the following train, the "Poole" train, to proceed along its tracks towards signal WF47 and thus towards the back of the Basingstoke train which was concealed behind a left-hand curve.

Chapter 2: The Morning of the Accident

2.1   On a typical Monday morning the peak hour could have been expected to build up relatively normally. The only difference from any other weekday would be that the trains could be expected to be a little fuller. In addition to all the regular commuting travellers, there would also be passengers who had been spending the weekend in the country with parents, relatives or friends. Trains were due to run regularly through the Clapham cutting and on into Waterloo on the Up Main line during the peak hour that morning. In the two hours between 06:10 and 08:10 the timetable called for twenty-nine trains to pass through the cutting, five in the first half-hour, six in each of the next two half-hour periods and doubling to twelve in the half-hour to 08:10 as the pressure of traffic built up.

2.2   With so many trains running before 08:10 it may at first sight seem surprising that an accident did not occur before then. The signalling system which was designed to keep trains from entering the same section of track had a potentially fatal fault within it. However, as long as there was a large enough interval between trains running into London no train would be close enough to the one in front to be affected by the faulty signal, or for its drivers to conclude that there was anything wrong with it.

The earlier drivers and their recollections

2.3   With an average of a five minute gap between the earlier 17 trains running on that line in the hour and half between 06:10 and 07:40, it is perhaps understandable that their drivers would have noticed nothing amiss about signal WF138. If the preceding trains were each that far ahead then it is likely that most of those drivers would have seen only green aspects as they passed the signals: they would have been "running on greens" on their way into London. They therefore would have passed WF138 when it was showing, perfectly properly, a green aspect.

2.4   Most of the drivers who had travelled the route that morning were asked next day to recollect the signals they had seen on the morning of the accident. This was for the purpose of statements they then made to British Transport Police. Soon afterwards they gave their recollections at British Rail's internal inquiry: this was held within a week or so of the accident. There would have been, in general, nothing in particular to stick out in their memories as they completed their routine journeys into Waterloo and started on the next part of their rotas for the day.

2.5   However, the recollections of five of the twenty-eight drivers who preceded Mr McClymont along the track, need to be examined to see whether the aspects which they recollected seeing at relevant signals could have had any significance in relation to the accident. Those five drivers were booked according to the timetable to pass Clapham Junction "A" Signal Box at:

   – 06:41 (Driver Keating)

   – 07:13 (Driver Mansbridge)

   – 07:46 (Driver Malone)

   – 08:01½ (Driver Christy)

   – 08:05½ (Driver Priston).

The last three travelled the route in the thirty minutes before the accident.

2.6   Each of those drivers would have had duties in relation to his driving imposed on him by the BR Rule Book. Certain of those duties related to the reporting of any unusual event. It is therefore necessary to look at the Rule Book to see whether any previous driver should have reported any irregularity in relation to signal WF138. If such a report should have been made, then it is understandable that a further question should also have been raised as to whether such a report could have prevented the accident. That question too, must be considered.

The provisions of the Rule Book

2.7   The current edition of the British Rail Rule Book was revised in June 1988. In Section H which is entitled "Working of Trains" certain duties are set out. The section starts with a fundamental statement:

"1.   PRINCIPLE

Safety must be the first consideration of each employee involved in the working of trains . . . ."

Rule H.7 reads:

"DUTIES OF DRIVERS AND GUARDS – IRREGULARITIES OR EXCEPTIONAL INCIDENTS DURING THE JOURNEY.

7.1   **Observing any irregularity or obstruction**

7.1.1   If a Driver or Guard observes anything which may endanger his train, he must stop his train immediately but should avoid stopping where it may be difficult to deal with the emergency.

7.1.2   If he sees any irregularity affecting another train, he must immediately inform the Signalman, stopping specially if necessary. If possible, he must also alert the Driver of that train by sounding the horn and exhibiting a red light.

7.1.3   If he sees anything which may endanger other trains he must inform the Signalman and alert the Driver of any approaching train as shown above . . . .

7.1.4   If he observes something not of immediate danger to trains . . . . he must report it at the first suitable opportunity."

2.8   Thus, a driver who observes "any irregularity affecting another train" is under a duty immediately to inform the signalman so that such information is passed on into the system. Further consideration of the meaning of these words and other words omitted from the quotation above can be left until a later chapter as can other words from Section C. It will be necessary to look later at the way in which the Rule Book may be generally understood (or misunderstood). For the moment it is necessary only to consider what signal aspects were noticed by drivers of earlier trains than that of Driver McClymont as they passed through the Clapham Junction cutting on the morning of 12 December. The diagram at Appendix K.13C will assist for this purpose. The distinction between a controlled and an automatic signal referred to in Chapter 1 paragraph 14 will also need to be borne in mind.

Driver Keating

2.9   Driver Keating was taking the 06:37 "empties" from Wimbledon Park to Waterloo. His recollection was that he had "all greens" from WF152 through WF148 to WF142 and that as he came to WF142 it changed from green to two yellows. When he came round the curve and was first able to see WF138 it was showing one yellow. The next signal WF47 was at green and thereafter he had greens all the way.

2.10 He had thought that for WF142 to change from green to double yellow was unusual but considered that the signalman might be sending his train into the loop platform at Clapham Junction, platform 7. The thought did not cross his mind that anything was wrong in any way with the signals and he did not consider any report about the signalling sequence to be justified. He said that there was nothing which put his or any other train in danger and therefore nothing to cause him the need to report to the signalman under the terms of the Rule Book.

Driver Mansbridge

2.11 Driver Mansbridge's train was the service described in the timetable as the 05:15 Poole to Waterloo and therefore running about an hour ahead of Driver Rolls's train. He had been running on green signals from Bournemouth to Wimbledon. As he passed signal WF152 at green, the aspect on WF148 went to green. WF142 further ahead was also at green, but turned to one yellow or two yellows as he went past it. Although the WF148 change to green was a quick one, he just thought that the train in front had moved on and perhaps had been put into the loop. WF138 was showing a single yellow as he passed, as was WF47 which took him into the loop where he stopped.

2.12 None of the signalling aspects he encountered on that journey caused him any concern and he did not consider there was anything to report as a result. When WF142 changed from green to yellow, he thought that the signalman's intention was to put him into the loop at Platform 7 which would have been his proper route.

Driver Malone

2.13 Driver Malone drove the 05:14 from Bournemouth. He had green aspects at WF152 and WF148 with two yellows at WF142. WF138 was green as he approached and as he passed it. WF47 was green. He found nothing unusual about the aspects he saw. He thought that a change from yellow straight to green at WF138 would not have been considered unusual. He believed he was following a semi-fast train which would have stopped at Clapham Junction in the loop.

Driver Christy

2.14 Driver Christy took over the driving of the 06:06 from Bournemouth once it reached Basingstoke at about 07:26. He took over from the previous driver, Driver Guy. That change of driver was an unauthorised change in that it was not known of and therefore not approved by BR. Comment will need to be made later in this Chapter on the unauthorised nature of the change and its possible effects.

2.15 Driver Christy said that the three signals, WF152, WF148 and WF142, all changed to green at the very same moment, but that the far signal, WF142, went back to one yellow: he was only assuming that it was one yellow because there was some smoke in the cutting at the time. He said that the change from green to one yellow was "rare" but that "it does happen" and he had seen such things before when approaching Clapham Junction: "It was not too uncommon". WF138 was showing one yellow when he first saw it and when he passed it. The same was true of WF47. He did not report the change of WF142 from green to one yellow, nor was it something he considered he ought to report.

2.16 He said that he thought the signalman at Clapham Junction had his reasons for setting the signals and that the signals in the rear would react accordingly. He said if there had been anything obviously wrong he would have reported it, and nothing placed his train or any other train in danger. He said that he dismissed these signals from his mind once he had passed them, as he did for most days work, because once he had passed them he had forgotten them and "it was history".

Driver Priston

2.17 Driver Priston was in charge of the 07:20 from Guildford, the last train to pass signal WF138 before Driver McClymont. He had all greens to Earlsfield.

WF148 was green and he then saw that WF142 was at one yellow. This was out of sequence and he checked his cab indicator (the Advanced Warning System known as AWS) which confirmed that WF148 had in fact been green.

2.18 He assumed that the signalman in the Clapham Junction signal box had "put the road back", which meant changing it from being a clear road for him to one on which he was checked. WF138 was showing one yellow as was WF47, but from then on he had all greens. He saw no need to make any report, seeing nothing of danger to his train or any other train. The single yellow light he had seen at WF142 he put down to nothing specific, assuming it was the action of the signalman.

The expert evidence

2.19 Two expert witnesses were called before the Court to give evidence on the aspects of signals reported to have been seen by individual drivers and as to whether in any individual case such aspects should have been reported. They were Mr Roy Bell and Mr John Morgan.

Mr Morgan's evidence

2.20 Mr John Morgan, a Train Crew Projects Officer, had considerable experience as a driver and as a drivers' instructor, and gave evidence both on driver training and on the aspects of signals reported by individual drivers. He said it was part of drivers' training that, although they would not be taught to expect signals to become more restrictive, they would know that there were circumstances in which signals could indeed become so. They would also know that this was not an indication that there was anything wrong with the signalling.

2.21 He gave evidence as to how drivers react to the two relevant Sections of the Rule Book, Sections C and H. We have already seen Section H at paragraph 2.7. We must now look at Section C, which deals with signals and starts with the principle:

"1.1.   The aspect/indication of each signal must be obeyed by the driver of the train or movement to which it applies."

Section C, Rule C.6.7.1 says that:

"6.7   **Signal not shown or imperfectly shown.**

6.7.1   The Driver must consider a stop signal to be at Danger and a distant signal at Caution in the following circumstances:

(a) the absence of a signal where one should be shown;

(b) a signal imperfectly shown;

(c) a white light shown where there should be a red, yellow or green light.

....

6.7.3   The Driver must report the circumstances to the Signalman."

2.22 Mr Morgan was unable at first to think of circumstances in which that rule could apply to a colour-light signal rather than a semaphore signal. He thought that the Rule Book, generally speaking, dealt with signals in Section C and with obstructions on the line at Section H. As to Section H he said:

"... here primarily you would be looking at obstructions to the line which .. would endanger the train ... but ... this could include signals as well"

2.23 It is fair to him to point out at this stage that Rule H.7.1.3 of Section H refers specifically to "the obstruction" as well as to "irregularities".

2.24 Though he considered that Section C would be the part of the Rule Book which would cover any query about signalling procedures and the signalling process, he accepted that there was no reference in that section to the type of signalling sequences sometimes seen.

2.25 As to whether there was anything in the Rule Book telling a driver to report something that was unusual about the signalling, he thought that there was nothing within Section C, but Section H and in particular Rules H.7.1.3 and H.7.1.4 would cover anything odd or unusual. It might be helpful at this stage to set out that rule in full:

> "7.1.3 If he sees anything which may endanger other trains, he must inform the Signalman and alert the Driver of any approaching train as shown above. He must also place a track circuit operating clip and three detonators 20 yards (or 20 metres) apart on each line affected at least 1¼ miles (or 2 km) from the obstruction. If he sees animals within the boundary fence, he must comply with this clause whenever:
>
> (a) a cow, bull or other large animal is within the boundary fence, **whether or not trains are immediately endangered or**
>
> (b) any other animals are on or near the line and he considers that trains may be endangered.
>
> 7.1.4 If he observes something not of immediate danger to trains (other than a cow, bull or other large animal within the boundary fence), he must report it at the first suitable opportunity."

2.26 At one stage, Mr Morgan said that a signal becoming more restrictive was an irregularity in itself. He suggested that such an irregularity should be reported by a driver, either orally at the first occasion on which he would normally stop, or by a report in writing at the end of the day. On that approach, Mr Morgan concluded that Mr Mansbridge should have reported what he had seen at the end of his shift. At the same time, however, he accepted that Mr Mansbridge's conclusion that the signal aspects he saw were the results of the signalman's action was perfectly justifiable.

2.27 Mr Morgan was at one stage in his evidence suggesting that each of drivers, Mr Mansbridge, Mr Keating, Mr Christy and Mr Priston, should have reported what they individually saw as an irregularity, but he later accepted that their interpretations of the signals they saw were reasoned and reasonable in that they did not consider their train or anyone else's train to be endangered. Mr Morgan's evidence was confused and far from persuasive which, in fairness to him, was hardly surprising in the light of the way in which the Rule Book itself is worded.

Mr Bell's evidence 2.28 Mr Bell, a BR Signal Engineer, gave a contrary view. He would not have expected any of the drivers of trains before Mr McClymont to have reported the signal aspects they saw as being so unusual as to indicate a problem with the signal. He concluded that this was a reasonable conclusion for Driver Mansbridge to draw, that none of the aspects Mr Mansbridge saw indicated danger to his train or to any other train and he came to the same conclusions in relation to the other drivers.

2.29 As to Driver Christy's recollection, the unchallenged technical evidence of Mr Bell established that, even bearing in mind the faulty condition of WF138, it was not electrically possible for Mr Christy to have seen in relation to WF148 and WF142 the sequence which he recollected. WF148 could not electrically have been at green at precisely the same time that WF142 was at yellow. The technical explanation as to why this is so can be found at the conclusion of Appendix F.

19

2.30 Mr Bell concluded that in the existing faulty state of the wiring to signal WF138, there would have been a change to green on signals WF152, WF148 and WF142 as the preceding train cleared track circuit DK and moved on to track circuit DL, but signal WF138 would not have changed to red until that preceding train occupied track circuit DM. When that happened, WF142 would change from green to one yellow and WF148 would change from green to two yellows.

2.31 Mr Bell had taken into account the increasing volume of trains using the track, as well as the slowing down of Mr Priston's train and the fact that the signal box levers for signals WF47 and WF45, those at the beginning and end of the loop, have to be operated for each train by the signalman in Clapham Junction "A" signal box. Similar levers also control the setting of the points at the beginning and the end respectively of platforms 7 and 8 at Clapham Junction station.

2.32 Mr Bell's evidence was that Driver Christy could thus have seen WF148 and WF142 both showing green at the same time, or he could have seen WF148 showing two yellows and WF142 showing one yellow at the same time. He could not have seen WF148 showing green at exactly the same moment as WF142 showed one yellow. He could, however, have seen those colours at those signals within a very short space of time. That evidence I accept, and it follows that Mr Christy's recollection which was, in any event, expressed only in vague and imprecise terms, I find to be faulty.

2.33 Mr Bell concluded that the traffic was building up in such a way that, as the line became more congested, sooner or later somebody was going to see WF138 go to red as Driver McClymont on the Basingstoke train did. He did not consider the fact that WF152, WF148 and WF142 all changed to green for Mr Christy at the same time to be unusual for a driver who was aware, from the restrictive aspects which he saw, that he was following another train and who knew that there was somewhere ahead, such as the loop platform, where the preceding train could be refuged.

Conclusions as to what the drivers saw

2.34 Where the views of Mr Morgan and Mr Bell conflicted the Court had no difficulty in coming to the conclusion that Mr Bell's evidence was to be preferred.

2.35 It is always difficult to construct with hindsight a clear mental picture of everyday events noted by the mind at the time but dismissed a second or so later as no longer relevant and of no historic value. Such was the nature of the signal aspects seen by drivers on a journey which at the time seemed to them to be a normal routine journey and involved danger neither to their train nor to any other. Once passed, the signals were dismissed from a driver's mind and forgotten as part of a routine which was now finished with.

2.36 The Court has come to the conclusion that there were no aspects seen by any driver before Mr McClymont which were reportable under the terms of the Rule Book. It follows that there was no failure by a preceding driver to report an irregularity in the signalling system which was in any way a cause of the accident itself.

2.37 It follows equally that the fact that Driver Christy was wrongly and unofficially driving a train which should have been driven by Driver Guy had no place in the causation of this accident. I respect the firm belief of Mrs Rolls to the contrary which was properly put forward on her behalf in cross-examination and in submissions to the Court. However, I find it to be misplaced, although completely understandable in all the tragic circumstances.

2.38 Had any of the earlier drivers in fact made a report to the signalman about any signalling irregularity, it must be a matter of speculation what would then have occurred. The problem of hypothetical situations is that by their nature they admit of alternative hypotheses. I would find it difficult to believe that any such report would have prevented the accident. I consider that there would have been insufficient time and insufficient understanding for the fault to have been identified and the appropriate action to have been taken of stopping all trains on the Up Main line.

2.39 In this context Mr Ivor Warburton, Director of Operations, British Railways Board (hereafter BRB) in his statement to the Investigation, dealt with the possible situation as it might have been if cab radios had already been fitted to trains. This conclusion is equally relevant to a situation where the report of a fault has to be made not from a cab radio but from a convenient telephone. He said:

> "If the driver of an earlier train had reported an irregularity the danger was unlikely to be realised immediately because the correct track circuit indications continued to be given in the signal box. This would have suggested to the signalman that a right-side failure had occurred."

2.40 No conclusive finding can be made, but it may be a comfort to express a firm belief that not only was there nothing known that morning to trigger off a report of the signal, but, further, even if a report had been made the accident would still have happened.

Driver substitutions

2.41 It is a cause for concern, however, that Driver Guy and Driver Christy should have been able so simply and so speedily to come to the arrangement they did that Driver Christy should unofficially substitute for Driver Guy from Basingstoke to London. The Court had no evidence upon which it could assess whether there was a widespread practice of such substitutions. It would, however, appear rather surprising, if this were an utterly isolated occasion, that it came about so readily.

2.42 Though the fact that Mr Christy was not a rostered driver had no adverse effect in this case and hence made no difference to the causation of the accident, the practice of unofficial substitution if it exists, is both undesirable and potentially a risk to safety. There are three clear reasons why this is so:

(i) it could inhibit the reporting of accidents;

(ii) it could mean that the substitute driver is not familiar with the contents of the current Weekly Operating Notice dealing with such vital matters as signalling changes; and

(iii) it could mean that a driver might exceed his rostered hours.

2.43 If and insofar as such a practice exists, it is essential in the interests of safety that it be stamped out.

The twenty-ninth and thirtieth trains

2.44 Of the twenty-nine trains which passed through the cutting in the two hours to 08:10, the last was in fact driven by Driver McClymont and was the Basingstoke train. His routine progress into London had received an unexpected set-back when signal WF138 had changed from green to red when he was almost on top of it, so that he had had no chance of coming to a halt before passing it. The reason for signal WF138 suddenly turning to red was because the preceding train had moved from the faulty track circuit, DL, where it was "invisible" to signal WF138, on to track circuit DM, which also controls WF138 and was working properly. (See paragraphs 1.21 to 1.23).

2.45 He had thus unwillingly become involved in an incident known in railway jargon as a SPAD (Signal Passed At Danger). That incident meant that under a rule in Section C of the BR Rule Book he had to stop and make immediate report to the signalman. Rule C.6.1.5 says that:

> "If the train inadvertently passes a signal at Danger, the Driver must stop immediately. He must not then proceed until authorised by the Signalman."

Driver McClymont had to comply with that rule. He stopped at WF47 to use the signal post telephone to speak to the signalman.

2.46 Behind Mr McClymont, Driver Rolls was driving the thirtieth train along the track that morning. He was driving his train in an exemplary manner and nothing he did was in any way a cause of the accident, a finding which I felt able, unusually, to announce at the conclusion of the hearings. He followed the dozen trains that had passed through the cutting during that last half-hour from 07:40 to 08:10. From the comparison of traffic density in those first four half-hour periods of that morning's traffic from 06:10, it is clear that the headway (the gap) between trains in that particular half-hour between 07:40 to 08:10 was then the smallest so far that morning and, while within perfectly safe bounds if the signalling system was working properly, the gap was narrowing.

2.47 Sooner or later that morning, as Mr Bell rightly said, a driver was going to see what Mr McClymont actually saw at signal WF138 and was going to have to report it. When he did so he would have been holding an instinctive belief that the signal behind him would necessarily and inevitably have gone to red. That belief would have been totally and tragically wrong.

Chapter 3: The Accident

The Poole Train 3.1   The 06:14 Poole to Waterloo train was due to pass Clapham Junction "A" signal box at 08:10½ on Monday, 12 December 1988. That day it did not in fact start its journey from Poole which is why it had been referred to as the "Poole" train. The rolling stock for the train was positioned as usual overnight in the sidings at Bournemouth up the line from Poole. On that Sunday night there had been a derailment caused by vandalism on the line between Branksome and Poole. As a result next morning the stock could get no further towards Poole than Branksome to start the service. Thus, the 06:14 Poole service to Waterloo effectively originated from Branksome at 06:21. Appendix K.1 shows the route the train took.

3.2   Vandalism did not therefore affect the make-up of the Poole train. It ran that morning with the rolling stock which had always been intended to be used for the service, namely, twelve Mark I coaches made up of three units of four carriages. The first unit was an REP (Restaurant Electro-Pneumatic) whose leading coach was a "Driving Motor Standard". The second coach was of a type known as a "Trailer Buffet" and the third a "Trailer Brake First". The buffet was not in fact open that day due to lack of staff and its shutters were closed. The leading part of the third carriage consisted of a large luggage cage. The fourth coach was another "Driving Motor Standard".

3.3   The remaining eight coaches of the train consisted of two four-coach units, known as TCs (Trailer Composite). The guard, Mr Paul Hayward, was in his van in the seventh coach. Normally he would have travelled the length of the train checking tickets. However, his ticket clippers had dropped between the train and the platform at Winchester and he therefore took the decision to stay in his van from Winchester to London. To him the train was not crowded. He believed if it had been, he would have seen people walking past his position looking for seats further towards the front. Equally, he believed that if the train had been crowded he would have had people in his luggage van and there was nobody there. The train left Basingstoke at about 07:38 and the next scheduled stop was Waterloo.

3.4   Sitting in the guard's seat of the rear guard's van in the tenth coach was an off-duty train driver, Mr Robert Flood. As a matter of habit he was watching the EP gauge which registers the brake pressure on the electro-pneumatic brake and also the auto gauge which measures brake application on the auto-brake. Having driven steam trains and electric trains without speedometers he was a reasonable judge of train speeds.

3.5   In the third carriage from the front was Mr Ernest Staton who was now an ASLEF district secretary. As a former driver himself, he became very aware of other people's driving techniques and he thought it a "perfectly normal journey" with the driver driving the train in "a perfect way with no jolting or harsh stops".

The Basingstoke train   The 07:18 Basingstoke to Waterloo train was being driven by Mr McClymont with Mr Simon Fritsche as his guard. It too was a twelve-car train, comprising three VEP units (Vestibule Electro Pneumatic). The train was on time until Woking when it lost a couple of minutes at the station. Guard Fritsche was in the sixth coach from the front. Like Guard Hayward on the Poole train he was not moving about the train. He said he could not collect tickets because the train was too crowded, and therefore he did not leave his brake-van between Woking and the accident. There were about fifteen to twenty passengers standing in the cage of his brake-van. This was the normal situation, as the train was usually full.

3.7 Driver McClymont was doing just over 60 mph and running on all greens from Earlsfield. As he came round the bend at about 65 mph to 70 mph to WF138 it was showing green. Before WF138, the automatic warning system (AWS) in the cab gave him the correct sound and visual signals for a green aspect at WF138, namely a bell and a black disc, but in the 200 or so yards between the operation of the AWS and the signal, WF138 changed from green to red. He was about a coach-and-a-half (or 30 yards) away from WF138 when the signal changed. He could not stop before the signal but made an emergency brake application. He then realised he would stop short of the next signal WF47 where he wished to telephone to the signalman to report the incident in accordance with the Rule Book. He therefore eased off the braking to bring the train to a halt at signal WF47 which went from red to one yellow as he stopped. To achieve perfect compliance with the Rule Book it might be suggested that he should have completed his emergency stop without easing off the brake. That would be pedantic and unhelpful and Driver McClymont is not to be criticised for his actions on the day, nor was he criticised at the Investigation.

3.8 He got down from his train, tried a telephone nearby which was not working and then climbed up a short ladder to the brand new telephone on the wall behind the signal. He picked the telephone up and was answered "more or less immediately" by Signalman Cotter in Clapham "A" signal box, whom he told what had happened. Mr Cotter said (as, of course, was the case) that his indication in the Box was that nothing was wrong with the signal. Mr McClymont was a little aggrieved, said he was going to report the signal at Waterloo, replaced the handset, and turned to go back to his cab.

The Haslemere train 3.9 Meanwhile a third train, driven by Mr Joseph Alston, had completed its journey into Waterloo. It had originally been the 06:14 Farnham to Waterloo. It was an eight-car train consisting of two units of VEPs. Once its passengers had disembarked at Waterloo it became the 08:03 ECS (Empty Coaching Stock), the "empties" to Haslemere. Since there were no passengers, the guard, Mr Richard Baker, joined Mr Alston in the cab after leaving Waterloo. The train was proceeding out of London and had all greens to Clapham Junction which it went through at 50 mph. It was travelling on the Down Main line and had the Up Main line on its immediate right. Driver Alston saw the Basingstoke train standing at signal WF47 and saw the driver of that train, Mr McClymont, telephoning from the signal-post telephone.

The first impact 3.10 On the Poole train, Driver Flood, sitting in the rear guard's van, noticed that the speed of the train between Wimbledon and Earlsfield was about 60 mph and may have been slightly more. This was a perfectly proper speed for that section of track. More than 200 yards after Earlsfield the driver reduced speed to about 50 mph and Mr Flood noticed that this was done with a 20lb./sq.in. application on the EP brake. There was then a full emergency application of the brakes. The EP brake went round to 50 or slightly over and the auto-brake dropped to zero. The emergency braking was very harsh and Mr Staton, travelling in the third carriage from the front, described it as "violent".

3.11 Mr Flood put the speed at point of impact at about 35 mph, an estimate which the Court accepted. He said:

"I heard a muffled bang and then a lot of the slack had been taken up by all the coaches like a machine gun and at the same time another bang. Afterwards I realised this must have been where we hit the empties."

The Poole train had run straight into the back of the Basingstoke train and had veered off to the right in the path of the Haslemere empties.

The second impact

3.12 Driver Alston, in the cab of the Haslemere empties, had already noticed the Basingstoke train and its driver at signal WF47. As he was getting to the rear of the Basingstoke train he saw another train approaching on that train's line and realised it was on a collision course. The collision between the Poole and Basingstoke trains happened when the Haslemere "empties" were just coming level with the rear coach of the Basingstoke train.

3.13 Before the second impact in which the Poole train and the Haslemere empties actually collided, debris, including a brake handle, came through the right-hand windscreen of the Haslemere train. Driver Alston felt the train running rough as if it were off the lines and running on the ballast. The actual impact was with the second coach of the Haslemere train and as a result Driver Alston's first carriage became separated from the rest of the Haslemere train and derailed. He stopped level with signal WH165 (see Frontispiece).

The final positions

3.14 The impact of the front of the Poole train on the last carriage of the Basingstoke train caused that last carriage to be thrown up above the concrete wall on the side of the cutting, which is some 10ft high. It came to rest lying on the embankment above the wall on its nearside at an angle of about 45 degrees from the norm. That impact had derailed some of the coaches and pushed the whole Basingstoke train forward a distance of 10ft in fact, but thought at the time by Mr McClymont to be between 4ft to 6ft. The first two coaches of the Poole train had veered to the right where the Poole train had struck the Haslemere empties a glancing blow and continued on in the gap between the other two trains.

3.15 All three trains had now come to rest in the position in which they can be seen on the cover of the Report, in the aerial photographs at Figures 1 and 2 and in particular in the Frontispiece. The accident had happened.

The fourth train

3.16 There was, however, still another Waterloo-bound train running on the Up Main line towards the cutting and about to pass signal WF138. It was being driven by Driver Barry Pike. He had received no indication from any earlier signal than WF138 that he should stop. When he approached WF138, despite the presence on the track ahead of it not only of Driver McClymont's Basingstoke train but also Driver Rolls' Poole train, it was, nonetheless, still not showing a red but instead a single yellow aspect and failing to prohibit entry to those very lines. Driver Pike was about 250 yards from the signal when he was first able to see the danger ahead of him. Fortunately he was able to bring his train to a stop just 60 yards from the rear of the Poole train. Had there been a further collision, even at a very slow speed, the Poole train would have been pushed forward: the effect on those already injured in the first impact, many of whom were trapped in the wreckage, does not bear contemplating.

Chapter 4: The Immediate Aftermath

At Clapham Junction
4.1   As Driver McClymont put down the telephone at signal WF47, he heard the crash and saw his train physically pushed forward several feet. He at once picked up the handset again and told Signalman Cotter that his train had been rammed in the rear, that there would be casualties and that Mr Cotter should call up all the emergency services.

4.2   Mr Cotter immediately placed to red all the signals that he could control in the Clapham Junction area. WF47 was the last signal towards the accident site that could be turned to red. The automatic signals from WF138 to WF148 would only respond to the red at WF47 in the single yellow, double yellow, green sequence. Driver Pike's train could not therefore be stopped by Signalman Cotter's actions and had already passed the last Wimbledon controlled signals.

4.3   Mr Cotter then used the "block bell" system to send an emergency alarm signal, six bells, to the Wimbledon "A" and West London signal boxes. After that he spoke on the telephone to staff at both boxes to tell them why he had sent the alarm signal. On the personal radio he then contacted Mr Noorani, the Station Manager at Clapham Junction, to alert him to what had happened, and to ask him to call out the emergency services.

4.4   Until now, in the first minute or so after the accident the communications to and from the signal box had worked perfectly satisfactorily and as they were meant to: unfortunately that situation was not to continue for long.

Trackside
4.5   Out on the tracks Mr McClymont had climbed back into his cab, for a number of reasons, one of which was to collect a set of track-circuit clips. Their function in an emergency is to be clipped to both of the running rails on a section of track in order to put the signal behind that track immediately to red. They thus have exactly the same effect as that of the wheels of a train in shorting out the track circuit. While he was still there he spoke to a British Transport Police Inspector whom he knew, Michael Foster.

4.6   Inspector Foster had been a passenger in the fifth carriage of the Basingstoke train and had jumped down onto the tracks immediately after the accident. He had first run back to Battersea Rise Bridge to assess the situation, and then forward to the front of his train at signal WF47.

4.7   There Driver McClymont told him that he had already telephoned Clapham Junction "A" signal box, but Inspector Foster decided to make a second call to the Box because he realised that Driver McClymont could not have been fully aware of what had happened at the rear of his train.

4.8   He used a signal telephone on the Up Local line in the middle of the tracks. He told the signalman that it was the police speaking and said that it was a "major incident" which he enlarged by saying: "You have a major train crash. Summon the emergency services". He emphasised particularly the need for the fire brigade and ambulance services, because he had seen the severity of the collision. He also told Signalman Cotter of the involvement in the crash of the Haslemere train of which Mr Cotter had been previously unaware.

27

4.9   Inspector Foster then ran back towards the rear of the Basingstoke train and climbed up into the empty stock of the Haslemere train because his path was blocked. He was then able to see the full severity and horror of the accident. He ran back to the front of the train where he met Mr Derek Hayter, another member of BR staff who had been a passenger on the Basingstoke train.

The traction current

4.10   Between them, Inspector Foster and Mr Hayter placed a short-circuiting bar from Driver McClymont's cab on the line. This is a metal device with a long wooden handle which is applied both to the conductor rail carrying the traction current and to one of the running rails. Its function is to short out the traction current and make the track safe to walk upon. Because there was no arcing when they used the short-circuiting bar Mr Foster and Mr Hayter concluded that the current was off. In fact they were correct: the traction current was off and had gone off at the time of the collision. However, this important information was still not generally known for some time. Indeed it was not until 08:35 that BR actually answered an enquiry by the Fire Brigade by telling them that the current was off and that "it had been turned off at approximately 08:20". This failure to establish that the traction current was definitely off, and to give that information to the emergency services is an aspect of the matter to which I shall return later.

Control of the traction current

4.11   The electrical current which provides the power to drive British Rail Southern Region's electric trains is taken from the national grid. It is known as the "HT" which stands for "High Tension" and is sometimes also described as the "33 KV" because the supply voltage is 33,000v. At this stage the current is Alternating Current (AC), but it is fed to sub-stations and is then rectified to 660 volts Direct Current (DC). This provides the power to the traction circuit and the running rails which is carried along the third rail, the conductor rail. The track signals current is carried between the two running rails. It was 110 volts 50 cycle AC but was in the process of being changed as part of the resignalling to a higher, audio frequency. (See Appendix F).

4.12   The traction current is controlled from the Raynes Park Electrical Control Room where Mr Ronald Reeves was working that morning. At 08:10 he heard the selectors on his diagram start to move. The alarm bell then rang and flashing lights appeared on his board for all the tracks on the Up and Down main lines at Clapham and at Earlsfield, followed shortly after by the Windsor section. He found that the current had tripped at the National Grid supply and at Point Pleasant Sub-Station. He thought this unusual and when the grid feeder went out he concluded that there had been a derailment by the cross-over on the Up Passenger Loop at Clapham Junction. In that he was extremely perceptive, and only a few hundred yards out.

4.13   His first reaction was to get the High Tension electricity supply back to normal so that trains could continue to run and be safely signalled on the Windsor side. When that was done he proceeded to create neutral electrical sections around the Clapham and Earlsfield lines to isolate the area in question so that no traction current could flow through it, either directly or as a result of a train spanning the gap between isolated and live tracks. He had done all that work by 08:12 and his next task was to try to contact others to tell them what he had done. To do that he had to rely on the communications equipment just as had Signalman Cotter at Clapham "A".

4.14   One of Mr Reeves's two internal telephones had been out of service since the previous Friday. He used the other internal telephone to try to contact Clapham "A" signal box which was engaged. He tried to contact Wimbledon "A" signal box and was unable to contact them for the same reason. He tried to get Waterloo traffic control on the direct line, but failed. In his own words: "It was just a blank".

4.15 The first time he was able to speak to anyone away from Raynes Park was at 08:17 when he was telephoned by Signalman Spencer from the Wimbledon "A" signal box. Signalman Spencer had meanwhile had his own communications problems. Before this call Mr Spencer had had a delay of about one minute in trying to talk to Waterloo Control on the direct line telephone. Only then was he able to advise them of the incident and ask them to summon the emergency services. It was then he tried on the direct telephone to get through to Raynes Park Electrical Control. This produced no response despite several attempts and so he used a dialling telephone and managed to get through to Mr Reeves after about a further 30 seconds.

4.16 Mr Reeves told Mr Spencer that the current was off between Queens Road and Durnsford Road. Mr Spencer in turn told Mr Reeves that there was a collision and derailment on the country side of Clapham Junction station. This confirmed what Mr Reeves had suspected. Mr Reeves had commendably assessed the situation correctly and had, on his own initiative, taken out the traction current from all four lines in the cutting, including the Up and Down Local, rather than merely the two Main lines which had tripped out. In this he said he was going a little bit further than the Rule Book because, as he explained, it looked a serious situation to him and he was taking every course of action he could.

4.17 Instructions for electrical control operators suggests that in the event of circuit breakers opening, they should attempt, at regular intervals of a set number of minutes, to close the breakers and therefore restore current. It is clear that in the event of an accident the current should remain off to ensure the safety of passengers, staff and rescue workers. If a short-circuiting bar is in place at the scene of an accident, this will prevent the electrical control operator from restoring current to the track. However, short-circuiting bars in use on Southern Region could be relatively easily dislodged and would, therefore, not prevent the electrical control operator from restoring current should he attempt to do so. A short-circuiting bar that could be applied and then clamped into place would reduce the risk of this eventuality.

The Wimbledon controlled signals

4.18 Mr Spencer at Wimbledon "A" signal box had been able to telephone Mr Reeves at Raynes Park Electrical Control because he had been alerted to what had happened by the driver of the Haslemere empties. Driver Alston's now disconnected first carriage had stopped level with signal WH165 and he therefore rang from the signal-post telephone. Just as all the signals whose wiring runs to Clapham Junction "A" signal box bore the prefix WF, so those wired through to Wimbledon "A" have the prefix WH. Thus, the telephone at signal WH165 went through to Wimbledon "A", not Clapham Junction "A". Mr Spencer's evidence was that Mr Alston told him very calmly that there had been a derailment but did not mention that there had been a major collision. Mr Alston asked Mr Spencer to place all signals at danger, to summon emergency services and to arrange for the traction current to be switched off. Mr Spencer first placed to danger all signals which he could control from Wimbledon on the Up Main Through and Up Local lines. This must have been at or about the same time that Mr Cotter at Clapham Junction "A" was dealing similarly with his controlled signals. Again like Mr Cotter, Mr Spencer had no means of putting the automatic signals to red.

4.19 The controlled signal furthest from him on the Up Main line and therefore the nearest to the accident was WH56 which was a few hundred yards to the country side of Earlsfield station. Signalman Spencer's action was sufficient to, and did, stop any train which had not so far reached the relevant signal. But it was not sufficient to stop any train on the Up Main line which had already passed WH56, the last of those Wimbledon controlled signals.

4.20 Thus, although the current was in fact already off on that stretch of track and although Signalman Spencer had put signal WH56 to red, neither of those factors stopped the onward progress on the Up Main line of the fourth train driven by Driver Pike which was closely involved in the accident but not the subject of any impact. This train was the 06:53 Waterloo to Waterloo service which travels in a loop out along the Windsor lines and comes back to Waterloo via Hounslow, Staines and Weybridge. It was an eight-car train and its last scheduled stop was at Surbiton.

4.21 As it stood there on the Up Local line, the Poole train passed by on the Up Main line. Driver Pike then followed the Poole train out of the station and crossed onto the Up Main line, behind the Poole train. He had left Surbiton station on yellow signals but by the time he got to New Malden he was on green signals. He went on through Wimbledon and approached Earlsfield at something between 65 and 70 mph. Signal WH70 at Wimbledon had been green, so had WH60, as was WH56.

4.22 The first of the Clapham Junction area signals was WF152 just before Earlsfield. It is an automatic signal and as we have seen could not be controlled from the signal box. It had not therefore been turned to red by Mr Cotter's actions; it, too, was showing a green aspect. As he approached signal WF152, Driver Pike was able to see the two next signals ahead of him, WF148 and WF142, both also automatic signals. WF152 and WF148 were showing green and WF142 was showing two yellows. He passed by signal WF152 at green and shortly after that he lost traction current. In his own words: "The juice went off".

4.23 Though it is now obvious that the loss of current was caused by the accident, there was nothing to tell Driver Pike this. His initial thought was that he had an electrical fault on his train, rather than on the track, because he had noticed slight arcing under his cab on the nearside. Thinking that this was the problem he decided to try to coast as far as possible to Clapham Junction station because at least there, trains would be able to get past him. He believed that the current might come back at any moment and had been doing about 65 mph when he lost the current.

4.24 He coasted past WF148 at green, WF142 at two yellows and approached WF138. Because of its position he could not see it as early as he could some of the previous signals. His evidence was that you could not see beyond signal WF138 until you were 250 yards from it. When he was first able to see beyond the signal and was travelling at about 60 mph, perhaps a little less, he suddenly saw ahead of him the last two or three coaches of the Poole train on the same line. The distance between his cab and the rear of the Poole train he put at 500 to 600 yards and in his own words:

> "I immediately applied the emergency braking and just kept my fingers crossed. That is all I could do."

4.25 His whole train passed WF138 before it came to its emergency stop. He estimated he was then only about 20 yards from the back of the Poole train. In fact the distance when measured was 187 feet, or just about the length of three carriages. The yellow front of his train can be seen behind the Poole train in the cover picture and in Figure 3. This train and its shadow are just visible at the bottom of the Frontispiece. The guard of the Haslemere train, Mr Richard Baker, had been at the back of the Poole train in order to get more track circuit clips and detonators and had seen Mr Pike's train "coming round the corner". Once he stopped, Mr Pike wanted to get the back of his train protected and spoke to his guard Mr Evans on the "loudaphone" link between them and asked him to go back to WF138 to see what aspect it was showing and to protect the train.

4.26 Guard Evans went back to WF138 which was still showing one yellow. At a nearby signal on the Up Local line, the Chessington to Waterloo train was stopped. Guard Evans collected some detonators and track circuit clips from the driver of that train and walked back towards WF142 laying detonators as he went, in order to protect the rear of his train because he "could not take for granted that signal WF142 was at red". There was, of course, no fault at WF142 and so it was indeed at red; Mr Evans therefore returned to WF138 at about 08:36, and waited there. Sometime later he saw a group of S&T personnel looking at the signal and the location cases at the trackside.

4.27 In addition to the train protection duties carried out by Guards Baker and Evans, all the guards attempted to give information to assist passengers but this could only be done by word of mouth repeatedly to individual groups of people. Public address systems on the passenger trains would clearly have been of benefit in informing passengers of what had happened and instructing them to remain in the train until it had been confirmed that traction current had been switched off.

4.28 Driver Pike used the signal-post telephone at WF138 to contact the Clapham Junction signalman. He told him which train he was, that he had passed signal WF138 at one yellow, and that there was a train standing in front of him. Mr Cotter's response was that WF138 was an automatic signal and should be showing a red aspect, to which Driver Pike replied:

"Red aspect be damned. There are three trains standing in front of it, and it is still showing one yellow."

Mr Cotter told Mr Pike that there had been a major incident and expressed surprise at the aspect the signal was showing. He told Mr Pike to stay where he was.

4.29 At that stage Signalman Cotter still did not know whether or not the electric traction current had been turned off. Neither he, nor his colleague Mr Coates in Clapham Junction "A" signal box, had been able to get through to Mr Reeves at Raynes Park Electrical Control by using the normal telephone links and eventually they had to go through the traffic controller at Waterloo in order to make the contact. He thought the delay must have been nearly ten minutes.

4.30 It was Mr Coates who actually tried to contact Electrical Control at Raynes Park. At this time there was no direct line from Clapham Junction "A" to Raynes Park Electrical Control Room and so he tried to use an ordinary telephone. (As a result of the accident a direct line has now been installed). Each time he tried there was silence and then a continual tone indicating number unobtainable. He then tried to make a British Telecom call from the same telephone by pressing 19 first. He met with the same continual tone each time he tried.

4.31 After about ten minutes he decided to use the direct line to Traffic Control at Waterloo. He told them of the major incident and that he was unable to get hold of Electrical Control and asked the Traffic Controller to get the Electrical Controller to ring him. So it was that one or two minutes later contact was made when the Electrical Controller, Mr Reeves, rang him and confirmed that the traction current was off on all four lines. Mr Coates had started this attempt to get Raynes Park much earlier, immediately after being informed of the accident and at the very same time as Mr Cotter in the same signal box was first talking to Mr Noorani the Station Manager on the personal radio.

4.32 Just after 08:10 Mr Noorani was in a subway at Clapham Junction when Mr Cotter first put out the call, telling those listening that there had been a major accident and that emergency services would be required. Mr Noorani immediately used the radio to direct the Station Control Room on platform 13 to call the emergency services. He then went up to the station platform to speak further with Mr Cotter on the radio. Mr Noorani thought that Mr Cotter told him that there was a rear end collision in the cutting on the approach to the station, but his memory of this part of the morning was " .. a little bit hazy". He then contacted Supervisor Cole to get the station car out to go to the site with members of the British Transport Police.

4.33 By the time he got to the scene of the accident at about 08:25 the emergency services were already active and he made his presence known to a senior fire officer on top of the wreckage. He spoke on the radio telephone to Traffic Control at Waterloo describing the condition and location of the various trains and advising that heavy lifting gear would be required. He went to signal WF138 and saw it was still showing single yellow. He then spoke to Wimbledon "A" signal box to find out what trains were immobilised elsewhere by the accident.

The traction current again

4.34 As to whether or not he knew at this stage that the traction current had been switched off, Mr Noorani was both completely frank and understandably vague. He recollected that before he had left Clapham Junction he had seen a Shepperton train at platform 11 showing only emergency lighting. He said that with hindsight all he could say was that he believed at the time he had spoken to the signalman about the current, but in fact he had not. He believed his memory of that section of events was not good by reason of the trauma of the actual incident.

4.35 Under paragraph 2.3.(a)(ii) of BR Southern Region's booklet "Accident Procedure", it was the duty of the Area Manager or his qualified deputy (and thus Mr Noorani at this time) to proceed to the site immediately and on arrival:

> ". . . . check that traction current has been switched off and that Electrical Control is aware of incident."

Mr Noorani did not, in fact, take these two steps. However, that did not in the circumstances of this accident exacerbate the situation. Nonetheless, this failure to ensure that the traction current had been switched off and that Electrical Control was aware of the incident is a matter I shall have to refer to later in the context of this and also of the Purley accident.

4.36 Mr Noorani organised a diesel train from Wimbledon to try to remove passengers from the site and also tried to contact the Area Manager's Office at Waterloo on the radio telephone but got no answer. He was joined at the scene by more senior BR officials who took over control from him. Thereafter he remained at the scene until about 10 p.m. dealing with the positioning of the breakdown vehicles and the removal of the wrecked carriages.

4.37 The immediate aftermath so far as British Rail employees was over, but work had to go on to clear the line and to investigate the accident. Such matters fall to be considered in Chapter 6. However, all the while that the events described in this Chapter were taking place, the Emergency Services were attending to their duties in relation to the extrication and movement away from the site of the dead, the injured, the distressed and the uninjured who had been involved in the accident.

Chapter 5: The response of the emergency services

The first calls

5.1   The tremendous noise made by the crash and the sight of dust rising from the cutting brought instant reaction from nearby members of the public. Householders and passers by hurriedly dialled 999: others rushed towards the scene to see if they could help. A passing AA driver used his radio to contact the emergency services. It was therefore partly by reason of the heavily populated and busy nature of the area surrounding the accident that members of the public got through to the emergency services before BR. However there were additional reasons for BR calls being later in time which had more to do with the routes chosen by BR staff for the passing on of their information.

5.2   At Clapham Junction "A" signal box, once Signalman Cotter had been told of the accident by Driver McClymont on the signal post telephone, the signalman used his radio to contact Mr Noorani, the Station Manager, to inform him what had happened. Mr Noorani then used that radio to contact the Station Control Room to tell them to call out the emergency services. That led in turn to a call to Waterloo Control and from there the emergency services were contacted by BR at 08:15. That 08:15 call was the fifth in the chain from Driver McClymont and five minutes had passed before the BR message got through.

5.3   In just the same way Signalman Spencer at the Wimbledon signal box, had first to digest the information from Driver Alston of the Haslemere train and to replace six controlled signals to danger before dealing with the request for the attendance of the emergency services. There is a BR procedure for contacting a BR emergency operator by dialling 19. Like Mr Cotter at Clapham Junction, Mr Spencer elected not to use that BR procedure. He said that he knew from experience that precise and detailed information would be required which he did not consider he had and so he decided to use his direct line to Waterloo Control. He did not have to dial but he had to wait for probably a minute before he was answered and was able to advise them of the incident and ask them to summon the emergency services.

5.4   It was by then probably three minutes or more after the accident had happened. In relation to the Clapham Junction accident calls from members of the public were almost bound to have got through to the emergency services before any from BR and thus no delay in fact occurred. An accident in a rural, rather than an urban, area would be likely to be a different matter, however, and in that case avoidable delay could result from such over-complicated procedure.

The first call to the Fire Brigade   5.5   It was in this way that the London Fire and Civil Defence Authority (hereafter called the London Fire Brigade or LFB) were alerted to the accident at 08:13 by a call from a member of the public, but had received their first call from British Rail Waterloo Control at 08:20.

The first call to the London Ambulance Service   5.6   The London Ambulance Service (hereafter LAS) had its first call from a member of the public at 08:16. The emergency services have a duty to alert each other once they have such a call. Six minutes later at 08:22 the LAS records show a call from the London Fire Brigade to "make ambulances 8 – medical team required". The LAS records do not tally with the records of the London

Fire Brigade which have the two requests made in two separate calls timed at 08:19 and 08:20. Such disparities are inevitable and understandable when the prime aim must be to get the emergency vehicles to the site. Attention to accurate paper work can naturally come lower in the list of priorities.

5.7   Some of the differences in timing that I heard in evidence were of little importance and need not be further examined. However, some of the time intervals between the receipt of a message and the passing on of that message have a greater importance, and call for further consideration. As an illustration of a significant delay, even accepting the earlier LFB timing of 08:19 for their first call to the LAS, that still leaves a gap of six minutes between the LFB's receipt of the information that an accident had happened, and the passing on by them of that information to the LAS.

5.8   In a detailed examination of all the circumstances surrounding the accident, it would be surprising if mistakes and failures of communication of one kind or another did not emerge, some of them with significant effects. Where such matters assume importance, in that there are clear lessons for the future, then those mistakes must be considered later in this Chapter.

The first call to the Police   5.9   The first notification to the police that an accident had happened came from Mr Brill, the licensee of the Roundhouse Public House. He did not, in fact, make a 999 call but telephoned direct to Battersea Police Station. The controller there immediately put out the message on personal radio to local units and passed the information on to Scotland Yard. It was thus that local units were quickly present at the scene. They were in fact already on their way to the accident when they heard the contents of the first 999 message received at New Scotland Yard at 08:12 being relayed from there by radio telephone.

5.10   That first message to come in on the 999 system was a call from Miss Lisbet Tolson who had been on a 77 bus when she heard the sound of the crash and saw that there had been an accident. She immediately jumped off the bus and used the telephone box on the corner of Spencer Park to alert Scotland Yard. A passing motorist, Mr Michael Matthews, had heard what he thought was an explosion and had seen what seemed to be smoke coming from the railway embankment. Before abandoning his car and going down the embankment to assist passengers he telephoned 999 from his car-phone and was put through to Scotland Yard at 08:13.

5.11   In the same minute, Scotland Yard was receiving a report of the train crash from the London Fire Brigade and two minutes later at 08:15 there came a similar report from British Transport Police in a radio call from Waterloo. This was passing on a message from a supervisor at Clapham Junction which was presumably the result of Mr Noorani's instructions to the Station Control Room.

5.12   The pattern of emergency calls by members of the public to specific emergency services whether fire, police or ambulance, preceding calls from BR can readily be seen. So can the pattern of those individual emergency services seeking to alert each other. The detail of what went right and what went wrong must come later.

5.13   In the meantime, however, it is right to point out that all the evidence called before me indicated that the rescue operation carried out by the emergency services was done in an exemplary manner. It was effected with total cooperation between those services. There was in the main speed and efficiency in the organisation of the response. There was total skill and dedicated devotion to duty at the trackside in difficult and dangerous circumstances. There was sustained concentration directed towards the best interests of the members of the public for whose assistance the emergency services exist.

5.14 The cooperation between the public and the emergency services was illustrated by the evidence of one of the first to the scene, Mr George Cannon, a schoolmaster at Emanuel School. He was in the Staff Room when he heard "a tremendous bang". He ran out and down to the bridge. He jumped over the edge of the parapet and worked his way back down the side of the embankment until he was able to climb into the third carriage of the Poole train. This was the coach with a large luggage cage; passengers in the coach had received serious injuries and some were trapped in the wreckage. He was there for some time assisting passengers. It seemed to him that "the rescue services" as he called them were there within about three minutes. He said:

"I thought they were marvellous. They seemed to restore order, provide help. The whole organisation seemed to be very smooth and efficient."

5.15 I turn now to examine the scene of the accident and the circumstances which helped and those that hindered the rescue operation.

The scene

5.16 There were problems in getting access to the site. There were tall metal railings, a steep wooded embankment followed by a 10 foot high concrete wall to be negotiated before it was possible to get down to the track. The first three carriages of the Poole train had suffered enormous damage. The first carriage had totally collapsed. The second carriage, the buffet car, had been devastated more particularly upon its left near-side. The close proximity of all three trains on the track made for great difficulty. So did the position of the last coach of the Basingstoke train which had been thrown by the impact above the concrete wall and onto the embankment. It was lying on its left near-side at an extreme angle, with its offside doors open to the sky. Figures 1 and 2 show the difficulties the rescuers had to face.

5.17 It was such difficulties that the emergency services had to face in coming to the aid of almost 1,500 passengers estimated to have been on the Poole and Basingstoke trains. Many passengers were trapped both within and underneath the wreckage. Great care had to be taken to ensure that moving one piece of wreckage or releasing one casualty did not cause greater pain or danger to those still trapped. The rescue workers in carrying out their task of extricating passengers from the wreckage in the face of all those constraints were taking on a task which was for them difficult, delicate and dangerous.

5.18 Rescue operations can sometimes be badly hampered by the weather, the time of day, and vehicular access, but this at least was not the case for access in the Clapham Junction accident. It was a bright, clear December morning with no problems of visibility. The accident was in a highly populated urban area, where the reporting to the emergency services could be expected to be almost instantaneous. The accident happened about ten minutes after 08:00, a time when ambulance crews had just arrived at their base stations and had not yet been committed to their normal duties. Road access to the site was not difficult and the green triangle of Spencer Park was readily available to accommodate the establishment of the control units and equipment stores for all the services. The Local Authority had a particularly efficient contingency plan in order to deal with major emergencies.

The scene

5.19 The Court heard many tributes to the courage, dedication and professionalism of all the emergency services. Having heard the evidence and seen videos of their work at the scene, I wish to endorse the deep sense of appreciation which ran throughout the evidence of passengers on the trains for the outstanding work of the men and women who did so much to ensure a safe, swift and successful operation. They include, not only members of the emergency services, but all those other people who provided support, direct or indirect. I would especially mention the pupils and teachers of Emanuel School who helped passengers from the scene in the first few moments of the incident.

The school quickly provided a casualty centre for the injured. There was a universal effort to help in this disaster from such people as the staff of the Roundhouse public house, the Salvation Army, local businesses who offered the use of their premises and their telephones and the many members of the public who rushed to help in any way they could. A deep debt of gratitude is owed to them all.

5.20 I turn now to the roles of each of the emergency services and the local authority in turn and in no order of priority. Most of these services will be familiar to the reader, but this chapter must include appropriate appreciation of the part played by a less familiar name, that of BASICS, the British Association for Immediate Care. This is a group mainly consisting of General Practitioners who have attended many tragic incidents and who provided invaluable medical care on site at the accident.

The role of the London Fire Brigade

5.21 The London Fire Brigade received its first call at 08:13 from a member of the public informing them of a train crash, just prior to Clapham Junction at Spencer Park. The message was clear and precise. Within four minutes the first fire appliance had arrived at the scene, followed almost immediately by the second, carrying Temporary Station Officer Mills who took charge of the incident. As he crossed the railway bridge before Spencer Park, he was able to look down on the accident and immediately sent a request that the number of pumping appliances attending the scene should be increased to eight.

5.22 He then ordered his crews to use short extension ladders to get to the scene and authorised the use of all first-aid kits. He sent further messages at 08:19 and 08:20 requesting the attendance of eight ambulances and a surgical unit. He climbed down the embankment to assess the situation and directed fire brigade, ambulance crews, and police as they arrived. He decided to allow those passengers around him who could walk unaided to leave the train. He saw more and more injured passengers and then became aware of the many fatalities. The full extent of the incident was now clear and thus his message declaring a "MAJOR INCIDENT" was sent at 08:27.

5.23 This message should have ensured that from that moment all emergency services and the designated and supporting hospitals put into immediate effect their major incident plans. I shall consider later in this chapter how this message and the earlier 08:20 message requesting a surgical unit were actioned. In each case the totally accurate, vitally important, speedily despatched information from a trained officer at the scene was subjected to unacceptable delays in the communications system.

5.24 TSO Mills then went on to request further emergency rescue tenders. These included the fire brigade's specialist cutting and lifting equipment. He detailed a crew to remove a section of the railings to give better access. Steady progress was being made in de-training the more mobile passengers trapped by the wreckage. TSO Mills also assisted with stretcher handling before he made contact with senior officers.

5.25 Station Officer Beauchamp, who had been ordered to the scene following TSO Mills' first call requesting increased attendance, arrived at 08:28. He had heard on his way the message declaring a major incident. Both officers were convinced, rightly as it turned out, that the traction current had been switched off and that there would be no danger to passengers.

5.26 SO Beauchamp sent a message at 08:32 requesting confirmation from BR that this was in fact the case. Confirmation was given at 08:35 in a message in which it was stated by BR, interestingly but erroneously that the current was "turned off at approximately 08:20 hours". The current had not been turned off, it had gone off by reason of and at the time of the accident at 08:10. Normal procedure where it was not known definitely that the traction current was off would have been to establish "look-outs" to warn rescue workers of any approaching train but this was not done. This procedure was put into effect at the Purley accident until it was confirmed very much later that traction current was off. This was the sole omission in the LFB handling of accident procedure at the initial command of the incident. It is to TSO Mills's credit that he achieved so much in his 10-minute period of command.

5.27 Senior officers arrived shortly after SO Beauchamp. Deputy Assistant Chief Officer Ash arrived at 08:44 and Assistant Chief Officer McMillan at 08:47. DACO Ash ensured that all three emergency services set up their forward control vehicles in close proximity on Spencer Park and that liaison was established between them (see Frontispiece, Figures 1 and 2 and Appendix K.4). On ACO McMillan's arrival, he was briefed by DACO Ash. ACO McMillan assumed command of the whole incident leaving DACO Ash in control of the trackside. Mr McMillan's role was to ensure that there were enough human and material resources on site and to liaise with the other emergency services and media. He kept in touch with the operation on site by making regular visits to the trackside.

5.28 DACO Ash's role at the trackside was to establish a forward command post at the foot of access "A" and to detail his officers to liaise with the medical services to establish the number and location of casualties. Priorities for their removal could then be determined. Two other access points, "B" and "C", were opened up: Local Authority workers and heavy equipment assisted in this operation. Officers were then instructed to set up an equipment pool at the top of access "A"; to establish field telephones and radio communication links with the forward control unit; and to maintain from the forward command post a list of all personnel and equipment arriving on site.

5.29 The rescue operation continued with particular concentration on the passengers trapped in the wreckage. Five passengers were trapped for a substantial length of time and the full range of the fire brigade's cutting equipment was used to free them. After nearly five hours a message was sent at 13:04 to confirm that the last live casualty had been removed from the scene. The last body was removed from the wreckage at 15:40.

The role of the London Ambulance Service

5.30 The LAS role in such an emergency is to ensure that there is sufficient manpower and equipment to care for and evacuate injured and trapped passengers. They have also to ensure that casualties can be speedily conveyed to hospital for treatment. It is their task too to alert the designated and supporting hospitals who will care for the injured in accordance with the Major Incident Procedure of the London Emergency Services Liaison Panel.

5.31 LAS staff are trained in advanced first-aid and some members (approximately 30%) have received extended training in intubation and infusion. Once they have completed that extended training, they become what is known as "Millar Trained" and must wear an appropriate badge so that their special skills are readily identifiable in emergencies. Not all staff who had that training were wearing the appropriate badges at the site, and this was unfortunate.

5.32 The scale of the accident meant that extra equipment had to be called for at an early stage. That equipment included extra stretchers, blankets, oxygen, Entonox (an analgesic gas for pain killing purposes), and Haemaccel (a fluid given to stabilise patients where necessary).

5.33 The first ambulance arrived on the scene at 08:21 five minutes after the first emergency call to LAS. The second ambulance arrived at 08:26 and by 08:36 twelve ambulances had been despatched to the scene.

5.34 Mr Chambers, Assistant Chief Ambulance Officer with the London Ambulance Service, arrived at the scene at 08:32 and assumed the role of Ambulance Incident Officer. Mr Chambers was briefed by his junior officers. Their first estimate of casualties ran into hundreds and Mr Chambers' first action was to declare a "Major Incident". This message was timed at 08:36, some 9 minutes after TSO Mills of the London Fire Brigade had sent a message: "This is a Major Incident , Implement Major Incident Procedure". It follows that Mr Chambers cannot have been informed that the "Major Incident" procedure had already been set in motion.

5.35 There is thus already a nine-minute gap between 08:27 and 08:36 when no action was taken under the Major Incident Procedure to alert designated and supporting hospitals, to prepare for the receipt of casualties nor to send for a medical team. This action is the responsibility of Central Ambulance Control. It goes without saying that it is vital that such steps are taken with the utmost speed. We shall see that there were, in fact, further delays.

5.36 Meanwhile, Mr Chambers established contact with the other emergency services and with the cooperation of the police ensured that ambulance service vehicles could have ready access to and exit from the scene. With the number of casualties now becoming apparent, Mr Chambers summoned additional equipment and established three equipment pools at the top of each access point to the site. This was to allow ambulances to be re-equipped as they left for the hospitals.

5.37 Mr Chambers requested further manpower from LAS training centres so that trainees could help with stretcher bearing, which posed a particular problem. The Court heard of some injured Poole passengers being passed through the Basingstoke train and being carried up the rather steep embankment. Photographs, such as that on the cover and Figures 1 and 2 illustrate the difficulties. The Training Centre was also able to supply instructors with extended training, providing essential help to the mobile medical teams on the track-side.

5.38 The forward control vehicle arrived at 08:33, only one minute after Mr Chambers, and was therefore available as a centre from which he could command the ambulance operation. In total 67 vehicles were committed to the scene during the incident. Such extensive cover was possible because ambulance crews had only just come on duty at 08:00 a.m. and few, if any, had left their station to carry out their normal duties. Equally 6 ambulances, 1 control unit and 3 Training School vehicles were provided to assist by the neighbouring Surrey Ambulance Service.

The role of the Metropolitan Police

5.39 The first call to any emergency service about the train accident was, as we have seen, made at 08:10 to Battersea police station and was not a 999 call. This call was immediately relayed to local units who started to arrive at the scene at 08:17. Under Inspector David George, initial traffic diversions were established to allow the fire engines and ambulances immediate access to the rendezvous point at Spencer Park. The first officers on the scene helped to rescue passengers from the wreckage and escorted walking wounded and the uninjured to Emanuel School. As more fire brigade and ambulance crews arrived the police were involved in stretcher bearing and cordon control.

5.40 The first call to Scotland Yard through the 999 system at 08:12 was immediately passed on through Scotland Yard's Control Centre. Metropolitan Police Officers' duties were then directed to:

– traffic control

– supervision of the casualty centre at Emanuel School

– supervision of the casualty collection point at Spencer Park

– establishing hospital liaison teams of officers to record details of casualties arriving at the hospitals

– setting up and control of the temporary mortuary

– establishing the casualty bureau.

5.41 The police were therefore responsible for ensuring that a proper record was maintained of all those injured and those who died in the accident. The first priority in the rescue operation was, of course, to rescue the trapped and injured. At the casualty centres at Spencer Park, Emanuel School and the Roundhouse public house, the walking wounded were cared for and their names and addresses taken. Police officers at the hospitals took details of those arriving and the severity of their injuries. A temporary mortuary was established at an early stage and details and descriptions of the deceased recorded.

5.42 All this information was being passed to the casualty bureau at New Scotland Yard which had opened shortly after 09:30. The decision had been taken at 08:29 to open the casualty bureau; within the hour police officers were drafted in to be briefed on the incident and on their work in manning the bureau's 20 telephone lines.

The Metropolitan Police Casualty Bureau

5.43 The casualty bureau's function is to match the information from the scene and the information received from telephone enquiries: the purpose is to collate that information to establish as quickly as possible a list of those injured and those who have died so that friends and relatives can be informed with the minimum delay.

5.44 In the early stages of an incident details of time, place and the trains involved may be sketchy. The number of people anxious for news will be high. The casualty bureau, by careful questioning, can reassure many people that their relative or friend could not have been involved.

5.45 For others, in the initial stages, all that can be done is for the operator to take details and a description. Only when information comes back from the scene and from the hospitals and is matched up with a particular inquiry can the police inform the caller whether their friend or relative has been involved and, if so, to what extent. The police have to strike a balance between delay in informing callers and ensuring that the information is accurate. It is a very delicate balance. In the Clapham Junction accident there were four people on one train with the same name, two in one carriage: three survived and one did not. There were two passengers with the same first and surname: both survived.

5.46 If the person involved has suffered only very slight injuries, information is passed to the caller by telephone. However, if the news is worse, the casualty bureau contact the local police station and an officer will visit the relative or friend identifying the hospital they will be able to visit. In the saddest eventuality, they will seek their agreement to identify the deceased.

5.47 It goes without saying that identification is a very distressing task. The police at Lavender Hill Police Station made every effort to attempt to relieve that distress. Most of the bereaved were asked only to identify jewellery or clothing. Very many of the statements of the bereaved record grateful tributes to the police for their sensitive and tactful approach at such a distressing time. I can only repeat and underline those tributes here.

5.48 Since the operators in the casualty bureau have to assess the likelihood of any particular individual being on the trains involved in the collision, that process takes time. Each call takes 4½ to 5 minutes on average to complete. The casualty bureau received about 8,000 calls in its first 30 hours of operation, including those from members of the public hospitals and other agencies. There was no queuing system and a caller who got an engaged signal would have had to redial and take his chance. That too, is a matter which needs looking at and will be dealt with in my recommendations.

5.49 The police are considering the introduction of a queuing facility. I know that under the auspices of the Association of Chief Police Officers (ACPO), the Bedfordshire Constabulary are also conducting a trial operation, known as Comtest, to double the number of lines available and to test whether the 40 operators need necessarily be in the one place.

5.50 The Court heard evidence of a number of passengers' relatives having difficulty in contacting the emergency services number which was constantly engaged. Just before the casualty bureau was opened at 09:30 the media obtained the telephone number being used by the police at Emanuel School. This number was published as the number to contact for casualty enquiries. As a result the telephone system at the school was overwhelmed, the number was constantly engaged and when callers did get through, they were frustrated to find that no information was available. It took about two hours to correct this error. This must have been the origin of many of those complaints and it clearly hampered police efforts at the scene.

The Metropolitan Police Helicopter

5.51 The Metropolitan Police Force offered the use of its helicopter to BASICS to convey their doctors to the scene. This proved to be invaluable in ensuring that more medical teams arrived promptly at the site. At 08:43 the police helicopter made an initial reconnaissance of the scene. From there it went to a rendezvous point with the BASICS doctors on the M11 in Essex and took off at 09:08 depositing them at Wandsworth Common at 09:14. Those BASICS doctors were therefore on the scene at exactly the same minute that the Medical Incident Officer, Mr Calvert, arrived. They had come from their practices in Essex. He had come from the designated hospital two miles away. The fault was not his, but that of the communications systems.

5.52 By 09:40 the helicopter had made another round trip to bring in a second team of BASICS doctors.

The role of the British Transport Police

5.53 Three British Transport police officers, Assistant Chief Constable Buckle, Inspector Foster and Inspector Innes, were travelling in the fourth carriage of the Basingstoke train when the collision occurred. None of them was hurt. Some of Inspector Foster's evidence to the Investigation has already been summarised in Chapter 4.

5.54 It was agreed with the Metropolitan Police that BTP's role was one of command and coordination. ACC McGregor assumed the role of coordinator of the incident on his arrival at 09:45. (He had been on a train out of Paddington and had had to get to the site from Reading). BTP was to be responsible for the police investigation into the cause of the accident, for preparing reports for the Coroner and the Railway Inspectorate and, as it turned out, for this Investigation.

5.55 I visited the British Transport Police incident room on 9 January 1989 and saw the detailed and difficult work which was necessary in order to seek to identify where passengers had been sitting or standing at the time of the accident. I am deeply grateful to Superintendent Stoppani, to Detective Chief Inspector Taylor and to the rest of their team in the Incident Room for that work and for all their help to the Court in this Investigation.

The role of BASICS

5.56 The British Association for Immediate Care is a medical charitable association which provides skilled medical assistance at the site of an incident and during transport to hospital. These doctors are skilled in a wide range of resuscitation techniques and work alongside the statutory emergency services in planning and rehearsing disaster procedures. BASICS was set up over ten years ago and initially received a pump-priming grant from Government to allow the organisation to get off the ground. The grant has now expired and BASICS is funded principally by charitable donation.

5.57 Greater London is served by the North East Metropolitan Accident Unit with eight medical members, mostly GPs with up to 25 years experience each in major incidents including many in London. These include the Moorgate tube crash, the King's Cross fire, terrorist and dangerous chemical incidents, and events at Heathrow and Stansted, such as hi-jackings and crashes. They take part in regular simulated exercises.

5.58 The doctors are in radio contact with ambulance headquarters in London, Hertfordshire and Essex, and can be mobilised by any of the statutory emergency services at any time. They carry a full range of equipment in their cars, including protective clothing and identity cards. Protective clothing includes crash helmets with visors, a variety of gloves including protective medical gloves, day-glo dungarees, jackets labelled "doctor", and boots. A tabard labelled "medical incident officer" is carried and was lent to Mr Calvert of St.Georges who took that position at the scene for the first few hours of the incident. After this time he felt, rightly, that he could be better employed back at St.George's and his role was assumed by Dr Winch of BASICS.

5.59 BASICS' doctors carry in their cars radio equipment which can be switched to the emergency reserve channel. They also carry a supply of triage labels, which allow the classification of casualties by categorising priority of treatment needed. The administration of drugs, and the patient's condition at particular times can also be recorded on these labels.

5.60 Dr Judith Fisher, Chairman of BASICS, stated in her evidence to the Court: "The cardinal rule of emergency care is to look after the air-way, breathing and the circulation". BASICS therefore carry a range of rescue equipment, including a selection of air-ways, aspiration equipment, equipment to suck out the airway if it is blocked, infusion fluids, splints, drugs, pain relief, and heart equipment, such as a defibrillator monitor.

5.61 BASICS rely on the rapid response of the London Ambulance Service to supply further needs during an incident. BASICS doctors attended the five passengers who were trapped for a long time, the longest extrication taking five hours. All five survived after their release. Dr Fisher paid tribute to those passengers, which I would like to repeat here:

> *"Part of your duty in a way is to try to encourage the patients. But they were absolutely superb. The good humour showed by these victims was a lesson to us all."*

5.62 Dr Fisher's own role was to take charge of the temporary mortuary. Attending to the living must take priority in incidents such as these, but it is extremely important that the deaths of casualties are confirmed as soon as is feasible. Thus, the casualty bureau can inform relatives with a minimum of delay and the dreadful uncertainty can be resolved.

5.63 It is encouraging to note that BASICS doctors undergo specialist training and that the BASICS organisation offers many courses to both hospital doctors and general practitioners.

The role of the London Borough of Wandsworth

5.64 The local authority, the London Borough of Wandsworth, had developed a formal borough-wide emergency plan. It was developed following upon the Manor Fields gas explosion in 1985 in which the council became heavily involved in rescue and other ancillary works. The council received its first notification of the accident at 08:25. Two management staff were on site within ten minutes and designated the incident as Category 1, the gravest category. That designation triggered off an automatic call-out of staff and the execution of the overall plan. On arrival further Council staff began to assist the walking wounded passengers and acted as stretcher bearers.

5.65 By 09:15, ninety-eight Council employees were on site with an incident control vehicle and an enviable assortment of vehicles and equipment. Since the metal railings and steep slope of the embankment were a major hindrance to the rescue operation, the railings were cut away using oxyacetylene equipment (some had already been cut by the LFB). Trees and shrubbery were cut away with chain saws, steps were manually dug into the embankment and chestnut fencing laid over the steps to give greater purchase. By 09:30 many more staff were on site, giving general assistance by taking medical supplies to doctors, tending the injured and continuing to act as stretcher-bearers, removing both the injured and dead from the wreckage. Other staff were implementing traffic control measures by providing cones, signs and bulk timber barriers which closed the South Circular Road. They were also involved in arranging subsequent diversions. Social Services staff attended to assist survivors where possible both at the site and at St.George's Hospital.

5.66 In all, 134 council employees were engaged either directly on site or in a support capacity. By mid-day all save eleven had departed from the site, many of them going to give blood at St.George's Hospital. A mobile incident unit had been set up on site which was in contact by radio and portable telephone with the control centre at the Town Hall.

5.67 The Salvation Army quickly set up a mobile canteen and the council kept the canteen replenished throughout the day with food and drink.

5.68 During the afternoon, council electricians provided lighting units at the mobile incident unit and flood-lighting to illuminate the crash scene as well as electricity supply to the mobile police unit.

5.69 At later debriefings the emergency services were of the view that the local authority was unique in providing such a wide range of assistance. Their officers are to be commended for the speed and scale of the assistance they gave to the emergency services. It would be prudent planning if other local authorities which do not yet have such a plan were to act now to devise an emergency plan on similar lines to that of the London Borough of Wandsworth.

Alerting the hospitals and the failures in communication

5.70 The Major Incident Procedure of the London Emergency Services Liaison Panel places upon the ambulance service the task of warning those hospitals which may later be involved that there is the possibility of a major incident. When the Central Ambulance Control judge from the initial information which they have received that this is the situation, they must warn the potential designated and supporting hospitals through the hospital switchboards with the specific words "MAJOR ACCIDENT – YELLOW ALERT". (This is intended to be a warning order which should bring the hospital up to its maximum state of readiness. That message had been telephoned through to the designated hospital, St.George's, Tooting, at 08:23. We shall see what, if any, effect it had).

5.71 Thereafter, once a major incident has actually been declared by one of the emergency services, the procedure requires the Central Ambulance Control to notify the nearest listed hospital that it is the designated hospital. Ambulance Control must also notify the next listed hospitals that they are the supporting hospitals.

5.72 It follows that, when TSO Mills declared a major incident at 08:27 to the London Fire Brigade at Croydon Control, the procedure called for the fire brigade to contact the ambulance service, whose duty it was to notify the hospitals that they were designated or supporting hospitals. That should have been effected within a minute or so of TSO Mills' call at 08:27 and should have led, amongst other things, to the immediate despatch of a medical officer to the site.

5.73 Unfortunately, when the LFB Croydon Control attempted to contact the ambulance service, its call was caught in the queuing system for eight minutes. It was not until 08:35 that the message got through and by now it was only one minute ahead of Mr Chambers own LAS declaration of a major incident at 08:36.

5.74 By 08:36 Ambulance Control had received two messages declaring a major incident, but nine minutes had already been lost. Sadly a further twelve minutes were to be added to this delay in that it was not until 08:48 that St.George's Hospital, Tooting, was notified that it was the designated hospital. It was now twenty-one minutes after the major incident had in fact been declared, and such a delay cannot be acceptable.

5.75 What appears to have happened in those twelve minutes at ambulance control is that the dockets in relation to Mr Chambers' and Mr Mills' calls became submerged amongst the other dockets which bore other messages requiring action, so that it was not until 08:47 that Miss Healy at Ambulance Control was asked to, and immediately did, declare a major incident to St.George's, the call being received by the hospital one minute later.

5.76 There were communications problems and delays earlier in relation to Mr Mills' 08:20 call to the LFB Croydon Control requesting the attendance of a surgical unit. Fire Brigade Control passed the message on to Ambulance Control at 08:22. There the message got from the person who received it to Miss Healy within two minutes. She was asked at 08:24 to request a medical team from St.George's Hospital. She tried to make contact with the hospital switchboard, but after holding on for approximately one minute without an answer she decided to dial casualty direct. This telephone was answered straight away and Miss Healy explained that following the Yellow Alert (sent to St.George's at 08:23) she was now seeking a medical team. The speaker at the casualty end was not aware that a Yellow Alert had been called and explained that a new switchboard operator had not completely understood the message. Miss Healy confirmed the Yellow Alert and again asked for a medical team at which the speaker indicated doubt and went away to check.

5.77 Miss Healy held on until she saw from her timer that she had been connected to St.George's for about four or five minutes. She kept the line open but contacted St.Stephens' Hospital, Fulham, on a different line to request a medical team from them. She had no difficulty contacting St.Stephens' who agreed straight away that they would provide a team. The time was now 08:35. She then returned to her call to St.George's: the line was still open. They agreed to send a medical team. At 08:42 a Surrey Ambulance Service vehicle was diverted to collect the medical team from St.George's.

5.78 The St.Stephens' medical team went mobile at 08:52 and were in fact the first medical team to arrive on site at 08:58. There was therefore a gap of some fifteen minutes between TSO Mills' first request for a surgical team at 08:20, ten minutes after the accident, and the call to St.Stephens' at 08:35 when they agreed to send a team. Not only that but it took from 08:24 until sometime after 08:35 for St.George's Hospital to confirm to the ambulance service that they would send a medical team. That team left St.George's at 08:56 and arrived on site at 09:08. The first two medical teams arrived therefore 38 minutes and 48 minutes respectively after the request for them had been made, nearly 15 minutes of which period was pure communications delay.

5.79 It must be said that had TSO Mills' message got through to the hospitals as quickly as it should, those medical teams would have been alerted about 15 minutes earlier and would have been on the site that much sooner. Whilst those people already at the site of course included doctors and nurses who had been on the trains and ambulance men who had recently arrived, the hospital medical teams would have consisted of the first doctors at the site able to alleviate suffering by the use of drugs. It goes without saying that the earlier such suffering can be attended to the better: no unnecessary delay can be tolerated. The failures of communication that led to the slowing down of the alert are to be regretted; they are a matter which must be dealt with in my recommendations.

5.80 A further failure of communications was, of course, that the Yellow Alert message that had been sent to St.George's at 08:23 was not understood by the new switchboard operator there and thus the hospital was not alerted by the call and the whole point of the Yellow Alert procedure was negated in relation to St.George's. The Yellow Alert calls to the supporting hospitals, St. Stephens' and St.Thomas's, were made at 08:33 and were effective.

5.81 It has also to be pointed out here that these problems in relation to the Clapham Junction accident have been shown not to have been isolated ones. The evidence given to the Railway Inspectorate Inquiry into the Purley Accident showed that after the accident happened at 13:44, the LFB initiated the Major Incident Procedure at 14:07 and a message to that effect was passed to its Croydon Control. Human error meant that this message was simply not passed on to the LAS who initiated its own Major Incident Procedure at 14:20. In the Purley case therefore, thirteen vital minutes were lost before the LAS were able to alert the designated and supporting hospitals to their roles. Once these hospitals got that message their response was instant and effective. It could have been instant and effective thirteen minutes earlier.

5.82 Better systems, better organisation, better training and better equipment, may prevent a repetition of such failures of communication and I will deal with these matters in my recommendations.

Communications between the site and St. George's

5.83 For the first few hours of the incident, Mr Calvert, an Orthopaedic Surgeon from St.George's Hospital, was the Medical Incident Officer on site. He arrived on site at 09:14 and contacted the Senior Police Officer and Ambulance Officers and went down to the track to survey the scene. Mr Calvert surveyed the scene of the crash to locate the positions of trapped casualties and direct medical teams to them. There were five casualties trapped in the first three Poole carriages.

5.84 In his view the major deficiency was that he did not have direct two-way communication with St.George's which he regarded as essential. His communication was therefore very difficult because the obvious place to go was to the Ambulance Control Centre or the Police Control Centre and the various lines were extremely busy. He said that it was actually impossible to get through and that matters were being conducted by messages and "people going backwards and forwards", which was less than satisfactory.

5.85 Mr Calvert did not think that these problems altered the outcome for anybody, but it would have been very advantageous for the base hospital to know precisely what was going on at site and it would have been advantageous for him to know the numbers and severity of the casualties arriving in the hospital. St. George's was large enough not to have been saturated and to be able to cope with the substantial numbers of patients, but in other circumstances things might have been different.

5.86 Communications were equally important in relation to getting blood or drugs quickly from a base hospital. He thought that they were: "Very adequately staffed in terms of medical personnel on site", and that the "rapid evacuation was done superbly by the emergency services". It was the trapped casualties who required first and foremost that their airways be maintained; they also required intravenous infusions of resuscitating blood or other fluids, and appropriate drugs for pain relief.

5.87 The absence of a radio link in this case between the St. George's hospital and the Medical Incident Officer was the consequence of the very recent opening of the accident and emergency department at that hospital. The fixed aerial at the old site had not been moved to the new premises. Such links are clearly essential as is the provision of a hand-held radio for the Medical Incident Officer to give him mobile communication. It is desirable that those who are likely to act in that capacity should have had training in the use of such radios and I was pleased that the LAS in their evidence to the Court were able to offer such training. It would also assist those at such hospitals who are likely to be called upon to act as Medical Incident Officers, were to be given some form of training in their potential duties.

5.88 Mr Calvert also pointed out that it was almost impossible for him to tell at any one moment the number and nature of the medical staff on site. At one stage he was aware that there were more medical personnel on site than was required and despatched some staff back to their hospitals where they could be used more effectively.

Liaison between the emergency services

5.89 All emergency services agreed that the operation at Clapham Junction had gone well. Early command at the trackside had been established by the LFB and that role had not been challenged. It is often the case that the LFB needs to take control at the site because they are best placed to evacuate passengers. They assess the danger of the situation and can best decide if, at any point, the situation is so dangerous that everyone including rescuers should leave the site. Such an evacuation was not necessary during the Clapham Junction accident.

5.90 Regular meetings were held between the emergency services and BR to ensure coordination. These were held at 10:20, 12:00, 14:00 and 16:00 hours. The 10:20 meeting set out the ground rules and agreed the respective roles of each service. The conclusions of the 10:20 meeting on command and control issues were that:

- the senior London Fire Brigade Officer would remain in control of the rescue operation on the track;

- the cause of the accident would be identified by British Transport Police;

- the Metropolitan Police would be responsible for identification of the deceased;

- the Metropolitan Police were to have initial control of property found at the scene, such property to be handed over to BTP at a later stage;

- a coordinated approach was to be taken towards the media ensuring a regular flow of accurate information.

5.91 The London Fire Brigade in assuming command of the incident took on responsibility for the well-being of all rescue workers at the trackside. Conditions were cramped and difficult. LFB expressed concern that a number of rescue workers were on site without even the minimal protective clothing of hard hats and gloves. While these might have been issued, rescue workers neglected their own personal protection. I welcome the LFB's decision to purchase a further 100 bump helmets to distribute from a central pool on such occasions, but this should not be seen as a substitute for each service providing for its own personnel.

5.92 The LFB also drew attention to the possible confusion arising from the various coloured tabards used at the incident and the fact that some rescue workers could not be identified from their clothing. Local authority workers wore green tabards; BR staff orange tabards; the fire brigade yellow day-glo surcoats; the ambulance service green. The police were in normal uniform or wearing yellow jackets with "POLICE" printed on them. The medical teams were either wearing different colours or no tabards at all. BASICS doctors, however, wore clearly identifiable protective clothing.

5.93 The Investigation heard of the regular exercises that take place involving all the emergency services and the use of table-top exercises as an addition. These obviously have an important role in emergency planning. In view of the comments I have already made future exercises should specifically test communications and in particular the call-out procedures between the services.

5.94 The LFCDA made representations to the effect that consideration should be given to amending the Fire Services Act 1947 so as to recognise command and control duties and responsibilities of the Senior Fire Officer at any incident to which the fire brigade dedicates equipment and personnel.

5.95 The overall command of the Clapham Junction incident at trackside was not disputed by the other services. However, the general principle of a statutory command and control role for a fire brigade at any incident where it commits personnel and equipment is not agreed by all the other services. Discussion would need to continue at national level to ensure that all relevant types of incident are considered.

5.96 Looking at the Clapham Junction accident alone, I cannot make a recommendation to create an extended statutory role for the fire brigades throughout the country on the basis of that rescue operation.

The media

5.97 Chief Superintendent David Ray was in charge of Battersea Police Station on the day of the accident and attended at the scene. He was also responsible for the conspicuously considerate and well-planned operation organised at Lavender Hill Police Station to assist the relatives of the bereaved through the distressing procedure of identifying the victims on the day after the accident. He gave evidence that outside Lavender Hill Police Station:

> ".... people having come at a rather distressing time on the day following the accident, found themselves besieged by the press outside."

He also told the Court that many relatives of the deceased expressed severe displeasure and concern about a small minority of press representatives, particularly around their homes. He said:

> "*A number of instances were given of irresponsible and quite outrageous behaviour by a few reporters which caused considerable distress by harassing relatives and their families.*"

There were occasions when police were called to protect relatives from harassing attention by some reporters and police also had to assist in this way outside Lavender Hill Police Station.

5.98 It is distressing to have to observe that it should be axiomatic in a civilised society that people under the strain of recent and tragic bereavements are deserving of the maximum consideration. This they got from the dedicated consideration of the police, the Social Services and the Salvation Army, who were all on hand at the Police Station to help, comfort and counsel. This maximum consideration they significantly did not get from a small minority of the press whose lack of common humanity and decency at such a time was and is deplorable.

5.99 It is fair to state that Chief Superintendent Ray was at pains to point out that these were the actions of only a small minority and that "the media themselves generally were cooperative and acted very responsibly at the scene of the accident". As in so many situations, however, it is the actions of the small minority that do most harm.

5.100 It is not within the ambit of this Investigation to make any recommendations in relation to such conduct. It is necessary, however, that it be publicly recorded and publicly condemned: this I do now, and express the hope that such conduct be not repeated and that those who have it in their power to prevent these practices should act firmly to prevent them.

48

Chapter 6: British Rail – The immediate response and investigation

6.1   The immediate response of members of BR staff most closely connected with the accident has already been dealt with in Chapter 4 up to the level of the Station Manager at Clapham Junction, Mr Noorani. This Chapter concerns itself with the response of other BR staff at higher levels than Mr Noorani and in particular of the Signal & Telecommunications Department (S&T).

6.2   It is necessary and proper to point out straightaway that those British Rail officials who attended at the scene at Clapham Junction and were responsible for such duties as evacuating passengers from trains stranded as a result of the loss of current, for the restoration of services to other lines and for the clearing of the wreckage and the restoring of normal services, carried out those duties in an efficient and totally effective manner.

6.3   Soon after the accident a number of senior staff were in attendance at the site, including Mr Aynsley, the Relief Manager at Waterloo, Mr Turner the Area Train Crew Manager, Mr Futter, the Area Manager at Waterloo, Mr Pettitt, the General Manager, Southern Region, Mr Maurice Holmes, Director Safety, and Sir Robert Reid, Chairman of the BR Board.

The immediate procedures

6.4   BR put in evidence a document containing a number of procedures to be followed in the case of an accident. It was the Southern Region booklet "Accident Procedure" which was published in November 1984 and is some twenty pages long. It is expressly stated that it is not intended to take the place of the contingency plans of each Area Manager for his own area, but is:

> "rather to promote a common basis on which Departmental Officers may plan, so that in the event of serious mishaps and other incidents which can seriously dislocate traffic, the necessary arrangements can be made swiftly and effectively."

It is directed principally at the Area Manager or his qualified deputy and lays down specific duties to be discharged on arrival at the site of an accident, both for that person and for Operations Control. The Area Manager or other designated representative is to be in overall charge of the operation and to be designated "mishap controller".

6.5   At para. 4.5. the booklet requires that:

> "A senior member of the Regional Signalling and Safety Section should attend to gather information which may be required for subsequent inquiries into the cause of the accident."

6.6   The cover of the booklet bears the message from the General Manager that:

> "This booklet must always be readily available. It is intended to be a convenient reminder to Operations and M&EE Department" (Mechanical and Electrical Engineering Department) "staff who are required to deal with major accidents . . ."

With one notable exception in relation to the preservation of evidence, it performs that function very well. It acts in the main as an aide memoire to the many duties which British Rail employees have to perform when an accident such as the Clapham Junction accident occurs.

6.7 The first priority is, of course, the calling out of the emergency services and the booklet stresses the importance of their being given the exact location of the accident. Another high priority is the switching off of the traction current to protect passengers who may be dismounting from the trains and rescue workers who may be coming to their assistance and also to prevent other trains running into the wreckage.

6.8 In addition to the reference to traction current and its switching off, already mentioned in Chapter 4 there is an earlier reference at para. 2.2. which reads:

"Staff should be made aware that:–

> (c) In electrified areas the traction current must be switched off as quickly as possible to minimise the risk of fire or other injury."

6.9 It is a cause for concern that as we saw in Chapter 4 there was a lengthy period when there was uncertainty as to whether or not the traction current was still on. That uncertainty unhappily was repeated at the Purley accident.

The booklet rightly stresses at paragraph 1.2 that:

> "The speed with which emergency services are brought to the site and the effectiveness and success of the operations mounted, depends very largely upon reliable information being passed forward correctly and without delay to everyone concerned, both staff and public."

6.11 As we have seen in the previous Chapter the emergency services were alerted speedily and effectively in the case of the Clapham Junction accident by members of the public. No avoidable delays took place in the arrival at the scene of the fire brigade, the police and the ambulance service. BR staff, though they took a little longer, were soon in touch with the emergency services.

6.12 It is necessary, however, to point out that this sadly could not be said of the Purley accident where staff of BR Southern Region should have been adopting the same accident procedure as is laid down in the Southern Region's booklet.

6.13 In the Purley accident, a railway driver who was a passenger on one of the trains, used a signal-post telephone to call the signal box, which happened to be at Three Bridges in Sussex and told the signalman what had happened and to block all lines. The signalman telephoned an operator at Waterloo to ask for the emergency services to be called. He did not say where the services were wanted, and the telephonist assumed that the assistance was needed at Three Bridges. She therefore contacted the Sussex Police at Brighton who, when Purley was mentioned, pointed out the error. The telephonist then dialled Scotland Yard and was caught in the queuing system so that her call took a long time before it was answered.

The investigation at Clapham Junction that morning

6.14 At about 08:10, Mr Ian Harman, Signal Maintenance Engineer at Wimbledon, was talking on the telephone to his assistant at Feltham, Mr Eggar, when Mr Eggar commented that the alarm had just gone off on the operating floor and he would find out what had happened. Mr Eggar rang back shortly and reported that the cause of the power failure appeared to be a collision in the Clapham cutting. Mr Harman confirmed with the Duty Line Manager at Waterloo Operations Control that there had been such a collision and was told that all four lines were blocked. As a result he decided to go to the scene with his Maintenance Assistant, Mr Robert Bradley, and his WARS Liaison Supervisor, Mr David White.

6.15 He thought it was about 08:40 that he arrived by car with his party. They went first to signal WF47 and he spoke to Signalman Cotter on the signal post telephone to find out about the circumstances of the accident. After conferring with his colleagues, his party then went to signal WF138, which was showing a single yellow aspect. There he spoke to Driver Pike who told him: "it came round the corner and I nearly ran into this lot". It was obvious that something was very sadly awry and as a result he spoke by radio telephone to Mr Roger Penny, the Area S&T engineer at Wimbledon, who said he would come to the scene.

6.16 Mr Harman then went to the location case a few yards away which controls the relays to WF138. He saw through the clear perspex case of relay HR, that it was in the energised position. If a train occupies the track sections controlling WF138, HR should, of course, be de-energised. By now not one but three trains were occupying these tracks and thus there was clearly a fault present. A voltmeter reading was taken at the contacts controlling the coil of relay HR which registered 43.5 volts, a little below the rating of the relay. He hand-traced all the wiring in that apparatus case and found that everything was correctly wired according to the wiring diagrams in the location case. In that location case there was a transformer rectifier which converted to 50 volts DC the 110 volts AC which emanates from the electrical supply at Clapham Junction "A" signal box. He then moved to a location case 20 yards to the London side of WF138, known as location 3/4, and found that the wiring there was also in accordance with its diagrams.

6.17 Having adjusted the circuit to place WF138 at red, Mr Harman and his party followed the line-side multi-core cables all the way back to Clapham Junction "A" signal box, stopping at each location case to check the voltage and that the cables were correctly connected. They arrived back at Clapham Junction "A" signal box at about 10:30 a.m. and at 10:51 they withdrew a fuse, which controlled the supply of electricity to that circuit. When they did that the electricity supply to WF138 was lost and they accordingly concluded that the fault was within the relay room and not external to it.

6.18 By now they had been joined by Mr John Deane the Area Signalling Engineer (Works), Mr Geoffrey Bailey, the Signal Works Engineer, and Mr Peter Christie, a supervisor. They took out the wiring diagrams kept in the relay room and started to trace out the circuit. Mr Harman examined the position of a relay TRR DL. By looking through its glass he could see that it was de-energised, which meant that as far as the signal box was concerned the presence of Driver McClymont's Basingstoke train *was* recorded in the signalling equipment. It followed that if the circuit was working in accordance with the wiring diagrams, the aspect shown at WF138 should have been red, not one yellow.

6.19 It was at this stage that they found that although the wiring diagram indicated that only one wire should be connected at the fuse end, there were in fact two. Meanwhile, at the other end from the fuse, namely at the relay TRR DM, Supervisor Mr Alfred Court found an extraneous uninsulated wire. Members of the team at the fuse end were using a voltmeter to check the voltage going out to signal WF138. Every time Mr Court pushed the extraneous wire away from the contact on the relay TRR DM, the voltage going out to signal WF138 was lost. Mr Harman recalled that the wire seemed to go back onto the contact of its own volition when moved away from its position.

6.20 The fault which was causing signal WF138 not to show a red aspect when it should have done had been identified. The wire connected at fuse 107 on row 12 at one end and in contact at the other end with terminal 4-Arm on relay TRR DM was permitting current to flow out along the circuit. That current was flowing to the relay HR in the location case near to signal WF138, thus keeping that relay energised and keeping signal WF138 at yellow when it should have been at red.

6.21 Mr Harman then left the relay room to see if Mr Penny had as yet arrived. He said that he: "Was anxious straight away to seek recourse to higher authority to ensure the information was properly disseminated and to seek guidance on how the evidence should be preserved". Those words reflect with some exactitude, not to say pedantry, a recognition of the clear duty on anyone in authority in British Rail to pass on the information and to preserve the evidence. Fortunately the information was in fact passed on: unfortunately the evidence was not in fact preserved.

6.22 The importance of the retention of evidence in an unaltered, unmodified state in any situation as grave as faced those people in the relay room that morning cannot be overstated. It was obvious that here was the electrical equipment in the actual condition that had caused the terrible tragedy out on the tracks less than three hours before and less than a mile away. It should have been equally obvious that the equipment *had* to be left untouched, so that it could be seen in that state by the eyes of others who would have to carry out an independent investigation. It should have been equally plain that it needed to be photographed then and there.

6.23 In fairness to Mr Penny, it has to be pointed out that the Southern Region Accident Procedure booklet would have given him no guidance whatsoever on how to deal with the acquisition and retention of evidence which might be needed in any investigation into an accident. Further, no BR instruction in existence at the time of the accident would have assisted him. He had therefore only his own thoughts and feelings to go on.

6.24 Wrongly, but for what I find to be no improper motive, Mr Penny instructed Supervisor Court to cut off the eye of the extraneous wire and to tape up the end. Mr Court carried out the instruction. Equally, wrongly, but again as I find for no improper motive, the bare eye at the end of the wire was not retained and has never been available as evidence. Surprisingly, no search was made then or later in the area of that relay for loose insulating tape which might previously have been attached to that wire. A photographer was called and later that day photographs were taken of the state of the relay, but the damage had already been done.

6.25 Mr Penny frankly admitted to the inquiry that: "It was a very big mistake. We should have actually taped up the wire with the eye on it and put it out of the way, but I was very concerned about the safety of the thing obviously". His concern was that, with the bare eye on, the end of the wire was obviously dangerous and he wanted to make absolutely sure that this situation should not persist. He said that the essential importance of that particular item had not occurred to him at the time and that they were all in a state of shock.

6.26 What Mr Penny should have done was to arrange immediately for the attendance of a photographer (that much at least is included in the instructions in the Southern Region Accident Procedure booklet, but the booklet is intended for the Operations and Mechanical and Electrical Engineering Departments only and not the S&T department). Both ends of the wires should have been photographed and the wire then made safe by removing it from the fuse end, insulating it and securing it away from the fuse. He should also have arranged for the attendance of a police officer. Whether that officer was provided from the Metropolitan or BT Police Forces he would have been aware of the need to preserve the scene for proper investigation and that the relay end of the wire should have been sealed within a transparent cover.

6.27 Having said that, it must be remembered that Mr Penny would clearly have been strongly affected both as a human being and as a signalling engineer by the sight of the appalling tragedy involving loss of human life and injury on the scale which he had just seen with his own eyes. It was in that light that he would have looked at the offending wire. The wiring error was so bad and so contrary to all that was good in signalling practice that I can understand his feelings that he wanted to have done with it. Nevertheless his action in giving that instruction was mistaken and regrettable. It was also, though not intended so to be, an obstruction to the proper investigation of the causes of the accident.

6.28 I am totally convinced that he took that action in utter good faith. I have to conclude however that the failure to preserve the wire in its then state and the disappearance of the eye have plainly obstructed the investigation of the accident, in that they have made it impossible to conduct any forensic tests which might have established conclusively whether that eye had ever been in contact with insulating tape, but some other means should have been considered such as tying it back to the tree after appropriate tests had been carried out.

6.29 Mr Penny's failure to ensure that vital evidence was retained in its existing state was sadly and surprisingly not a lone example by BR staff in this case. At this time at the fuse end, the extraneous wire was still connected as the second wire on fuse 107 row 12. That was also vital evidence for any investigation. That evidence came very close to being interfered with. That wire came very close to being cut off. Mr Bradley and Mr White at the fuse end came to a joint decision that they had better cut it off and Mr Bradley uttered aloud some such words. They were crouched over the fuse end of the wire and Mr Harman had come and stood behind them. He overhead Mr Bradley's words and said: "Well don't, we need it as evidence". As a result they put the second wire back onto the fuse. Mr Bradley and Mr White, again as I find without any hint of impropriety, seem to have reacted on the same sort of basis as had Mr Penny. Mr White said: "It seems to be bred into us that safety comes first and it was just a natural instinct to cut the thing away".

6.30 The interference with evidence was still not over. The next day Mr Kenneth Hodgson (Director S&T Engineering) and Mr Deane (Area S&T Engineer) were in the relay room with Supervisor Court, when he cut back the offending wire from which the eye had already been removed by a further foot or so. In taking this action according to a number of conflicting accounts given in evidence, he was either acting on or alternatively totally misunderstanding the instructions he had been given. A finding of fact in relation to this matter is not vital to this Investigation, but I consider it more likely that Mr Court was in fact carrying out his instructions, rather than misunderstanding them when he cut the wire. The consequences of this interference with the existing evidence were that although the piece of wire was retained, and preserved safely. The fact of its detachment meant that it was impossible to establish forensically whether there was or was not a tendency in that wire, when pushed away from the terminal, to return to its old position.

6.31 The final and least important alteration of the status quo at the accident happened as part of the same visit to the relay room on 13 December 1989, when Mr Court, on Mr Deane's instructions, took both the two wires off the end of fuse 107, cut off the end of the old wire and replaced the new one. The only adverse evidential effect of this alteration of the situation was that no photographs had been taken before this operation which would have recorded the true position at the fuse end at the time of the accident.

6.32 The British Rail Southern Region Accident Procedure booklet is silent as to the important matter of the retention of evidence. It is perfectly apparent that little thought had been given before the Clapham Junction accident to the essential significance of securing and retaining the available evidence to allow proper investigation before and proper scrutiny during an investigation. It was perhaps as a result of these failings and their identification that by the time of the Purley accident the wheel had turned full circle in an unfortunate manner. Immediately after that accident the initial investigation team was unhelpfully denied access to the site of the accident for nearly three hours and therefore prevented from getting evidence which could have had an important bearing on the investigation, namely, evidence of brake pressures of the vehicles. This is vital information of a "perishable" nature and proper proceedings must be laid down for the speedy and efficient collection of such information and the acquisition and retention of all types of evidence.

British Rail's Internal Inquiry

6.33 British Rail set up a Railway Joint Inquiry in order to "to ascertain the facts appertaining to the event, find the cause and take steps immediately, if necessary, for the safety of the railway". The inquiry sat at Waterloo on the 14 December 1988 and concluded on 21 December 1988, having interviewed thirty-four witnesses. A Joint Inquiry is so called because of the participation of different departments in the panel investigating the accident. The panel members were:

- Mr Maurice Holmes, Director Safety, British Railways Board who was in the Chair;

- Mr Hodgson, Director Signal & Telecommunications, British Railways Board;

- Mr Vine, Mechanical & Electrical Engineer (Resource Management), British Railways Board; and

- Mr Galley, Regional Operations Manager, Southern Region.

6.34 The Joint Inquiry completed its report before Christmas and made twenty-five recommendations, which was not the normal practice. Recommendations are ordinarily dealt with under separate procedures, but in the circumstances surrounding this particular tragedy the inquiry thought it pertinent to comment within the main body of the report. Those recommendations were categorised as either "immediate", "current" or "less immediate" in relation to their urgency and comment will be made later on some of the recommendations.

6.35 It was recognised at paragraph 6.3 of the report that:

"The majority of the recommendations refer to normal quality assurance procedures. We understand an appointment has recently been made within the S&T function at Board Headquarters that this post should concentrate on safety matters."

6.36 The report's findings were in certain respects modified by an Addendum dated 3 February 1989. I should like to pay tribute to the care, skill and expertise which went into the preparation of that report and to the speed and diligence which made it available so early. It proved of invaluable assistance to all those who were representing parties before this Court and indeed to all members of the Court. We are grateful to the Joint Inquiry panel for the quality of their report.

PHOTOGRAPHS

Fig 1.
Fig 2.
Aerial views of the accident site.

Fig 3. Driver Pike's train stationary approximately 60 yards from the rear of the Poole train.

Fig 4. An interior view of a Driver's Cab showing the controls.

Fig 5. An interior view of the type of Buffet Car on the Poole train, showing the non-fixed seating, facing forward in the direction of travel.

Fig 6. A further interior view of the type of Buffet Car, again facing forward, showing the closed shutters on the left, behind which are the kitchen and serving areas, and the passenger space on the right.

Fig 7. A view of the Buffet Car of the Poole train taken on the evening of Monday 12 December, showing the destruction of the kitchen and serving areas on the left (nearside) of the coach, and the damaged loose seating.

Fig 8. An interior view of Mark 1 rolling stock similar to some carriages of the Poole train, showing lateral luggage racks.

Fig 9. An interior view of a carriage of the Basingstoke train, showing damaged transverse luggage racks.

Fig 10. A view of Clapham Junction 'A' Signal Box with the relay room at the extreme right above the first third of the leading coach of the passing train.

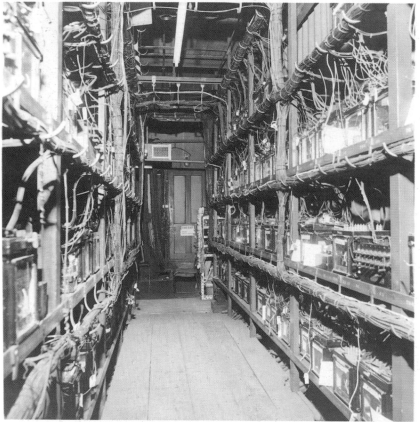

Fig 11. A view of the relay room, looking towards the entrance, showing the relay racks, and the trees of the wiring. Relays TRR DM and TRR DN are on the bottom shelf on the right in the last section towards the door.

Fig 12. Relays in Clapham Junction 'A' relay room, showing track relay 'DN' adjacent to track repeater relay 'DM'.

Redundant "black" wire running to fuse end

TRR DM TERMINAL 4A

Fig 13. Relay TRR DM taken on 12 December at approximately 14.00 hours.

Fig 14. Fuse racks. Row 12–f107, taken on 13 December.

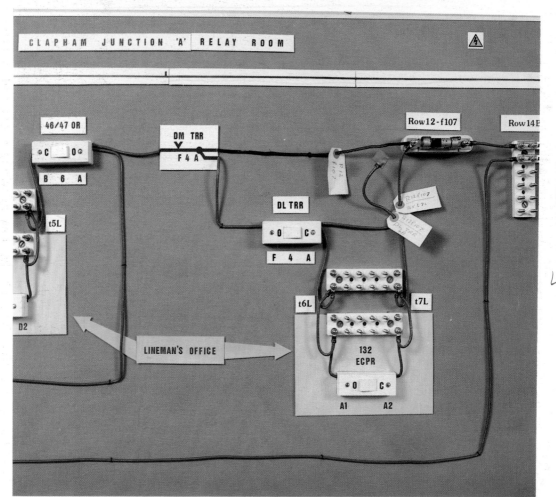

Fig 15. Extract from the working model demonstrating jobs 104 and 201 and the wiring errors made. The black wire along the top of the diagram connected at DM TRR and Row 12–f107 should have been disconnected at both ends but was wrongly left connected at the fuse end at Row 12–f107. Although disconnected at the relay end the wire was left loose and made metal-to-metal contact at DM TRR allowing a false feed of current to by-pass DL TRR. Hence the occupation of track circuit DL by a train had no effect on signal WF 138 and it did not turn back to red as it should have done.

Fig. 16. Working model of the relevant signalling circuits, showing wiring errors; and topographical model of the crash site.

PART TWO: THE IMMEDIATE CAUSES

Chapter 7: The wiring errors which caused the accident

7.1   It has already been established that the electrical "culprit" for the false feed of current to signal WF138 was an old wire in the relay room at Clapham Junction. One end was lying in contact with a terminal on relay TRR DM and the other was actually connected to a fuse. The current was permitted to flow out to the signal. This situation was the result of electrical work done in that relay room on two Sundays in the fortnight before the accident. This chapter will concern itself with that electrical work and in particular with the wiring errors which brought that situation about. It will deal with:

(i)   why the work had to be done in the first place;

(ii)   how it was prepared; and

(iii)   how it was actually carried out.

WARS and why the work had to be done

7.2   By the late 1970s and early 1980s, it had become clear that the electrical wiring which controlled the signalling in the Waterloo area had aged badly, was continuing to age and could not be allowed to remain as it was. Most of it had been installed in 1936 and its replacement had become imperative. Out of the need for that replacement the Waterloo Area Resignalling Scheme (WARS) was born. In Chapter 12 I shall look closely and, it has to be said, critically at the planning and execution of WARS as a whole. This chapter will confine itself to the work which needed to be done in order to carry out just two jobs, Job Nos. 104 and 201 of stage 7B of WARS. It will look particularly at the work done by Senior Technician Hemingway in the relay room at Clapham Junction "A" on those two Sundays, 27 November and 11 December 1988.

7.3   Those two jobs were only a tiny proportion of the installation needed for Stage 7B, let alone for the overall WARS scheme. They were but a part of the work involved in creating a particular new signal, WF138. They involved the creation of new circuits to control the new signal. To do this:

(i)   the old wiring running from the relay TRR DM to the fuse had to be replaced by new wiring; and

(ii)   the circuit had to be redesigned to include the relay TRR DL on its way to the fuse.

How the work was prepared

7.4   It was always the practice of the S&T Department that the work of connecting up new signalling installations was done at weekends. This was clearly sensible in that it involved the minimum of disruption to services while the line was taken out of use for the new connections to be made. It followed therefore that it was equally the practice of the S&T Department to have all the preparatory work completed during the working weeks that led up to the commissioning weekend and in particular in the last week before that weekend.

7.5   Thus, the new wires which would be needed in order to commission the particular part of the scheme would be prepared and laid during the working week and by the weekend they would be lying ready, but unconnected, for the installation work to take place. Frequently, but far from always, it would be the technicians who had done the preparatory work during the week who would be responsible for the final connections at the weekend. They would be working to wiring diagrams which had been drawn up in the Design Office at Southern House, Croydon, some time before.

7.6   The relevant wiring diagram for Job Nos. 104 and 201 had been issued by the Drawing Office on 10 August 1988. It is numbered 74F 10/45. The relevant detail from that drawing has been extracted and appears in larger and redrawn format at Appendix K.3.

7.7   The proper procedure was that once the drawings were ready, the Design Office would issue three copies to the Signal Works Assistant. He retained an office copy for later use by the Testing & Commissioning Engineer and passed a second copy on to the supervisor and the third to the senior technician. The evidence showed that this proper procedure was frequently not followed.

7.8   If any problems arose "on the ground" in translating the intentions of the Design Office as shown on the wiring diagram into the reality of the wiring in the relay room, then a practice of informal consultation between the Design Office and the particular supervisor or technician involved came into operation.

7.9   This was certainly the case in relation to Job No. 201. It appeared to the installer, Mr Hemingway, that there was not physically enough room in the relay room for the additional relays for Job No. 201. He therefore worked out a scheme whereby multicore wiring would be run out of the relay room to a room on the far side of the signal box which had once been the lineman's office. From there the wiring would return to make the connection at fuse 107 on row 12 in the relay room. (A general view of the relay room can be seen at Figure 11. It occupies the far end of the Clapham Junction "A" signal box and can be seen at Figure 10).

7.10 This change in the original design was accepted and agreed to by members of the Design Office staff. They did not issue an amended drawing. It would have been good practice to do so. Mr Hemingway kept in his notebook a detailed record of the necessary further connections which were not shown on the drawing. That information had not yet been passed back to the Design Office at the time of the accident.

7.11 The informality and imprecision of these arrangements meant that the arrangements themselves had within them a potential for confusion and misunderstanding. They also had the potential for creating future problems if, as in this case, the wiring diagram (which is kept in the relay room after the work had been done) did not accurately record the wiring which had actually been carried out on installation. None of these features were in any way instrumental in the causing of the Clapham Junction accident. They are, however, examples of a failure of proper communication and of the accurate dissemination and recording of important information, which was far too prevalent in the S&T Department. I shall deal with these and further examples of failure of communication in Chapter 11.

7.12 The work originally called for by the wiring diagram and the additional work of the wiring to the lineman's office had been prepared by the end of the working week which finished on the afternoon of Friday, 25 November 1988. All the wires which would be needed for Job Nos. 104 and 201 had been prepared and run. They were ready to be connected by Mr Brian Hemingway when he attended for work on the commissioning day for new signal WF138 on Sunday, 27 November 1988. That day he was to be under the supervision of Mr Derek Bumstead, a supervisor who knew his work well and had allocated to him one assistant, Mr Patrick Dowd.

How the work was carried out

7.13 So far as signal WF138 was concerned, the work which Mr Hemingway had to do in the relay room at Clapham Junction "A" on Sunday, 27 November 1988, on Job Nos. 104 and 201 was not difficult. Before he started work that day, the track circuit which was in operation included a wire running from the relay called TRR DM to the fuse at Row 12 – 107. (This is the black wire which is also the top wire in the diagram Mr Hemingway had, an extract from which can be seen at Appendix K.3. The diagram shows the design of the old wiring and the new wiring involved in the two jobs).

7.14 That was a simple direct route for the wire connecting the relay and the fuse and was the way in which the old signalling system had worked. In order to carry out the resignalling work, however, that connection was to be made by a different route. In the description of the work which follows, I shall use to describe the various wires the colours in which they appear in that wiring diagram extract at Appendix K.3. Thus I shall use the diagrammatic colours of "brown" and "yellow" for that new wiring although, as will be seen from the photographs, the actual colour of the insulation on the new wiring is blue.

7.15 Instead of a single wire running from TRR DM to the fuse, the new system required the running of a wire from TRR DM to TRR DL and of a further new wire on from TRR DL back to the fuse. That was Job No. 104, which was coloured brown on the diagram Mr Hemingway had. To carry out that job all he had to do was to disconnect at both ends the old "black" wire running straight from TRR DM to the fuse, and replace it by one new "brown" wire running from TRR DM to TRR DL and another new "brown" wire running direct from TRR DL to the fuse.

7.16 Job No. 104, however, was itself only a half-way house on the way to the completing of a slightly more elaborate wiring system which was to be effected by the next job, marked in yellow on Appendix K.3, Job No.201. Job No. 201 was to change the route between TRR DM and the fuse still further. It left in place the new route from TRR DM to TRR DL, which had been created by the first of the two "brown" new wires on Job No. 104, but it changed the route back to the fuse from TRR DL. Instead of being a direct route back from the relay TRR DL to the fuse as achieved by the second "brown" wire on Job No. 104, there was now to be a more complicated "yellow" route making other electrical connections on the way. The second "brown" wire of Job No. 104 which had just been connected between TRR DL and the fuse had to be disconnected at either end and replaced by a further new "yellow" wire running the new route from TRR DL to the fuse, by way of other electrical connections to the lineman's office and back.

7.17 Mr Hemingway had been with British Rail for sixteen years. He had been a senior technician since January 1981. He had worked before on large resignalling schemes in relation both to London Bridge and to Victoria. The work he was to do that day was the type of work he had always done. He was held in high regard by his colleagues and his superiors. His attitude to his work was that he had always thought he had done a good job. As far as he knew there was no criticism of his work. He booked on at 8:00 on the morning of Sunday, 27 November 1988 and started work at about 08:45. He felt just as he usually did : "alright".

7.18 Mr Dowd arrived at about 09:00, Mr Hemingway did not give him a lot of work to do, although he did ask him to disconnect some wires on the new cable termination panel in the lineman's office to help with the buzz test of the wires. He had worked with Mr Dowd before on two or three weekends, but did not feel comfortable in having Mr Dowd for an assistant because Mr Dowd's hands "shook too much for" Mr Hemingway's "liking". These factors made Mr Hemingway decide that he would have to do most of the work himself because he did not know Mr Dowd's capabilities.

59

7.19 In addition to Job Nos. 104 and 201, Mr Hemingway that morning had two further tasks in Job Nos. 226 and 111. He did those first and neither of them went as smoothly as he had expected. He then turned to Job Nos. 104 and 201 which he did together. His evidence was that he had finished them both by about 1 o'clock, early afternoon. The next time he had to do any work was much later in the afternoon. In the meantime, all he had to do was wait until the stage was reached when testing work commenced. As to whether there was any interruption while he was doing Job Nos. 104 and 201, he said:

> *"It is possible, but I can't really remember. If it goes like normal I generally get interrupted at times. It goes like that."*

7.20 Mr Hemingway said that the morning was unusual because the other jobs that he had been doing did not go well. He had worked out in advance that he should have been able to complete all of his work in two hours, but actually took twice as long and so he did not keep to his forecast as he would have liked to have done.

7.21 He said that there was no question of anybody putting pressure on him to work quicker than he could properly and safely do. He did not consider that the hours he had worked in the week and the hours he had worked on the Saturday affected his ability to carry out the work on the Sunday. He gave a series of very frank and objective answers without at any time seeking to excuse himself for his errors. The series of answers ended:

> *"Q. .... You are certainly not seeking to blame tiredness or pressure of work yourself for the mistakes that occurred.*
>
> *A. No. Sir."*

7.22 He said that he did not think he was really being supervised that day because he was basically working on his own. He did not have a supervisor with him that day, because Mr Bumstead was working outside. He was not expecting anyone to check his work visually that day. He was not expecting anyone to do a wire count, that is to say, to do an independent check whether the right number of wires according to the wiring diagram were physically in place at each point in the installation. In his experience on the changeovers he did, nobody ever did a visual check of his work. Nobody ever counted the wires after him.

7.23 Mr Hemingway gave detailed evidence to the Court, which included an account of the work involved in the two Job Nos. 104 and 201. He gave evidence of the order in which he thought he would have done the two jobs and the steps he would have taken. This was clearly an exercise of reconstruction of events, rather than recollection from memory. He said in terms:

> *"I really can't remember the events, but I can see going from the drawings what should have been done."*

7.24 Since Mr Dowd was absent from the relay room for almost all the time Mr Hemingway was working in it, the Court therefore heard no evidence, given from recollection, of either the order or the manner in which Mr Hemingway carried out the work involved in Job Nos. 104 and 211.

7.25 To a competent technician with an accurate set of drawings the work on those two jobs should have been simplicity itself and have been carried out with total safety in under half an hour. Although they were incomplete there was no error made in the drawings, but there were errors made in the installation. Those errors created the potential for a false feed of electrical current along the line of the old "black" wire direct between relay TRR DM and the fuse. The potential for that false feed meant a potential for a wrong-side failure of signal WF138 preventing it from showing red when it should. Those errors and their potential for disaster were not discovered by Mr Hemingway himself, were not discovered by any supervision of him, and were not discovered in the testing process before the signal was commissioned that evening and the line put back into public use next morning.

7.26 Essentially what Mr Hemingway did was to connect up new "brown" and "yellow" wires following the new Job No. 201 route between TRR DM and the fuse, but to leave the old "black" wire, which had run direct between that relay and fuse almost untouched. He left it still connected at the fuse end. At the other end at relay TRR DM, although he did disconnect it, he left it close to and in a position where it was in imminent danger of making contact with its old terminal on the relay.

7.27 These were totally basic errors. That wire should have been disconnected at both the fuse and the relay ends. To remove the wire completely would not have been practicable. In the case of the wiring in Clapham Junction "A" relay room there was a perfectly understandable desire not to disturb the embrittled nature of the covering on other adjoining wires, which ran, as can be seen in Figure 11, out from the "trees". A perfectly safe alternative to total removal had been evolved which should have been employed. That alternative involved:

(i) the foreshortening of the wire by cutting it back, so that it could never again come into contact with its old home;

(ii) insulation by the use of tape over the foreshortened end; and

(iii) the securing of the end of the wire in a safe place away from the terminals.

7.28 In a disastrous departure from any acceptable standard of electrical work, Mr Hemingway did none of these. At the relay end, he did not cut back the wire at all. He did not secure it away from the relay by tying it elsewhere, he merely pushed it aside. Further, I have to say that, for reasons which are explained in the next chapter, I find that he did not even apply any insulating tape to it. At the fuse end even more surprisingly he did not disconnect the old wire at all.

7.29 All save the insulating error, Mr Hemingway frankly admitted in his evidence. As to the failure to tape, he said that he just could not see how that could happen. I shall deal separately with each of these failures and the possible reasons for each one in the next Chapter.

7.30 All Mr Hemingway did was to push the old "black" wire out of the way to the back of the relay. It was, in the relatively gloomy lighting in that relay room, not likely to have been immediately apparent to a cursory glance. Had the work been properly inspected, however, as part of the carrying out of the supervisor's duties the errors should have been detected.

7.31 Though Mr Bumstead had the responsibility for supervising Mr Hemingway's work that day, he carried out no such supervision. He spent his time out on the tracks leading a gang involved in the outside work. He worked long and hard with them, often carrying out the manual work himself. He was fulfilling the role of a senior technician rather than a supervisor. He got himself so fully involved in this role that he totally neglected his duties as a supervisor.

7.32 Mr Bumstead did not even enter the Relay Room that day. It followed that the errors made by Mr Hemingway, which should have been detected by the eyes of a supervisor checking the relay top and the fuse end, went entirely undetected. The old "black" wire went unseen.

7.33 Had the "black" wire been seen at the relay end, it would not have been immediately apparent where it ran to at its other end without the help of the wiring diagram. Thus, since the fuse is in another part of the relay room, the fact that not only the "yellow" wire, but also the "black" wire was connected to that

61

fuse would not have been immediately apparent. The presence of the extraneous "black" wire on the fuse would, however, have quickly been detected by a wire count.

7.34 The use of the wiring diagram to confirm that what is physically in place after an installation is what is in fact demanded by the diagram for that installation is an essential feature of good signal engineering. The exercise is known as a wire count. Such a wire count was demanded both by S&T practice, and by S&T written instructions. Such a wire count has to be done independently of the actual installer before the line is put back into service. Such an independent wire count properly conducted would have prevented the accident. Such a wire count was not done either by Mr Bumstead as Supervisor, or by Mr Dray, the Testing and Commissioning Engineer. It was not done by anyone else either: a vital safety check was entirely omitted.

7.35 With the bare end of the old wire lying near to the terminal which had once been its home and with its other end still being connected to the fuse, there existed a potential for disaster which was the total contradiction of British Rail's determined and understandable commitment to "absolute safety". That potential was tragically realised when other work came to be done in the same relay room two Sundays later on the eve of the accident.

The second Sunday

7.36 On Sunday, 11 December, further work came to be done in that relay room which had nothing to do with Job Nos. 104 and 201. However, by a coincidence that was to be catastrophic the job involved work in the immediate vicinity of the relay TRR DM. The task was to replace the adjoining relay TR DN with another unit. These relays are a little larger and heavier than a conventional car battery. They can be seen in Figure 12, TR DN being to the immediate left of TRR DM. This work involved not only the movement of individual wires in their transfer to the new relay, but also the physical movement of the old and new relays themselves. The existing relay was pushed bodily towards the back of the shelf and the detachable top of the new relay was placed on a convenient piece of wood at the front of the shelf. Once the wiring work was completed the old relay was moved out and the new relay moved into its place. It was again pure coincidence that it was Mr Hemingway who had to do this work: this time his assistant was not Mr Dowd.

7.37 The work involved wires which ran from the same "tree" as the wires to TRR DM. (The "trees" are the collection of wires that can be seen running horizontally along the racks and vertically along the upright divisions in Figure 11). The work also involved physical manhandling of the relays themselves. The work had the unforeseen and unwanted result of disturbing the wires in the vicinity of TRR DM. The most unwanted effect of all was to permit the bare uninsulated end of the old "black" wire, left in that condition by Mr Hemingway two weeks before, to revert to the natural position it had held over many years. It went back to lie against and in contact with the terminal which had been its previous home under the old system when it had been designed to pass current to fuse 107. It was still connected to that fuse and now it could and did again pass current directly to it, and out of the relay room down to the signal WF138.

7.38 Just as had happened two weeks before, neither the bare end of the rogue wire, nor its contact-making position was detected. It was even less likely to be detected this time because, of course, no one had been working on the relay TRR DM. Further, on this occasion there would be no supervisor looking at the work. Mr Hemingway himself was acting as supervisor on this Sunday and he was therefore in theory supervising his own work. Again, as the work was simple and involved only the replacement of one relay by another, known in railway jargon as "like for like", there was no requirement for the intervention of a Testing and Commissioning Engineer.

7.39 Thus it was that Mr Hemingway's errors on Sunday, 27 November 1988, went unnoticed. Thus it was that they had no harmful consequences at the time. Thus it was that by disastrous coincidence two weeks later further unrelated work had to be done next to relay TRR DM. Mr Hemingway again, by coincidence, was the person who had to do that work. It was pure misfortune that an unidentifiable wire must have tugged at and moved the rogue wire while the old and new relays for TRR DN were being switched. It was, however, a misfortune which created what was to be a calamitous condition in signal WF138.

7.40 It is inevitable in this chapter that the name of Mr Hemingway has repeatedly been at the centre of the factual description of the wiring errors which caused the accident. He must and does carry a heavy burden of responsibility for the accident and its consequences. As the evidence at the Investigation developed, however, it became abundantly clear that such a responsibility was not his alone. The evidence which the Investigation heard demonstrated that such responsibility must be shared by the many others who had permitted a situation to exist in the S&T Department in which, not only could such errors be made in the first place, but they could be permitted to remain undetected when the work was inspected, tested and commissioned back into public service.

Chapter 8: How those errors came to be made – the workforce and their working practices

The Characteristic errors

8.1   Mr Hemingway was considered by his superiors to be a very good worker. He was the sort of person who could be left alone to get on with the job in his own way. He would make his own assessment of the task in hand. He would consider it carefully. He would make a plan in his head, and then put it into effect. There were no complaints about the standard of his work. At all times over the years, months and weeks, leading up to the accident, the general picture of Mr Hemingway in the eyes of his colleagues and superiors was that of a thoroughly competent and efficient senior technician.

8.2   The reality, sadly, was very different from the picture. Many of the errors Mr Hemingway made in the relay room on Sunday, 27 November 1988 he had been making all his working life. They were not isolated momentary lapses, they had become his standard working practices. In addition to these characteristic errors, there were two further totally uncharacteristic mistakes made by him that day which were of vital importance in the causation of the accident.

8.3   As to the characteristic errors:

(i) It is proper and safe practice when disconnecting an old wire to cut the wire back so that it can never again reach its old position: it was Mr Hemingway's practice not to do this.

(ii) Once such a wire is cut back it is proper and safe practice to secure it by tying it back out of the way: Mr Hemingway's practice was not to do this, but merely to push the wire aside.

(iii) When insulating the bare ends of a wire it is proper and safe practice to use only new insulating tape: it was Mr Hemingway's practice frequently to use tape that had already been used.

The third factor was not involved in the causation of the accident because no tape at all was in fact used by Mr Hemingway.

8.4   The fact that there were such errors of practice was enough to have created a potential for disaster whenever Mr Hemingway was dealing with old wires. That he could have continued year after year to follow these practices, without discovery, without correction and without training, illustrates a deplorable level of monitoring and supervision within BR which amounted to a total lack of such vital management actions. Further, that deplorable lack of monitoring and supervision did not confine itself to Mr Hemingway's immediate superiors.

8.5   Still more disturbing was the fact that these errors of practice were not Mr Hemingway's alone, but were, as I find, part of a widespread way of working, almost a school of thought, at technician, senior technician and even supervisor level within the S&T Department of Southern Region BR.

8.6　In fairness to Mr Hemingway it must be emphasised that from the beginning of the Investigation (and indeed from immediately after the accident) he has accepted a burden of responsibility for this accident amounting almost to totality. In that he happens to be wrong and to do himself an injustice.

8.7　Mr Hemingway had the right to expect that those who monitored, those who supervised, those who managed staff at his level would have had sufficient regard for safety to have ensured:

(i) that the quality of work carried out on the installation of new works was of an acceptable standard; and

(ii) that staff were given appropriate instruction and training to ensure improvement of standards and the maintenance of those improved standards.

Just as those charged with responsibility for monitoring and supervision fell down completely on their tasks, so did management and so did those responsible for the issuing of instructions, both oral and written, and for the provision of training, both "on-the-job" and in the classroom.

8.8　To see how these criticisms are reflected in the errors involved in Mr Hemingway's work, I shall deal first with Mr Hemingway's experience and qualifications, then with the specific errors he made on an individual basis and finally with the more widespread implications.

Mr Hemingway's experience and qualifications

8.9　Mr Hemingway joined BR in June 1972. After a year he did a preliminary course of about seven weeks and later in the 1970s when he was at New Cross he did a basic signalling course of four weeks. He also did two short courses at Derby Training School and a course on level crossing equipment. Apart from that he had no other training in electrical engineering and technical matters although he had been working on technician's duties ever since 1973. He got to his grade as Senior Technician Scale A in January 1981, not by taking any examination, but because of a change in staffing arrangements. Before he started on WARS he had worked on the London Bridge Resignalling Scheme and throughout the five years of the Victoria Area Resignalling Scheme. When WARS started he was at the South Lambeth depot and he worked continuously thereafter on WARS work from that depot until the Summer of 1988 when he was relocated to Wimbledon in a wholesale reorganisation of the S&T Department. He still, however, continued to work on WARS.

8.10　In the months leading up to the accident, Mr Hemingway worked normally during the week with a regular crew consisting of himself, and two other technicians. They worked happily together and Mr Hemingway knew their abilities. However, the other members of his normal crew did not work overtime at weekends and so Mr Hemingway would then end up working with different individuals whose abilities he knew less about. Sometimes he would end up working on his own.

8.11　Mr Hemingway said he had learned the job through experience, through watching his predecessors as senior technicians. He had never had a job description, nor any training on how to be a supervisor before he came to act as supervisor on various weekends. A job description, which in fact existed for a Senior Technician (Installation) and came into effect as part of the Pay and Grading Agreement of 1974, described the senior technician as:

"A man in charge of installation of complex equipment . . ."

and went on to say that he:

". . . must have passed the appropriate departmental test."

Mr Hemingway had not passed any such test in that as we have seen he obtained his grade before such a requirement came into force. As a senior technician he would receive the drawings, plan his work and tell the technicians what to do. He said that his method of doing a job was that he "just made a plan out himself in his head and then went and did the job".

8.12 From this brief summary of Mr Hemingway's career in the S&T Department, it can be seen that he had a bare minimum of training on courses and no training for any technical qualification whatever. It is in the light of that experience and that lack of training and of qualification that one can begin to understand his working practices as reflected in what I find to be completely truthful answers of Mr Hemingway:

> "Q: Is it your practice to cut back the wire?
> A: No.
>
> Q: Have you ever been told to cut back the wire as a matter of practice?
> A: No.
>
> Q: You have worked with other technicians and senior technicians, have you ever seen them cut back wire?
>
> A: I have never paid much attention to other technicians, to tell the truth, but I believe a lot of them work the same way as I do.
>
> Q: If the wire is pushed away from the terminal where it has been resting, in your view is it necessary to cut it back?
> A: No.
>
> Q: If you have not cut it back but have put it to the side as you say, have you left the wire safe?
> A: I believe so, yes."

8.13 It can be seen that not only did Mr Hemingway have a practice of omitting to cut back the old wire, whether by cutting off merely the eye, or by cutting it back still further, but also that he believed it was perfectly safe to leave the wire at its former length. He had worked on that basis for a long time and nobody had ever told him that what he was doing was wrong.

8.14 The same was just as true of his practice of simply moving the wire to one side, rather than securing it by tying it back to other wires coming off the branches of the tree. Again nobody had ever told him that this was wrong. As to the re-use of insulating tape rather than using fresh tape on all occasions, again nobody had ever suggested that this was an error and that he should correct it.

8.15 It is completely clear that this was the way Mr Hemingway had worked throughout his sixteen years in the S&T Department without there ever having been an occasion of complaint by any supervisor or other technician that what he was doing was not only contrary to proper practice, but obviously unsafe. Had any of those who supervised him, whether at the Wimbledon depot after the reorganisation in Summer 1988, or at South Lambeth in the seven years before, or indeed at any earlier stage in his railway career, looked properly at Mr Hemingway's work they ought to have detected and corrected these errors in his working practices.

8.16 It follows therefore from Mr Hemingway's long continuing of these errors that it is not merely at the quality of supervision by Mr Bumstead on the day in question that criticism must be levelled, but in effect at the quality of supervision throughout Mr Hemingway's railway career. That such criticism was perfectly justified and on such a wide ambit was inherent in a concession very frankly made by Mr Roger Henderson Q.C. for BR, at the start of his cross-examination of Mr Hemingway on Day 14 of the Investigation. He said:

67

"Mr Hemingway, before I ask you any questions, can I just make one or two things absolutely plain so that people understand what British Rail's stance is. You have said that it was not your practice to shorten wires, nor was it your practice to cut off eyes. You said it was your practice to re-use insulating tape. You have described your method of doing it. You said it was not your practice to secure the wires back in the sense of tying them back, but instead to push them aside and you have used the word to "flick". I make it quite plain to you that in relation to all those matters we recognise that those are not satisfactory and indeed bad practices but that the blame for that does not lie with you, it lies with British Rail. Either it should never have been allowed in the first place or once it had happened and the practice had become your practice and indeed was commonplace, it should have been stopped because the matter should have been monitored. So, there is no criticism of you for those failings which we recognise are our failings and not yours . . . "

We shall move to specific criticisms in relation to the supervising of Mr Hemingway later in this chapter, but in the meantime it is necessary to look at other mistakes Mr Hemingway made on the day in question.

The uncharacteristic errors

8.17 The errors which have so far been described have all fallen into the category of errors which were consistent and continual in all that Mr Hemingway did as a senior technician: they arose out of his normal practice. There was, however, a second category of error made by Mr Hemingway that day which had nothing to do with his normal practice and was totally uncharacteristic of his work.

8.18 The first of these was that two wires, not one, were left connected at fuse R12 - 107, the old "black" wire being connected underneath the new "yellow" wire. One thing which should have been utterly clear to Mr Hemingway from looking at his wiring diagram was that the old "black" wire at the fuse end had to be removed as an essential part of the jobs he was doing. Indeed he said in evidence:

"It is still beyond me how it did not get done."

The fact that it remained on that terminal had nothing to do with perpetual errors in working practice. It was a different and major error with disastrous implications.

8.19 The second error was that Mr Hemingway failed to insulate the bare end of the old wire at the relay end at all. I have earlier found in Chapter 7 at paragraph 7.28 that the reason for there being no tape on the relay end of the "black" wire on the morning of the accident was not Mr Hemingway's habit of re-using insulating tape. It was rather that Mr Hemingway failed to use any insulating tape at all on that wire. This again was totally uncharacteristic of him. How did these uncharacteristic errors come to be made by Mr Hemingway?

8.20 The one thing which is clear about Mr Hemingway's method of work is that he is both meticulous and consistent in his approach to that work, whether his practices are right or wrong. Thus, the aspects of his bad practices described in paragraph 8.3 are constant in their repetition. Quite different, however, are the failure to remove the old "black" wire at the fuse end and the failure to insulate the same wire at the relay end. They are completely out of character.

8.21 I am satisfied that it was indeed Mr Hemingway and not Mr Dowd who added the "yellow" wire to and on top of the "black" one already connected to fuse 107. I am satisfied that, at the moment he did that, he intended to deal with the "black" wire at a later stage. It may be that he was in fact confused by the process of combining the two jobs, but whatever it was I am satisfied that he never came back to the fuse to put that intention into effect.

8.22 The only possible explanation for these uncharacteristic errors in work which was otherwise carried out to a set pattern with great consistency is that Mr Hemingway's concentration was broken by an interruption of some sort. That interruption caused him to have his mind diverted elsewhere and by the time he turned his attention back to his own work, he forgot that he still had more to do. His recollection told him wrongly that he had in fact finished his work for the morning. He had not, and he never returned to finish the jobs.

8.23 I am satisfied that such an interruption came and that the stage at which it came was when he had just connected the new yellow wire at terminal 4-Arm on relay TRR DM, had just moved the old "black" wire a little out of the way of the terminal and was about to tape it with insulating tape. As his next job he would have gone to the fuse end and disconnected or cut back the other end of the same "black" wire. It was at that moment that he was interrupted. The relay would then have been in the state it appears in Figure 13, save that what is there described as "redundant wire" would have been untaped and moved a little out of the way (that photograph was taken after the accident and after the eye of the wire had been cut off and the bare end then taped).

The interruption

8.24 Mr Hemingway could not, understandably enough, remember in what way he had tackled job numbers 104 and 201 that morning because they were "run of the mill" and, once done, were quickly forgotten. He thus could not say in what order he had done any particular tasks. However, again understandably, he was able to remember other people coming into the relay room from time to time. Apart from such every day matters as Mr Dowd bringing tea, there were other interruptions. There were, for instance, problems with the work outside the Box for the same Job Nos. 104 and 201: someone from the outside teams came in with a problem and Mr Hemingway tried to help. Mr Hemingway thought it was a Mr Percival, but was not sure and the identity does not matter. Mr Dray, the Testing and Commissioning Engineer, came into the relay room too, because he was looking at the outside drawings with that same member of the outside team.

8.25 Mr Hemingway accepted the possibility that errors could be caused by interruptions, but did not claim to remember them as a fact and did not for a moment seek to use them as an excuse. I find, however, that such an interruption did take his mind off the work he was then doing and that, once he had given his assistance in relation to the outside drawings, he had a moment of forgetfulness and believed he had finished his own morning's work. Such a mistake is perhaps the more understandable in that he had very nearly finished it in any event. As a result, he did not return to it, and did not realise that it was incomplete, and dangerously so.

8.26 Although Mr Hemingway never thought for a moment to blame the constant seven day a week working that he had been engaged in as the cause of any of his errors, it is more likely than not that such a work programme was the trigger for such a gross error. He was not normally troubled by interruption to his work, nor a man prone to lapses of concentration, rather the opposite. I find that this lapse of concentration and inattention to detail was probably caused by the blunting of the sharp edge of close attention which working every day of the week, without the refreshing factor of days off, produces.

The independent wire count that did not take place

8.27 Any worker will make mistakes during his working life. No matter how conscientious he is in preparing and carrying out his work, there will come a time when he makes a slip. It is those unusual and infrequent events that have to be guarded against by a system of independent checking of his work. This is true of any industry, but it is essential in such a safety-dependent industry as the railway and especially in the installation of new signalling. The installer who makes an error may, when he looks at the work, miss the error he has made. He may see what he thought he had done, and meant to do, not what he has in fact done.

8.28 The safety check done by an independent person which both good practice and written Departmental Instructions demand, is a check of the number of wires connected to each terminal in the circuit against the number appearing on the wiring diagram. Its purpose is to ensure that there are no extraneous connections giving false feeds of current. This independent wire check is a vital weapon in the armoury of safety.

8.29 Once Mr Hemingway had finished by lunchtime all his installation work for that day, there were then some hours of waiting until the testing could commence. The actual work content of a Sunday, if there was to be no main commissioning, would not be very much. There would therefore have been time for him to carry out a wire count on his own work. This would not have been an independent wire count, but it would have taken him back to the fuse end where he would have seen how his own work had been left unfinished. He could have looked at the wiring diagram while an assistant called out the number of wires on the fuse end. Both Mr Dowd or Mr Marsh (who was also waiting in the signal box for the testing to begin) were available to help him. If that exercise had been done, the rogue wire would have been discovered immediately and the accident would not have happened.

8.30 Mr Hemingway did not at that stage do a wire count of his own work. His practice was to do the wire count as he was doing the job, not to do one as a final check. He was not expecting anyone visually to check his work or to wire count his work that afternoon. Nobody ever had before. At his level he had no concept of how essential it was that there was an independent wire count by a third party not involved with the work. In fairness to him, nobody had ever taught him the importance of an independent wire count or instructed him to do a final wire count of his own when he had finished his work.

8.31 As to what instructions he considered that he needed for doing his own checking and testing he said:

> "I know what I have got to do. I have been doing it for quite a while now, so I have never really given it any thought . . . I mean I suppose there must be a set procedure to work to . . . if you have got a separate procedure written down in front of you then you follow it."

He had not given any thought to doing a wire count of his own and was not aware of any instruction or good practice which said he should. Thus, Mr Hemingway was not going to do a wire count of his own work that day. When he was interrupted and thereafter wrongly thought that he had finished his job, he had already looked his last at his work.

8.32 However, other independent eyes should have been looking at the work after he had finished it since it is actually an independent wire count that both good practice and Departmental Instructions called for. That independent wire count should have been carried out before the line was re-commissioned by one, other, or both of Mr Bumstead, the Supervisor, and Mr Dray the Testing and Commissioning Engineer. The actual responsibility for ensuring that it had been carried out lay with the Testing & Commissioning Engineer. It was a relatively simple procedure, and it would have been perfectly acceptable to have delegated it to supervisor level. Neither made the least attempt to carry out any such count.

8.33 An independent wire count could and should have prevented this accident. The responsibility for the accident does not for a moment lie, as Mr Hemingway seemed to believe it did, solely upon his shoulders. His were the original errors, but they should have been discovered and neutralised by the processes of supervision and testing.

Mr Bumstead

8.34 Though Mr Bumstead had the responsibility for supervising Mr Hemingway's work that day, he carried out no such supervision. He spent his time out on the tracks leading a gang involved in the outside work. In his favour it has to be said that he was not for a moment slacking. He worked long and hard with them, often carrying out the manual work himself. He was fulfilling the role of a senior technician rather than a supervisor. What was wrong with the way he approached his tasks that Sunday was that he got himself so fully involved in this role that he totally neglected his duties as a supervisor.

8.35 Mr Bumstead did not even enter the relay room that day. It followed that the errors made by Mr Hemingway, which should have been detected by the eyes of a supervisor checking the relay top, went entirely undetected. The old wire went unseen, both at the relay end and at the fuse end. Had Mr Bumstead used the wiring diagram to carry out a wire count, even if he had not spotted the state of the old "black" wire at the relay end, he could not have failed to notice its extra unwanted and disastrous presence on fuse 107. Had the old black wire been disconnected from that fuse and properly secured the accident could not have happened.

8.36 Thus Mr Bumstead's work that day was energetic, and continuous, but it was pointed in the wrong direction. As a result of the limited numbers available to work and because of his good opinion of Mr Hemingway's quality, he left Mr Hemingway unsupervised in the relay room and led one of the external gangs himself. It was, no doubt, part of his own style of leadership that he involved himself so closely with the physical work that had to be done. The limited workforce available contributed to the problem, but I find that he over-involved himself in carrying out tasks rightly the responsibility of technicians and under-involved himself in the tasks essential to his role as supervisor. Just as the limitations of the available workforce and the demands of constant weekend work had combined to blunt Mr Hemingway's edge of concentration, so had they distorted Mr Bumstead's direction of attention.

8.37 Mr Bumstead was a Temporary Supervisor at South Lambeth by 1976, a Supervisor by 1978, a Senior Supervisor soon afterwards and by 1984 was a Supervisor Grade E. He moved from South Lambeth to Wimbledon in the Summer of 1988 on reorganisation. He was therefore very experienced.

8.38 Mr Bumstead's reasons for not doing an independent wire count in the relay room were:

(i) that he was expecting Mr Hemingway to wire count his own work as he went along;

(ii) that the general practice for years back had been one of installers checking their own work; and

(iii) independent wire counts had not been mentioned by anyone as a requirement for WARS work and he had never known an independent count to be done in relay rooms on commissioning days.

Mr Bumstead and SL-53

8.39 On 11 May 1987 the S&T Department of BR Southern Region issued a Departmental Instruction No.SL-53 entitled "TESTING NEW AND ALTERED SIGNALLING" which had been signed on 3 April 1987. It should have been issued down to supervisor level and thus it should have reached and been studied by Mr Bumstead. One of its internal testing requirements at paragraph 4.4. was to:

"Carry out a wire count on all free-wired safety relays and terminations . . ."

71

Mr Bumstead said that he had not received a copy of SL-53 between its issue in May 1987 and the accident in December 1988. In this he was not alone among the supervisors and I find that although he should have received a copy of SL-53, he did not.

8.40 SL-53 had been preceded by an instruction described as SL-Provisional which had been issued in October 1985, and which we will look at later. Mr Bumstead should have been issued with that document too. He said in evidence that it had never been issued to him, and I accept that evidence. Nonetheless, since SL-53 was in fact and was intended to be a direction in relation to existing good practice in the S&T Department, Mr Bumstead and the other supervisors should have known that there was a requirement for an independent wire count whenever new works were being brought into operation. Since other supervisors were aware of the need for an independent wire count as a matter of good practice, so should Mr Bumstead have been.

8.41 He was not aware either of the requirement of SL-53, of SL-Provisional, or of the requirement of good practice. He would therefore not have been doing or arranging for an independent wire count, in that he did not believe the system called for such a wire count. In that he was at fault, but the fault of the system was graver. It was that fault that permitted Mr Hemingway's errors to go undetected.

8.42 Nor did Mr Bumstead regard it as his duty to check the quality of Mr Hemingway's work on Sunday, 27 November 1988. Thus another protection which might have assisted safety was ignored. Though it might have assisted safety in other circumstances, it is in fact unlikely that under Mr Bumstead's supervision it would have done so: that was because of the perfunctory and totally inadequate nature of the quality check Mr Bumstead used to perform. Thus, even had Mr Bumstead come back from his outside work into the relay room that Sunday and made a decision to make a quality check in that relay room, it is unlikely that his type of quality check would have detected anything wrong. Mr Bumstead himself described his practice. His evidence on this matter went thus:

> "*Q: When you did a quality check in the relay room perhaps you could describe what exactly you do with regard to the relays?*
> *A: The relays? Well, I walk round the relay racks and see that wires are not anywhere touching the live contact and see that the wires that are being run are taped.*
>
> *Q: Do you check the tops of relay boxes?*
> *A: Only if they are at your height. You have a hard job to inspect just on a walk round relays that are below the level of your height because you require a lamp to inspect them and I don't carry a lamp with me.*
>
> *Q: What are the lighting conditions like?*
> *A: Poor.*
>
> *Q: And the general condition of the wire?*
> *A: Poor.*"

As an example of the defective quality of the supervision effected by Mr Bumstead, such a description in his own words can hardly be bettered.

The wire count and the Testing & Commissioning Engineer

8.43 If Mr Bumstead's lack of supervision of Mr Hemingway had failed to pick up the dreadful errors that had been made in that relay room on the day in question, then there should have been a further safety net in the presence on the scene of a Testing and Commissioning Engineer, Mr Dray. I shall look more closely at the testing defects both of Mr Dray himself and of the system in the next chapter. For the moment, suffice it to say, that although Departmental Instructions and good practice in railway signalling demanded that the tester either carried out, or ensured that there had been carried out, an independent wire count, Mr Dray did no such thing. The wire count properly carried out would have prevented the accident. It was not carried out and the accident was not prevented.

8.44 Thus, what had originally been a perfectly reasonable system directed towards the safety of the railway and based sensibly on a three-level system of installer, supervisor and tester, degenerated into a series of individual errors at those three levels of staffing within the S&T Department. At each level, whether installer, supervisor or tester, it was the duty of the operative in accordance with BR's commitment to "absolute safety" and "zero accidents" to carry out his own work to the highest practicable standards. At each of those three levels that was not done: the standards of work had been allowed by BR to slip to unacceptable and dangerous levels. Despite the commitment to "zero accidents" the reality was one appalling accident. The intention of the system and the reliance upon a three-level method of reducing the risk of an accident to the lowest possible level had not worked.

8.45 That system was designed to produce a failsafe situation when new signalling works were installed. That it did not was the result of error compounded upon error. Again, however, it was not merely the three specific individuals who made these specific errors that were to blame, but also those who allowed an originally sensible and workable system to degenerate into an incompetent, inept and potentially disastrous way of working.

The planning of Sunday, 27 November 1988

8.46 There was incompetence, ineptitude, inefficiency and failure of management in the way it came about that on Sunday, 27 November 1988, that particular workforce were engaged in doing those particular jobs. Under the WARS programme of stageworks, that particular workload had been ordained years earlier for that particular weekend. The way in which that particular workload came to marry up with the particular workforce who chose to attend on that day is a matter which needs to be examined.

8.47 Very early in 1986, Mr Gordon Callander, then working in the comparatively junior position of Senior Construction Assistant at the South Lambeth depot, began to plan out the weekend "packages" of work on the WARS scheme which would run from first commissioning in April 1987 right through into the middle of 1989. Nobody told him that he was responsible for this task, but he very conscientiously took the job upon himself. At a meeting held at the South Lambeth depot on Wednesday, 11 February 1987, his proposals were approved and they included the specific work for the weekend of 26/27 November 1988, for what were said to be "track and signal conversions on Up Main fast" between Clapham Junction and Wimbledon.

8.48 Mr Callander had no experience of organising and planning such extensive works, but he did know from experience on previous jobs how much could be achieved in any one weekend. He therefore worked out how many weekends he would require. It is important to note that in working out that equation, he was using staffing levels at the time back in 1986 which were to deteriorate significantly over the next two years into 1988.

8.49 One of the reasons for staff leaving BR in that period was the unsociable hours aspect of weekend work. Such people by late 1988 would no longer have been available for weekend work. This matter will have to be dealt with in greater detail in Chapter 12. For the moment it is sufficient to draw attention to the way in which the weekend workload for the last weekend in November 1988 was originally decided upon, more than two years earlier, on the basis of how much work could be done in a 1988 weekend at 1986 staffing levels.

8.50 No adjustment was ever made later to those workloads in the light of changed circumstances in relation to staffing. Nobody in management at a higher level than Mr Callander ever reviewed the situation. It is true to say that shortly before the weekend in question Mr Callander, in his post-1988 reorganisation position as Area Testing & Commissioning Engineer did change the detail of the work to be done in relation to one particular set of points, but that was all. It was thus that the workload for the weekend was arrived at. How was the workforce for that workload selected? At what level in management were the decisions made which provided for the selection of that workforce?

8.51 The plain answer to that question is that the workforce was never selected: it merely selected itself. The identity of the persons who attended for work on any particular weekend depended entirely upon the wishes of the individual worker as to whether or not he wanted to do overtime. A sheet was put up on the depot notice board on the previous Friday and those who wished to do so had until Tuesday to tick the "Yes" column. Everyone who had said "Yes" by Tuesday when the sheet was taken down was ensured of work that weekend. Neither the particular size of the workforce, nor the particular mix of grades of supervisors, senior technicians and technicians bore any relationship whatsoever to the workload which had been decided in a relatively arbitrary fashion some two years before and had not been raised since, despite a reduction in the number of skilled staff available at the depots. If it was considered that there might not be enough staff then others had to be sought from other depots and, indeed, for the weekend in question seven extra staff were brought in from Eastleigh.

8.52 The result, of course, was that although during the week the men worked together in teams and knew the ability of their colleagues, at the weekend they would not be working in such teams and would have no idea of the ability of many of the other workers. No attempt was ever made by anyone in authority to monitor this unsatisfactory state of affairs or to regularise the position.

8.53 Even worse because the schedule of work on WARS became even tighter in the second half of 1988 when Stage 7B began, as will be seen in Chapter 12, commissionings had to take place every weekend. As a result there was overtime work every weekend. Overtime was popular for two reasons:

(i) it involved higher rates of pay being available to be earned so that, by constant overtime working, a man could double his annual basic salary; and

(ii) for a man such as Mr Hemingway there was the job satisfaction of carrying out the connection of wires that he had prepared in the week and thus of seeing the job through.

8.54 There was thus always available at weekends a ready source of supply of labour in the form of men who had already worked a full working week. Whilst this was satisfactory and could be tolerated for a number of isolated weekends it was not good for morale, for enthusiasm for the task, or for clearness of thought and sharpness of action that, week after week, the same men should be working seven days a week. Mr Hemingway was one such man who was very happy to work overtime, who did not feel that it affected him in any way, who liked seeing the job through and who was happy to double his annual income from £8,000 to £16,000 in this way. He was not alone in this and the Investigation saw sample figures which showed that in the thirteen weeks preceding the accident 28% of the workforce worked 7 days every week, and another 34% worked 13 days out of 14. Thus, nearly a third of the workforce were working every day over that period, and a further third had only one day off each fortnight.

8.55 Mr Callander accepted in his evidence that continuous working of seven days a week every week was affecting the ability of the staff in their mental alertness. He thought it would be human nature that there would be some slippage of the high standards that the job required. He thought that having just that one day in the week off made a tremendous difference, that "it took a time to reveal itself, the continuous strain of working every day".

8.56 The Investigation heard much evidence that the effect of constant weekend working was likely to dull the cutting edge of efficiency of those who undertook such work. It followed that it was a clear minus factor so far as safety was concerned. Although it should have been obvious that it was constantly the same individuals who were doing the weekend overtime, that fact was never monitored, nor was it ever registered by senior management. The result was that there was never an appropriate selection process of a suitable workforce to carry out the actual work involved on a particular weekend. Insofar as there was any selection it was self-selection by the workforce itself. Such a system necessarily involved an abdication of management's responsibilities at which we shall look more closely in later chapters.

8.57 It was submitted that two other factors affected the state of mind and efficiency of the workforce during this period. Neither of them do I find to have had any such effect in fact. First, it was suggested that there was an overall tiredness affecting the workforce, in that the week's work was so extensive that by the weekend the workers were overworked and exhausted. That I cannot accept: all the evidence showed that during the week the workload was not excessive by any means and that at a commissioning weekend the load was greater but perfectly manageable. There were also many hours of waiting during which no work was in fact being carried out. No question of exhaustion arises and indeed it was the evidence of Mr Hemingway that he was a man who had plenty of time to do the work, who felt perfectly fit to do it, who enjoyed the work and who thought he was doing it, not just to acceptable standards of competence within BR, but doing it well.

8.58 The second suggestion was that the wholesale reorganisation of the S&T Department in the Summer of 1988 had a lowering effect on the morale of staff which was reflected in a lowering of standards of work. Whilst I entirely accept that at certain higher levels this was regrettably so, that was not the position with the S&T staff actually doing the installation work. It was the same WARS work which they were doing from the Wimbledon Depot which they had in the main been doing from the South Lambeth Depot and they were in the main the same workforce. The men actually doing the work at the "pit face", that is on the tracks and in the relay rooms were less affected by the general disruption of the reorganisation of the Summer 1988 than were those above them. Reorganisation and its effects will be considered in Chapter 10.

8.59 Of those above them, one particularly adversely affected by the reorganisation of 1988 was the Testing and Commissioning Engineer on the day in question, Mr Peter Dray. He it was who should have ensured that an independent wire count was carried out in the relay room on the work done on Job Nos. 104 and 201 before he commissioned the line back into service. It is to the question of the testing of New Works that I now turn.

Chapter 9: The testing of new works: the last defence

9.1   As we saw in Chapter 8, an independent wire count to check the wiring work actually done against that called for by the wiring diagram would have revealed the two wires attached at the fuse at Row 12 - 107 when there should only have been one. The responsibility for ensuring that such a wire count was in fact carried out rested on the shoulders of the Testing & Commissioning Engineer. It is therefore necessary to seek to establish why Mr Dray did not ensure that such a wire count had been done. Departmental Instruction SL-53 requires that an independent wire count be carried out. If he had been working to that Instruction, the wire count would have been done and it would have disclosed the fault. This Chapter looks at first Mr Dray's background, his experience, and his attitudes and, in particular, the way in which he came to be doing the testing on Sunday, 27 November 1988.

Mr Peter Dray

9.2   In that month there was no permanent Testing and Commissioning Engineer for the South West Area of BR Southern Region. Mr Gordon Callander had held that post for the few months since reorganisation in May 1988 until October 1988. There was therefore a vacancy for a Testing and Commissioning Engineer working from Wimbledon, which was taken by Mr Dray on a temporary basis.

9.3   Mr Dray was living in the Ashford area and had been badly affected by the reorganisation in which his previous job as Site Engineer at the Ashford depot had disappeared. He had made four or five applications for other jobs, but had been successful in none. It followed that in railway terms he had become "displaced" and "unallocated". It was a situation in which he had been before. For a time he remained at Ashford, as he put it, finishing off the odd scheme which was still going on.

9.4   It was in these circumstances that Mr Dray was invited to take the temporary vacancy as the Testing & Commissioning Engineer at Wimbledon until Mr Callander's successor was appointed. Although he had been asked whether he was interested in applying for the job on a permanent basis, he had declined to do so by reason of the travelling involved: however, he felt he did not have much choice about taking the job on a temporary basis because he was displaced.

9.5   This was the way in which he came to be at Wimbledon as an Acting Testing & Commissioning Engineer for what was expected to be a six week period. He was doing a job which he had really no wish to do at a place where he had no wish to be. If he had little liking for the job, he had less enthusiasm.

9.6   He had no real induction training. Although both he and Mr Callander were at Wimbledon for some weeks before Mr Callander left, they were doing different types of work and only saw each other on some mornings. In any event Mr Callander regarded him as a caretaker in the job, and did not go into any detail about it with him. There was no discussion between them about

Mr Dray's duties or about SL-53. Mr Callander said that he did not realise until later on that Mr Dray was going to stand in his shoes when he left: had he realised that earlier, he would have endeavoured to provide Mr Dray with more in the way of induction. It has to be doubted that the situation would in fact have changed even if Mr Callander had arrived at that realisation.

9.7   Mr Dray had not done wire counts on British Rail work for perhaps ten or eleven years. He had been at Ashford in October 1985 when a document called SL-Provisional had been issued. It was entitled "TESTING OF NEW AND ALTERED SIGNALLING". He was himself doing some testing at the time but he did not regard the document as in force. When it was issued he thought it was a discussion document and he was asked for comments on it and made some on a scrap of paper. He did not receive a letter written on behalf of the Regional S&T Engineer, Mr Clifford Hale, on 15 November 1985, giving SL-Provisional the full authority of any other Departmental Instruction. In that he was not alone, and the failure of that letter to reach all those to whom it was directed is another example of the failure of communications on the part of the S&T Department which we shall need to return to in Chapter 11. If he had received that letter, he would have known that the Instruction was in force and that an independent wire count was essential. To him, however, SL-Provisional remained a discussion document.

9.8   Although Mr Dray said that at Ashford the Instruction was worked to "in the spirit of it", he said that he did not treat it as part of the testing procedure "because at Ashford my responsibility was the functional test". In fact paragraph 3.3 of SL-Provisional states:

> *"A wire count must be carried out on all free-wired safety relays and terminations and recorded on the contact/terminal analysis sheets."*

9.9   Had Mr Dray regarded SL-Provisional as in force and part of the testing procedure, he would have needed to comply with that Instruction. However, neither at Ashford nor at Wimbledon did he understand that wire counts were his responsibility. He thought that such work should be covered by the workforce, by the supervisors or leading technicians who were doing the actual changeover. He did not understand that he had any responsibility to ensure that an independent wire count had been carried out. So it was that his attitude mirrored that of Mr Hemingway and Mr Bumstead that any sort of wire count was no responsibility of theirs. Like them he had no concept of the essential importance of an *independent* wire count.

9.10   The arrival on the scene of Departmental Instruction SL-53 made no difference to his attitude. When it was issued on 11 May 1987, Mr Dray regarded it as a document which had merely arrived in his "In-tray" with no accompanying instruction from BR as to how it should be implemented or what it was about. He said in evidence that it had never been put fully into operation and that when he was at Ashford and when he later took over as Temporary Testing & Commissioning Engineer at Wimbledon, he did not think of himself as having overall responsibility for its implementation: nobody told him he had that responsibility.

9.11   This was accepted by Mr Callander who agreed that he did not tell Mr Dray that they were not implementing SL-53 at Wimbledon. That was, in fact, the case but Mr Callander did not regard it as significant enough to tell his temporary replacement.

9.12 That, then, was the situation on the morning of Sunday, 27 November, at about 09:30 when Mr Dray arrived at Clapham Junction "A" signalbox for what was only his third weekend of testing in his temporary position as the Testing & Commissioning Engineer for the South Western Area. As he waited in that signal box until just after 2:00 p.m. for the testing to start, he had in his mind no clear idea of what his duties were, or of any Departmental Instruction with which he should be complying in the work he was about to do in testing the New Works before the lines were restored to public use.

9.13 The very first words of Departmental Instruction SL-53 read:

"1. **Roles of key staff**

1.1 *Person in Overall Charge of Testing Scheme*

To assess, on a continuous basis, resources needed on schemes and produce a detailed testing programme. Define and control detailed requirements. Carry out final functional tests and certify installation ready for service. Agree detailed staging arrangements."

Despite those words, Mr Dray told the Investigation that he did not understand who was to be the person in charge and he never thought paragraph 1.1 of SL-53 referred to him.

9.14 He said he did not think he was a high enough grade and he had never actually worked to this part of SL-53. He did not in any event believe that the document was capable of being put into practice because of staffing levels. He did not ask the technicians or supervisors if they were applying SL-53, despite the fact that on the relevant Area Certificate of Test he was later to put his signature to the words:

"Work correctly installed to issued diagrams and approved amendments thereto and tested in accordance with Departmental Instruction SL-53."

The words on that Certificate had been drafted by Mr Callander. They were, in fact, not worth the paper they were written on because neither Mr Callander, the drafter of the Certificate, nor Mr Dray, its signatory, were making the least attempt to work to SL-53.

9.15 Mr Dray said in evidence that he made no attempt to put SL-53 into practice:

"Mr Callander wasn't and nobody senior to me was making sure I did."

He said that a practice had developed whereby he felt he could do his job simply by doing a functional test. He admitted, however, that a functional test could not ensure the safety of the equipment. He accepted that the document SL-53 played no part in his way of thinking and that he did not apply his mind to what tests were being carried out by others in the context of SL-53.

9.16 How it could come about that a tester on such safety-critical new installations as WARS could be happy to turn his back on so fundamentally relevant and important an instruction as SL-53 would seem inexplicable were it not for the realisation of how poor were BR's channels of communication and instruction in the S&T Department of Southern Region. This is a matter which will be dealt with in more detail in Chapter 11.

9.17 Departmental Instruction SL-53 requires the person in charge of internal testing to carry out all internal testing requirements (para.1.2). Those requirements include, under paragraph 4, the carrying out of a buzzer test (para.4.2) and the carrying out of a wire count (para.4.4). Mr Dray carried out neither. For the second time, and now at the testing rather than the supervisory level, an independent wire count was to be ignored as a safety check. Such a wire count would have revealed two wires instead of one at the fuse end, and would have prevented the accident.

9.18 Mr Dray's response to the suggestion that he might actually himself have done a wire count emerged in his evidence in chief:

"*Q: Back to the question of your responsibilities as far as wire counts are concerned, looking at the scheme of work as it was in operation at Wimbledon when you were temporary Testing and Commissioning Engineer, if it was suggested to you that the T&C could and should have gone into the relay room prior to changeover and conducted a wire count themselves, what would your response be to that suggestion?*

A: I would have wanted somebody, assistance to actually do it. As I was on the signalling floor, I do not like to leave the signalling floor, because of the phone, and people want to know where you are all the time. That is the kind of control point. So I would not really want to leave the actual signalling floor. If it had been my responsibility I would have had to have had a supervisor or a P&T (Professional and Technical) staff to come and actually do the wire count for me."

In cross-examination he at first persisted in that attitude:

"*Q: The fact is Mr Dray, there was no reason why you and/or Mr Marsh could not have ensured that the internal work in the relay room was checked in accordance with the full provisions of SL-53, paragraph 4, was there?*

A: I do not think I would have gone into the relay room to work, no. I needed to be by the phone."

Three questions later however, the question had to be faced:

"*Q: I would like you to help me. There was no reason was there, why the full provisions of paragraph 4 of SL-53 should not have been put into effect by you through either using yourself, or through Mr Marsh, on the morning in question?*

A: No."

9.19 Thus it came about that the *independent* wire count was never done. The careful testing of intricate newly installed signalling equipment upon which the lives of passengers and crew depended was not carried out. The proper carrying out of the duties of the Testing & Commissioning Engineer is intended to be the last line of defence in relation to any errors or omissions of first, the installers and second, the supervisors. That last line of defence failed totally on Sunday, 27 November 1988.

9.20 The criticisms made in this Report of Mr Dray are and are intended to be trenchant. Yet again, however, in fairness to Mr Dray we shall see that it was not an isolated failure on the part of one man. We shall see that even if others had done the testing that day the result would have been all too tragically the same. It will be necessary to look at how it could come about that there could be such an attitude to the work of testing of newly installed signalling work, not just in the mind of Mr Dray, but throughout the S&T Department.

Mr Gordon Callander

9.21 Had Mr Callander still been in post as Testing & Commissioning Engineer on Sunday, 27 November 1988 and been in charge of the testing that day, the concept of an independent wire count would have fared no better. Such an essential safety check would still not have been done.

9.22 Despite the fact that Mr Callander was appointed as Testing & Commissioning Engineer for the whole of the South Western area on reorganisation in May 1988 and served in that post until 3 October 1988, he had never even read SL-53. Although he had had a copy from about mid-1987, a year before his appointment, and although throughout that year he had been responsible for all the WARS testing, amazingly he had only ever glanced through SL-53. He did not like it and he did not attempt to work to it.

9.23 Before he moved to Wimbledon on reorganisation, Mr Callander was serving at the South Lambeth depot as Senior Construction Assistant. There he worked under the Signal Construction Engineer who was first Mr Flook, until his retirement in September 1986, and thereafter Mr John Deane. Mr Callander said that when SL-53 was promulgated in 1987, it dropped into his basket on his desk at South Lambeth. He realised it was a Departmental Instruction and that it would have to be read carefully and thoroughly, but he did not do so: he merely glanced through it. He said that he had no time to sit and study it: he did not give it any more thought because his mind was occupied with more pressing problems. He said he merely filed it and carried on with the mounting volume of work he had. He said that if he had read SL-53 he would have decided he was incapable of carrying out all of the duties. He would have sent somebody else to test because he could not do all of the work involved in it.

9.24 This evidence of Mr Callander as to the way in which he treated Departmental Instruction SL-53, virtually ignoring it and hoping it would go away, is profoundly disturbing on two counts:

(i)   for what it reveals about the way in which Mr Callander elected to carry out his testing duties; and

(ii)   for what it reveals about the lack of management skills and actions of those who permitted him to do so.

9.25 Until May 1988, and with the agreement of Mr Geoffrey Bailey, the Regional Testing & Commissioning Engineer, Mr Callander had been responsible for all the testing done by the South Lambeth depot. That involved, as we have seen, all the testing to be done on the WARS project. Although there had existed since August 1986 Mr Bailey's Regional Testing Team (at which we shall have to look later in this Chapter), that team did not involve itself in WARS testing.

9.26 It followed that both before moving from South Lambeth to Wimbledon on reorganisation in May 1988 and thereafter, until 3 October 1988, the entire responsibility for the testing of new installations on the WARS scheme was placed in the hands of a man who had never read SL-53 and had never worked to it. It further follows that at no stage throughout that period did any of Mr Callander's superiors enquire whether he was working to SL-53 or discover that he was not. Thus, not only was the tester not testing according to Departmental Instructions, but also management was not managing the tester.

Mr Callander and the Certificate of Test

9.27 As we saw in para. 9.14 despite his dismissive attitude to SL-53, Mr Callander in fact referred to it in an Area Certificate of Test he drafted for the purpose of certifying that testing had been done. The earliest such certificate the Court saw was dated 30 June 1988. We have already seen the words to which the tester had to put his signature. The technicians and supervisors in turn had to certify that the work had been:

"Correctly installed and tested in accordance with Departmental Instruction SL-53."

9.28 In drafting such a certificate in order that technicians, supervisors and testers should certify that they had done something in accordance with SL-53 which they had not, Mr Callander accepted before the Court that he was requiring them to sign something which was incorrect. He said he had to use the reference to SL-53, because old Regional Certificates of Test which were still in current use referred to a Rule 77 of the General Rule Book. That rule had ceased to exist in 1972. He therefore thought the wisest course was to refer to SL-53. This was yet another example of the failure of BR to organise an effective means of communication with its staff even in a document as central to the safe running of the railways as the Rule Book. Rule 77 had gone in 1972 but nothing had replaced it.

9.29 The old Certificate of Test required, amongst other things, a signature in respect of internal electrical equipment against the statement:

> "Tested and found correct in accordance with . . . wiring diagram number . . ."

Equally the tester had himself to certify that all apparatus had been tested:

> "As prescribed in Rule 77 - General Rule Book - . . . and found correct in all respects with the wiring diagrams . . ."

Mr Callander accepted that under that old certificate there was a requirement for an independent wire count. However, he insisted that he did not regard it as his function to carry out such a wire count, nor any part of the responsibility of his job to ensure that a wire count had been carried out.

9.30 It follows that insofar as any testing undertaken by Mr Callander on the WARS project was concerned, the issue of Departmental Instruction SL-53 by management had made not a jot of difference to the way in which that work was in fact tested. Appearance had nothing to do with reality. The issue of that document had had no effect whatsoever in ensuring that an independent wire count had to be done. The protection and degree of safety that such a wire count would have provided was therefore denied.

9.31 We have seen that it would not have made any difference, whether on 27 November 1988, the testing had been done by Mr Dray or by Mr Callander, there would still have been no independent wire count. We must now look to see whether it would have made any difference if the testing had been done by Mr Bailey.

Mr Geoffrey Bailey

9.32 Until the 1988 reorganisation, Mr Bailey had been the Regional Testing Engineer in charge of the Regional Testing Team which consisted of himself and two assistants, Mr Bassett and Mr Blain. He held that post from August 1986, until the 1988 reorganisation when he moved to the position of Signal Works Engineer at the Wimbledon depot. In that new position he had in fact been responsible for the testing of the works done on Stage 7B of WARS on another weekend in November 1988 when Mr Dray could not be present. Further, Mr Bailey was actually in attendance during the afternoon of Sunday, 27 November at the Clapham Junction "A" relay room.

9.33 We shall see that yet again, in a repeat of what is becoming a dismal pattern, it would not have made any difference if Mr Bailey had actually been the Testing and Commissioning Engineer for that work. Mr Bailey had to admit in his evidence to the Investigation that he had a "blind spot" on the subject of wire counts. Had he been in charge of testing, an independent wire count would still not have been done.

9.34 On 4 August 1986, Mr Bailey took up his role as Regional Testing Engineer working from Croydon. He was coming back to the Southern Region after a spell with the Western. He told the Court that at the time he regarded the golden rule of testing to be: "to make sure the railways were safe for trains to run on". He thought that "safety is the paramount consideration". Within two weeks of his appointment, Mr Clifford Hale, the Regional S&T Engineer spoke to him. Mr Hale made it clear that the primary function of Mr Bailey's position was to raise the standard of testing on the Region and particularly to attempt to avoid some of the failures that had occurred at or just after commissioning. Mr Hale did not then identify those failures which had occurred in November 1985 and which were referred to during the Investigation as "the Oxted incidents".

9.35 In that same month on 21 August 1986, a Construction Group meeting was held at Exeter chaired by Mr Robert Davies, the Signal Works Engineer, and at which Mr Bailey (described in the minutes as "C9") attended. He learned more of his responsibilities at that meeting, the minutes of which read:

"In terms of scheme testing, C9's principal responsibilities are:

1. to determine the extent of testing required, (limits, type and duration).

2. to determine the personnel to be used for testing

3. to ensure that all testing has been carried out

4. to train staff in testing duties, techniques, and disciplines

5. to audit the standard of testing."

Those minutes also contain the following strong, clear and unequivocal sentence:

"It was emphasised and agreed that testing must be of the highest standard and that C9 has the responsibility for ensuring that this is so."

9.36 Neither Mr Hale nor the Construction Group Meeting, briefed him on the particular way in which he was supposed to raise the standard of testing and thereafter Mr Bailey was left largely to his own devices. He had a heavy workload and only two assistants, Mr Blain and Mr Bassett. Mr Bassett had to be trained before he could assist. Mr Bailey's resources were clearly limited and this was well known to management.

9.37 At about the same time and within two weeks of taking up the job Mr Bailey had a meeting at South Lambeth with Mr Flook and Mr Callander to discuss the arrangements for WARS testing. As a result of that meeting Mr Callander was left to carry out all the WARS testing, since it was considered that the workload of the Regional Testing Team would not have allowed it to cope with WARS. As a result Mr Bailey effectively left Mr Callander to carry out the testing unsupervised. Mr Callander, too, like Mr Bailey, was effectively left to his own devices.

9.38 When Mr Bailey came to the Region in August 1986, nine months after the Oxted incidents, he became aware in August 1986 of SL-Provisional which he thought was a consultation draft, an impression he told the Investigation he was sure he got from his superior, Mr Davies. Like Mr Dray, he never became aware of the memorandum of 15 November 1985, which gave it the full authority of any other Departmental Instruction. He did, however, make written comments and drafted a check list to assist Mr Davies in the putting together of SL-53 for its eventual issue in May 1987. In drafting those check-lists he entirely omitted any reference to the wire count.

9.39 Mr Davies must have noticed the omission because he remedied it by himself writing in the reference to wire counts in Mr Bailey's draft check-list so that wire counts did appear in SL-53. Unfortunately, Mr Davies did not take up with Mr Bailey this surprising omission and thus a "blind spot" remained undiscovered. We shall see more of this "blind spot" and how it emerged in evidence before the Court, later in this Chapter.

9.40 As to his understanding of the status of SL-53, Mr Bailey said that he first received a copy some time in the middle of 1987. He could not be sure when. He said that he was under the impression that SL-53 itself was not in force. There had been discussions within the Construction Group about SL-53 and it had been decided that a trial would be carried out at Forest Hill to see how the finished document actually worked in practice. He referred to a meeting of the Construction Group held on 23 August 1987, where SL-53 was discussed. Mr Bailey was not present at that meeting, but saw the minutes which contained the entry:

> "It was agreed the full provisions of SL-53 would be implemented for the Forest Hill relay room job."

In fact the Forest Hill work had still not been undertaken by the time of the Court hearings and its completion, therefore, at the time of writing of this Report, still lies in limbo. If the implementation of SL-53 had needed to await the Forest Hill work, it too would still have been a matter for the future.

9.41 Mr Bailey said he had not received instructions from anyone that SL-53 was in force. He said surprisingly that in his role as Regional Testing Engineer he would have expected to have received some instruction concerning the implementation of SL-53 and that such instruction should have come from Mr Davies who was his boss.

9.42 He could not recall any discussion between himself and Mr Callander on the subject of SL-53. He accepted that SL-53 was supposed to be distributed down to supervisor level and that if it had been, then those who received it would treat it as a Departmental Instruction, but he still insisted that none of SL-53 was to be put into force officially until after the Forest Hill relay room work.

9.43 Mr Bailey conceded in cross-examination that SL-53 had a greater significance to him than to any other individual in Southern Region. It was fundamental to his duties. It followed that he was the one person in the whole of Southern Region who should not have been in any doubt as to its applicability. He also conceded that if he had any doubts on the subject he should have asked his superior, Mr Davies. He reiterated that his state of mind was that SL-53 was not in force at the time of the Clapham Junction accident.

9.44 It is a matter which the Court can only look upon with both alarm and horror (a word not usually suitable for the dispassionate analysis which is required for an Investigation such as this) that the man in overall charge of the testing of new works for the whole of Southern Region could have arrived at a conclusion that a Departmental Instruction which had as its very title "TESTING OF NEW AND ALTERED SIGNALLING" and had been formally and properly issued, was not in force, and that he could have persisted in that view for a period of one and half years between the issue of that document and the accident. That such a situation could have arisen is both alarming and surprising enough, but that it should have been allowed to persist in an organisation whose proper and avowed aim is "absolute safety" almost beggars belief.

9.45 How he could have been permitted by his superiors to remain in that state of mind is a question the importance of which cannot be overstated: this matter will be dealt with in a later chapter. When that was Mr Bailey's attitude it is easier to see how others carrying out the testing on the region while he was Regional Testing Engineer did not have any clear idea of their own duties.

9.46 Not only was Mr Bailey not working to SL-53, but he was not working to SL-Provisional or to good practice either. All demand that an independent wire count is carried out as part of the testing procedure. Mr Bailey, however, did not regard an independent wire count to be part of testing procedure at all. A "blind spot" had intervened.

9.47 Mr Bailey took that state of mind acquired as Regional Testing Engineer with him to his new job at Wimbledon as Signal Works Engineer. Thus, as we have seen, if he been doing the testing and not Mr Dray on Sunday, 27 November, there would still have been no independent wire count. Mr Bailey agreed that he was not aware of any arrangement at Wimbledon between testers and supervisors that the supervisors would have responsibility to carry out the independent wire count. He was asked:

"*Q: Who else would be doing it?*
A: As it transpired, sir, nobody I think.

Q: Is that really the position, that you thought that no-one was carrying out independent wire counts?
A: I think at the time sir, as I have said before, I did not fully appreciate the philosophy of wire counting. I do not believe that I had specifically thought about that aspect of it sir.

Q: So would this be right, when you came to manage your supervisors, you would not have considered it any part of your responsibility to ensure that they themselves carried out independent wire counts?
A: Yes, I think that may have been the case, sir."

That situation should never have been permitted to arise, nor would it have been if earlier lessons had been learned within the S&T Department.

The Oxted Incidents: November 1985

9.48 When, in August 1986, Mr Hale had told Mr Bailey about recent failures in testing, although he did not identify those failures by time or place, he was referring Mr Bailey in particular, to a cluster of different wrong-side failures which had occurred in the month of November 1985, at Oxted, Northfleet and East Croydon. We shall need to look particularly at the Oxted incidents in order to see what caused them and how they are relevant to this Investigation.

9.49 In 1985 new signalling had been installed on the line between Sanderstead and Oxted. The work was to be commissioned on 2 November 1985. At that time there was additional pressure on the management staff at New Cross Gate, the depot which had done the work, particularly in extra testing commitments since the Design Office was unable to provide all the additional testing staff.

9.50 Three separate incidents occurred in the days following the commissioning of that work. In all of those incidents the testing was at fault, but the most alarming was that at signal OD7. By reason of two separate wiring faults OD7 was allowed to show a green aspect when it should not have done. This happened because a relay out at the signal was irregularly energised. In other words it was receiving a false feed just as three years later signal WF138 was to receive a false feed. This fault would have been discovered by a wire count: no wire count had in fact been done.

9.51 One of the two errors which caused this Oxted failure was that two wires had wrongly been connected to the same terminal of a relay when there should only have been one wire. The similarities between the essential ingredients of this incident and what was to happen three years later at Clapham Junction need no further underlining.

9.52 The Oxted incidents, their repercussions, and those at Northfleet when a signalman noticed irregular aspects being shown by a signal, and at East Croydon, which involved an accident in which two passenger trains had a side-on collision, had all occurred three years and one month before the Clapham Junction accident was to happen. They all happened within a period of a week in November 1985. They should have provided the clearest possible lessons that all was not well in the S&T Department. They should have been used as clear pointers to what was going wrong in the installation and testing practices on Southern Region. They could and should have achieved the result which Mr Bailey had called "the golden rule of testing", namely, to make sure the railways were safe for trains to run.

9.53 Instead, all that those incidents produced was:

(i) A brief flurry of paperwork over three or four months which provided important information, but on a very limited circulation;

(ii) despite an immediate recognition that the need for a new testing document was urgent, the emergence as late as 18 months afterwards of a document SL-53 which was never to be properly understood or implemented and was not to change any of the existing working practices for the better;

(iii) despite the recognition of the importance of training staff, not a single training course on testing in the three years before the Clapham Junction accident; and

(iv) the appointment of the Regional Testing Team under Mr Bailey, with the objective of raising standards of testing and avoiding failures, but with a workload, a lack of resources, and a lack of management direction which meant that, because of the sheer weight of non-WARS testing duties, those objectives were never going to be met.

9.54 Had the lessons of Oxted been learned at the appropriate levels, both above and below those who actually investigated the incidents, and had any proper and vigorous attempts been made to ensure that those lessons were taught to the workforce and fully understood by them, then the Clapham Junction accident should not have happened. The Court believes that it would not have happened. It is to those lessons that we now turn.

The lessons of Oxted 9.55 An inquiry was held into the incidents on 20 November 1985, chaired by Mr Davies, the Signal Works Engineer. All the other members came from the New Cross depot. That report established the fact that:

"There was a historic practice used by some of the staff at New Cross Gate of having both old and new wiring terminated on equipment at the same time in order to speed changeovers . . ."

The Oxted report found that those two wires should have been discovered by a wire count and went on to say that wire counts must be carried out immediately and that:

"Old and new circuitry must never be mixed unless the most stringent precautions are taken to prevent non-operation."

9.56 In its "Conclusion" the report noted that:

"There seems to have been a downward drift in the standards of production and checking of BR's own work. This combines to put greater and greater pressure on the functional tester, whilst at the same time the numbers of staff both inside and out available to undertake functional testing had been reduced, either directly in the case of DO" (Design Office) "staff, or indirectly by reducing the numbers of supervisors and shifting their work upwards to the outside management staff."

9.57 Mr Davies enclosed a copy of his report into the incidents in a letter of 10 February 1986 to the Signal Construction Engineers at all four depots, South Lambeth, New Cross, Eastleigh and Ashford. In the letter he said:

> "While the incidents relate to staff at New Cross Gate, the lessons to be learned are fundamental and must be noted by all staff and I summarise the recommendations of the report below:
>
> ....
>
> 3.2   Full wire counts of new or altered installations must be made . . ."

9.58 There was a Construction Group meeting a month later on 6 March 1986 attended by all four of those Signal Construction Engineers (including Mr Flook from South Lambeth and Mr Deane then at Ashford). Under Mr Davies's chairmanship that report was discussed at length. The minutes record these words:

> "The following is a definitive statement of all the recommendations applicable to SCEs and amplifies and interprets the report in a covering letter . . ."

One of those recommendations read:

> "Following any installation work a wire count of all the affected equipment must be made before commissioning."

9.59 That wire count was, of course, one done independently of the installer. If there was one lesson which the Oxted incidents should have taught the entire S&T Department of BR Southern Region, it was just that: an independent wire count of affected equipment must be done before the commissioning. The lesson was never learned for the simple reason that it was never properly taught. Admittedly, the Departmental Conference chaired by Mr Hale, at its meeting on 30 January 1986, recorded the fact that:

> "Whole works function to be reminded that instructions must be obeyed"

Despite that injunction, those instructions were still not obeyed. Management failed in its duty to monitor whether the issue of that command had any effect on the workforce.

9.60 In the wake of Oxted, SL-Provisional had been given the "full authority of any other Departmental Instruction" by the letter of 15 November 1985 referred to at paragraph 9.7 of this Chapter. Paragraph 3.3. of SL-Provisional was in totally clear terms:

> "3.3.   A wire count must be carried out on all free wired safety relays and terminations . . ."

Neither Oxted, nor the question of wire counts, were specifically mentioned by Mr Hale in his conversation with Mr Bailey on his appointment to the post of Regional Testing & Commissioning Engineer on the need to prevent recent failures recurring, and although the Oxted papers were provided for Mr Bailey, he never took on board their lessons.

9.61 In his evidence before the Court it emerged that surprisingly and really inexplicably Mr Bailey had a "blind spot" about the importance of a wire count. That "blind spot" should never have been allowed to occur had the lessons of Oxted been fully learned and properly and widely taught. Those lessons should have been further reinforced by those from the Queenstown Road incident which happened only six months before the Clapham Junction accident.

The Queenstown Road Incident: The Final Lesson Not Learned

9.62 The next station after Clapham Junction on the way into London actually bears on the front wall two names, Queens Road and Queenstown Road. These two names were interchangeable in the documents and in the evidence put before the Court. Resignalling work was done in the area of Queenstown Road on 22 May 1988. Once the work had been done it was tested. The work passed that test and was commissioned into service that day.

9.63 Just over three weeks later on Tuesday, 14 June a driver of a Waterloo to Hampton Court train was stopped by a red aspect at signal WA28 on the Down Main Local line. He could see a train ahead of him on his line at the station. He was able to see that train move off towards Clapham Junction and so knew that his signal WA28 should clear to yellow. In fact it cleared directly to green before reverting to single yellow. He spoke to the signalman who immediately called in the S&T Department.

9.64 This was a wrong-side failure, but fortunately it had occurred on a straight stretch of track where the driver could see the train ahead and its movements, and could thus detect that the signal had a fault. That fault had two causes:

(i) design errors emanating from the Design Office; and

(ii) the failure to carry out proper testing procedure.

9.65 The Design Office had issued a drawing which completely omitted one track circuit from the controls of signal WA28. This was a repeat of what had happened at one of the Oxted incidents. Such a fundamental error should have been found in the Design Office checking procedure: it was not. It should have been found by subsequent Design Office checking: it was not. It should have been found in the testing: it was not.

9.66 Both the errors of the Design Office and of the Testing procedure which perpetuated the fault highlight important defects with vital safety implications in the S&T Department. The safety implications should have had wide circulation: the facts should have been assimilated, the lessons learned and the lessons taught to the workforce. None of this happened. Instead management interest seemed to be satisfied by the taking of disciplinary proceedings against the supervisor concerned with the testing. Those proceedings, as it happened, were ineffectual.

9.67 Mr Bailey in his new role at Wimbledon investigated the Queenstown Road incident, identified correctly the causes, and made a report. Here, too, was a "repeat" of the procedure which had followed the Oxted incidents. Once again, although the errors had been identified, no thought was given to two clearly important questions:

(i) how the lessons could be taught to the workforce at Technical and Supervisor levels; and

(ii) what lessons there were for management to learn from the errors?

9.68 In his report on the incident dated 20 June 1988, Mr Bailey noted that a member of the Design Office staff had commented:

"... that the fault escaped notice largely as a result of a lack of continuity among the checking staff. Whilst such changes cannot always be avoided it is obviously undesirable. This is particularly so in the case of a large scheme such as WARS where the stageworking arrangements are particularly involved.

It is not satisfactory to allow such discontinuity to affect safety standards and it seems that managerial control needs tightening in this respect."

9.69 Mr Bailey had actually identified lack of continuity as a problem, and a need to tighten managerial control. Although Mr Bailey's comments were directed to the fault on the part of the Design Office staff, the lessons were there to be learned equally well in respect of the testing staff. The particular tester had prepared no plan for his testing. He had not even functionally tested the work and had left part of the testing to another supervisor. The lessons were there to be learned too in the need to tighten managerial control in relation to the management of the testing staff. It had been Mr Callander who had appointed the tester concerned to do that work.

9.70 Mr Bailey was the man who had recently ceased to be the Regional Testing & Commissioning Engineer in charge of the Regional Testing Team. He was now the Signal Works Engineer at Wimbledon and was reporting to Mr John Deane, the Area Signal Engineer (Works). If ever a man should have been conscious of the lessons to be learned from the Queenstown Road incident and the importance of spreading them throughout the workforce, that man was Mr Bailey.

9.71 Further in his report to Mr Deane, Mr Bailey was at pains to point out that:

> "I am most concerned to note that" (the tester) "appears to have come on to the job without any preparation. He was told AT THE TIME what the job entailed and felt able to test it. In my opinion this is unlikely to be an acceptable way of doing things. There may be some jobs where such action will be adequate but, for any work where a change of controls is taking place, it is a perilous course to adopt. Furthermore, he does not seem to have done any 'functional' testing."

Mr Bailey had identified a lack of preparation and a lack of experience and expertise in the man sent to do the job of testing, and had recognised "a perilous course" but took the matter no further to ask how management would permit this to happen.

9.72 Mr Deane in his turn duly made a report to Mr Roger Penny Area S&T Engineer (SouthWest), on 22 June 1988. Mr Deane commented that the tester "must bear the brunt of the incident due to his sloppy methods" and considered that he should be severely reprimanded. He concluded his report by making a recommendation in relation to Design Office drawings and saying:

> ". . . otherwise we may find recurrences of this type elsewhere and with the pressures and tightness of the WARS programme coupled with a mixed bag of site staff our integrity will again be challenged."

Mr Deane, even while recognising the problems of the tightness and pressures of WARS in combination with "a mixed bag of staff" failed to ask how management was permitting this tester to do this safety-critical job.

9.73 Disciplinary proceedings followed against the supervisor who had done the testing. There was a formal hearing on 20 July 1988, in which it emerged that testing was not even included in his job description. Mr Porter, the Signal Engineer, wrote two days later to confirm his decision not to proceed further with the proceedings and told the tester:

> "As discussed, testing is a matter of some judgement: there are some black and white rules, but during stageworks particularly, the extent of testing necessarily requires planning and thought, and in future you need to ensure that you make adequate time available for this aspect of the work prior to having to carry it out.

> Arrangements are being made for staff required to carry out testing duties to be trained and certified as competent to test at certain limits and you will, with others, be involved in this."

9.74 It is significant to note that neither in the disciplinary charge, nor in the formal hearing, nor in this letter, was there any specific reference to SL-53 and its detailed provisions. Mr Porter had actually said at the formal hearing that testing had to be done "To Departmental Instructions" but did not identify them further. In his letter to the tester he was saying that there were "some black and white rules". Though the rules may have been black and white, the question of what they were, whether they were in force and if so to what extent, remained even after the Queenstown Road incident the grey area it had always been in the S&T Department.

9.75 The faulty testing and the work itself had been done on 22 May 1988, at or about the time of reorganisation. It had remained undiscovered until 14 June 1988, just after reorganisation. There remained six months, all but a day, before the Clapham Junction accident. In that period, despite what was said in Mr Porter's letter, no training whatsoever was offered to the tester in question, or more importantly, to any other tester at all. It was not until late February of this year that that tester was given a four-day course on SL-53, the first of such courses having taken place a few weeks earlier.

9.76 In that six-month period before the accident, no action was taken by management to examine the underlying reasons for what had gone wrong. It was Mr Callander who had detailed the particular tester to carry out testing which he was not competent to do, and for which no plan had been made. The fault did not lie merely with the tester's "shoddy work", it lay equally with the person who had sent him to do the job. Mr Bailey had noted in relation to the Design Office error in his report to Mr Deane, that: "... managerial control needs tightening...", but noted nothing about the slackness in Mr Callander's managerial control which had led to the incident.

9.77 Equally Mr Deane, to whom that report was addressed and to whom Mr Callander reported, saw no reason to examine the managerial breakdown which had permitted this situation to occur. No one in management took the good hard look which was the essential logical sequel to the Queenstown Road incident at what was going on and going wrong in the testing of new installations in the S&T Department. If they had done, the almost cavalier disregard for proper practice that was rife in the Department, with the consequent serious threat to safety, might well have been discovered.

9.78 If the lessons of Oxted should have been fully learnt by management and fully taught to the workforce, so too should the lessons of Queenstown Road. There was still a period of six months for that learning process to be achieved. The Court, on the clearest possible evidence and consciously rejecting the misleading light of hindsight, came to the conclusion that those lessons should have been learned and that had that happened there would have been no accident at Clapham Junction on 12 December 1988. Testing, the last defence of the S&T Department, had become no defence at all.

9.79 Management had failed to ensure that lessons which it had correctly identified and the importance of which it had rightly assessed were being followed by prompt, effective action to remedy the defects in working practices. That failure was compounded by a further failure to ensure by proper monitoring that those defects were never again allowed to repeat themselves. It is to the structure of management and the identity of those in post in management at relevant levels and times that I now turn.

PART THREE: MANAGEMENT AND THE UNDERLYING CAUSES

Chapter 10: Management and the signals and telecommunications department

Before reorganisation in May 1988

10.1   In the two years before the Clapham Junction accident the structure of management of the S&T Department was changed radically by a total reorganisation which took place in and about May 1988. We shall look later in the chapter at what was intended to be and what was in fact, achieved by that reorganisation. We must look first at the structure of management before that reorganisation.

10.2   When considering the bad working practices which were endemic in the S&T Department at the time of the accident it is important to realise that those working practices cannot have happened overnight. It is therefore necessary to be able to identify who was in which post at what time when considering what, if any, arrangements were made in the years before the accident for training of the workforce and the issue and distribution of the Departmental Instructions. Appendix K.7 sets out the structure and those in post from September 1986 to May 1988.

10.3   In relation to the more senior posts in management, it is necessary to look further back historically in order to put in context those who were in senior management positions at such relevant times as the Oxted incidents in November 1985 and the resultant period of the protracted eighteen-month drafting of SL-53.

10.4   Work of the S&T Department on Southern Region before May 1988 was distributed through four different depots at:

–   Ashford in Kent

–   Eastleigh in Hampshire

–   New Cross Gate in London

–   South Lambeth in London

Each depot was presided over by a Signal Construction Engineer. It was from the South Lambeth depot that most of the WARS work was done.

10.5   The Signal Construction Engineer from September 1986 until reorganisation in May 1988 at the South Lambeth depot was Mr Deane. He had moved there from the Ashford depot where he had held the same post. At South Lambeth, Mr Deane's Senior Works Assistant was Mr Dine and his Senior Construction Assistant was Mr Callander. As Senior Construction Assistant, Mr Callander was involved in the planning of the work, the liaison with contractors and additionally was responsible, as described in Chapter 9, for almost all testing on WARS from September 1986 until May 1988.

10.6   Among the supervisors reporting to Mr Dine were Mr Bumstead and Mr Court. Mr Hemingway was one of the installation staff who was at that depot. In looking at lines of management, therefore, in relation to individual members of the S&T Department staff most closely connected with the causes of the Clapham Junction accident, it is clear that at South Lambeth Mr Bumstead was the supervisor who had overall charge of Mr Hemingway's work. Mr Bumstead reported through Mr Dine, the Senior Works Assistant, to Mr Deane, the Signal Construction Engineer.

10.7   Mr Deane reported to Mr Davies, the Signals Works Engineer, who in turn reported to Mr D Graham Brown, the Signal Engineer (Works). Mr Davies' job title was changed in 1985 to Signal Works Engineer, previously it had been Construction Engineer when he took up post in May 1983. He was therefore in post at that level for the five years between May 1983 and the reorganisation of May 1988. It was at his level that an overview could be taken of all four depots and their respective practices. Mr Davies held regular meetings with the heads of the four depots and minutes of those meetings have been referred to at a number of points in this Report.

10.8   Mr Davies was also responsible for the Regional Testing Team, headed by Mr Bailey, which was not involved in the line management of the depots. It can therefore be seen from Appendix K.7 that Mr Davies was the first point in the management structure to have overall control of both new works and testing. It was Mr Davies who carried out the investigation and made the report into the 1985 Oxted incidents, referred to in Chapter 9, and it was to him that the depot heads reported that they felt SL-53 was unworkable. Additionally it was his task to supervise the work of the Regional Testing Team in its objectives of raising standards and introducing training for testers.

10.9   Mr Brown, to whom Mr Davies reported, took up the position of Signal Engineer (Works) in April 1986. In that post he was responsible for all projects involving resignalling or alterations to existing signalling systems. His responsibilities covered scheme development, project engineering, design, construction and testing. It was therefore only at Mr Brown's level that all the elements of the WARS scheme came together.

10.10 Mr Clifford Hale was promoted in November 1981 to become Chief Signal & Telecommunications Engineer of the Southern Region. The title of that post later changed to Regional Signal & Telecommunications Engineer. Before the 1988 reorganisation he was totally responsible for all S&T activities on the Southern Region, from planning and specification design to installation, commissioning and subsequent maintenance for all S&T systems and equipment, together with the direction of all staff associated with these activities.

10.11 That, then, was the structure of management in the S&T Department up to Regional S&T Engineer in the years before the May 1988 reorganisation. We shall need to look in later chapters at the way in which the duties of management were discharged over those years and after the 1988 reorganisation in the six months or so leading up to the accident. It is to that reorganisation and the changes it made in the structure of management that I turn now.

After the 1988 reorganisation

10.12 The Signal & Telecommunications Department of the Southern Region was reorganised in May 1988, to fit in with a wider reorganisation throughout BR, known as Administration and Organisation III (A & O III). The aims behind this large-scale reorganisation were three-fold:

–   further to reduce administrative costs;

–   to institute a large measure of delegation to a new tier of management at area level; and

–   to ensure a strong contractual relationship between the new area level management on the production (operations) side, and the sub-sector level of the businesses. This was important in ensuring that contracts were being drawn up with the person on the production side who was personally responsible for the delivery of that service to the business side at the standard required.

10.13   The S&T Department had already been the subject of major reorganisations in 1982, 1984 and 1986. The Department had thus been subjected to four reorganisations in eight years, with a resultant cumulative effect on both staff and management. All these reorganisations took place during Mr Hale's period as Regional S&T Engineer.

10.14   During the hearings the Court was at pains to stress that it did not consider that a detailed analysis of all or any of these reorganisations came within its terms of reference. In particular, and in relation to the 1988 reorganisation, the Court made it clear that it was not within its remit to consider and decide upon the question of which of various alternative forms of reorganisation might or might not have been preferable to that actually implemented. That remains the position. The 1988 reorganisation is only relevant to this Investigation if and insofar as the fact of the reorganisation impinged on the working of the S&T Department in a way which affected or might have affected the workforce involved in carrying out the work which caused the accident. It is only for that reason and in that light that the 1988 reorganisation will be considered in this Report.

10.15   When proposals for the 1988 reorganisation were originally put forward in the first half of 1987 the Regional S&T Engineer, Mr Hale, was concerned that an area level reorganisation would need additional staff and would therefore not meet one of the A&O III objectives of reducing costs. Mr Hale was also concerned that certain functions carried out then on a regional basis would not be performed as effectively if split up into areas. He quoted as examples the three-man Regional Testing Team, which was to be disbanded and replaced by one tester in each of the three areas, and the personnel function. The proposals, which contained a large element of delegation, also included the creation of central functions at Board Headquarters under the Director of S&T Engineering, Mr Kenneth Hodgson. This would have meant that Mr Hale would lose responsibility for the Design Office, the computer function, and Project Management. Whilst willing to accept the first two changes, Mr Hale said that he was reluctant to lose control of his project engineers, through whom he exercised responsibility for investment schemes and expenditure.

10.16   With the support of the General Manager, Southern Region, Mr Gordon Pettitt, Mr Hale produced alternative proposals which were aimed at achieving the Board's principal objectives, but in a way which would not involve increased staffing, which he called his "matrix" solution. The aim of the "matrix" proposal was to leave unchanged the management level responsible for each depot and insert above them a new tier of three area business liaison engineers, reporting directly to Mr Hale. In his view this proposal would have meant not only that local depot management, supervisors and technicians would be affected as little as possible by the change but that there could still take place reorganisation at senior management level. In addition, this proposal maintained the Regional Testing Team, but allocated design and computer functions to BR HQ.

10.17 Mr Hale thought that these proposals were going well and that they seemed to have gained some favour with the business sector managers. However, his proposals were then considered by the Director of Network SouthEast, Mr Chris Green. Mr Green believed that the matrix solution did not meet one of the aims of A&O III, namely to strengthen the contractual relationship between business manager and the engineer responsible for the provision of the work.

10.18 Mr Hale was sent in November 1988 a copy of a minute from Mr Green, which stated that the matrix proposal missed the whole principle of delegation and that Southern Region should fall into line with the other three regions which had a contractual relationship to provide services to Network SouthEast. In a meeting on 22 December 1987 with Mr David Rayner, Joint Managing Director Railways, Mr Gordon Pettitt, General Manager Southern Region, and Mr Kenneth Hodgson, Director Signals & Telecommunications, Mr Hale was directed to abandon his matrix proposal and introduce an Area S&T Engineer form of organisation on the Southern Region following the standard pattern agreed for other regions. At the meeting, it was agreed that extra staff would be needed to implement this form of reorganisation.

10.19 Meanwhile, the introduction of A&O III was progressing throughout the rest of BR. In order to ensure that national consultation should not be delayed because of Southern Region, and in order to give the required 14 days' notice to the Unions on the subject of consultation, it was necessary to issue the details of the proposals by 27 January 1988. Mr Hale informed his middle managers of the change in plan. He calculated the minimum number of extra staff that would be necessary to implement the proposals and he spent the next few months preparing for reorganisation.

10.20 For reasons already identified, the Court makes no judgment on which form of organisation should have been preferred. The particular form of the reorganisation could not be classified as a circumstance attending the accident, and the Court was unwilling to hear evidence as to the merits and demerits of alternative forms. However, the process of implementation of the reorganisation was clearly within the Court's terms of reference. There were three specific areas on which the Court took evidence:

(i) the disbanding of the Regional Testing Team;

(ii) the effect on staff morale; and

(iii) the administrative arrangements and their effect on the standard of work.

The disbanding of the Regional Testing Team

10.21 The Regional Testing Team set up in August 1986 consisted of Mr Bailey, Mr Blain and Mr Bassett. Their role had been intended to be the carrying out of testing on the whole of the Southern Region assisted by new works staff as required. (In fact, as we have seen by reason of the substantial workload involved, it was Mr Callander, the Signal Construction Engineer at South Lambeth, who in the end had done almost all the testing on the WARS scheme.) In addition to testing work, the team was charged with raising standards of testing and with developing training courses so that a list of qualified testers could be created. It has already been mentioned that virtually nothing had been done towards achieving the last two objectives.

10.22 By Christmas 1987, no plans had been made to run training courses. A one-page hand-written list of topics to be covered in a functional testing course had been prepared by Mr Bailey but nothing more had been done. The impetus for training which should have followed the Oxted incidents had long since been dissipated: there was no momentum to lose. Nothing was done in the early months of 1988 before reorganisation to develop courses. Knowing that the team was to be disbanded, there was little incentive for Mr Bailey to press ahead with something that he had scarcely begun.

10.23 The three members of the Regional Testing Team were to be replaced by three Area Testing & Commissioning Engineers. Therefore, in terms of numbers of testers, there was no change. In the South West area, where the accident took place, Mr Callander was appointed as the Area Testing & Commissioning Engineer. He was not completely content with the change because his new role was restricted to testing and had none of the planning involved in his previous post.

The effect on staff morale 10.24 The arrangements which were made for transferring staff in the course of reorganisation were particularly cumbersome. These arrangements were agreed between management and unions and both therefore must bear some responsibility for the problems encountered. The arrangements required that all employees received letters telling them that they were made redundant in the existing organisation: they were then asked to apply for posts within the new organisation. Effectively they were displaced, and needed to apply to be reallocated.

10.25 In the 1988 reorganisation, the only information available on each new post was a short sentence included in a long list of posts available. No interviews were conducted to ensure the suitability of the applicant for the new post. Job descriptions were not available in the May 1988 reorganisation to ensure that staff knew exactly what was expected of them. Many of the staff were not successful on their first application and were forced to spend a number of months as "unallocated" staff, attached to a depot but with no particular post of their own. Many experienced a change in the geographical location of their post and for a substantial number this was at some distance from their homes with resultant personal difficulties.

10.26 The May 1988 reorganisation affected differently many of the staff whose work is the subject of this Investigation. For the more junior grades, there was little change. Mr Hemingway and Mr Bumstead moved directly from South Lambeth to Wimbledon, but were essentially doing the same job as before. For them there would only have been the initial difficulties of going through the formal procedures of reapplying for the same job. Mr Bumstead did express particular dissatisfaction with the large number of staff brought in from other depots because he was not aware of their capabilities. Nor was he content with some of his supervisor colleagues or with the chain of command.

10.27 Mr Lippett had spent most of his career on maintenance work and his previous post was Area Maintenance Assistant at Wimbledon. He was due to retire in October 1989. He was not particularly happy with the job application he had made because of a number of important factors: he had little experience on new work, WARS was already well underway, and this was a completely new job with no-one to follow on from.

10.28 Despite all this and the fact that Mr Lippett was not available for weekend working, a disadvantage which was well known to his superiors, he was none the less appointed to the post.

10.29 Mr Bailey moved from Head of the Regional Testing Team to the position of Signal Works Engineer at Wimbledon. This was his first management post and he was responsible for the Wimbledon and Eastleigh depots. Mr Deane, as we saw earlier, did a direct exchange from being in charge of the South Lambeth depot to responsibility for Wimbledon. His job was much altered by the reorganisation in that he took on wider responsibilities on budget and planning as well as management of the works.

10.30 The new Area Signal & Telecommunication Engineer was Mr Penny. His experience was principally on maintenance and telecommunications. His only experience of the management of New Works was six months in 1978 as Project Engineer for the Gatwick Airport Resignalling Scheme. In that six months he had done some functional testing. It was Mr Penny's responsibility to get his new organisation up and running. Mr Davies and Mr Brown moved to BRB HQ, directly responsible to the Director of S&T.

10.31 The picture is therefore one of staff at junior levels being largely unaffected by reorganisation, but with management at junior and area levels being inexperienced in their particular fields of work. Although Mr Deane acted as an element of continuity, he now had a much larger scale of responsibilities.

Administrative
arrangements

10.32 A large amount of planning was necessary to implement the reorganisation in the timescale proposed. In fact, Mr Hale asked for a three week extension for implementation to allow more time for preparation. Although much had been done by May 1988, there were a large number of problems. The Personnel and Finance Divisions had not successfully been transferred from the Region to the Areas and were kept on at Regional Headquarters to ensure that the staff could still be paid. The computer system, too, had teething troubles and was not properly implemented until November 1988. Job descriptions were not issued to all staff. Permanent accommodation was not available and temporary huts were established at Waterloo and Clapham for parts of the Wimbledon depot staff. A number of individuals had been seconded full-time to implement the reorganisation, and their work had to be carried out by colleagues. No additional finance or staff had been made available to implement the changes.

10.33 As well as having to implement the reorganisation, managers were also involved in monitoring an industrial dispute which arose from the imposition of the Pay and Grading Agreement in May 1988. Mr Penny was actively involved in monitoring the response to the dispute and in conducting a hearts and minds campaign, yet he only had two personnel staff available to assist him when the complement should have been twelve.

Conclusions

10.34 It is clear that the 1988 reorganisation was a major upheaval for the whole of the organisation. Mr Deane summed it up in the expression: "all the uproar of being reorganised". Junior staff had to suffer the uncertainty of applying for different posts and some had to relocate to depots at some distance from their original workplace. Junior management were inexperienced in their tasks, while the roles of more senior managers had changed dramatically. Mr Penny was asked to take charge of an organisation which had not been properly prepared and which lacked the resources he needed in order to manage the change.

10.35 It is necessary to see whether the reorganisation had a place in the causation of the accident. Poor working practices, unsatisfactory training and incomplete testing had all existed before the reorganisation. The reorganisation did not make any of these three factors worse and therefore cannot in that way be seen as part of the cause of the accident. However, the reorganisation could have been an opportunity to come to grips with the existing situation. New brooms might have swept away old bad practices. That indeed is one of the underlying reasons for such a reorganisations.

10.36 Sadly it did not happen that way. Mr Lippett noticed levels of poor workmanship but did not want to "rock the boat" by intervening at an early stage. He was an outsider in charge of a workforce that had worked closely together for a number of years. He had to run that workforce through Mr Bumstead who was suffering from low morale because of all the newcomers. The opportunity for improvement was not grasped.

10.37 Mr Callander too was dissatisfied and anxious for a change. But, even if he had remained Testing & Commissioning Engineer, Mr Hemingway's errors would not have been picked up by his testing because he too would not have conducted an independent wire count. Mr Dray, Mr Callander's temporary successor, was unhappy in his job and had little contact with Mr Callander. He would not in any event have picked up Mr Hemingway's errors for exactly the same reasons as existed in Mr Callander's case.

10.38 The administration of the reorganisation is a further example of poor management and planning practice within the S&T Department generally. However, the reorganisation is also of relevance to the accident in that some of those individuals selected to take up the new posts were either not the right people for the job, or were insufficiently prepared for their new responsibility.

10.39 What was necessary was for the new appointees to be able to take a fresh look at their workforce, and to identify and remedy the defects in installation and testing practices which undoubtedly existed: to look afresh at the programme for WARS in the light of reorganisation and to see if reorganisation had affected that programme, and if so how. What was needed was for the organisation to undergo a renewal, with all the capacity for change and improvement that are inherent in that concept. It did not happen. The new brooms swept as little and as ineffectively as the old.

Chapter 11: S&T Departmental Instructions – the communication of information and training of the workforce

Basic concepts

11.1   The problem of communication between management and staff is one which can bedevil any industry. The quality and effectiveness of that communication is frequently a reliable guide to the health of that industry. Where the quality of communication is poor the messages which should be sent both down and up the structure of an organisation will begin to fail to get through. When those messages fail to get through, staff will no longer be working in the way that management wishes them to and management will not be able to react to the problems staff are facing and the errors they are making. In this way poor communication leads to poor control and management begins not to manage.

11.2   Thus, if management wish to ensure that work is carried out in a particular way, the usual procedure in an industry or business is to prepare and issue an instruction as to proper working standards to which management requires that its staff work.

11.3   It should go without saying (but sadly in the evidence the Court heard, it did not) that the issue of that instruction, with all the information contained therein, is of no use at all unless that information is actually communicated to the staff: the message that never gets through might just as well never have been sent. That is why management must not only issue the instruction, but must ensure that the information does actually reach the staff. Management must monitor the reaction to that information. For this purpose a good system of communication is vital.

11.4   Once the first two steps of the issue and the communication of the information have been taken there is still a third: the staff must be taught how to deal with the information, how to approach it and how to put it into effect. They must be trained to use the information properly.

11.5   It is only by the full and proper inter-relation of those three aspects of instruction, communication and training that the workforce will be enabled to work as management intends. While this is true for any industry or business, in one so bound up with and committed to the concept of safety as the railway industry it is essential that none of these three concepts be ignored if the workforce is to carry out its duties safely. Sadly, in the evidence presented to the Investigation, the Court saw failure after failure to observe these axiomatic principles.

Communications in the Signals & Telecommunications Department

11.6   How did these many layers of staff and management communicate within the S&T Department? The principal means of formal communication was a series of meetings penetrating down through the organisation. At the head of the Department, Mr Hale, the Regional S&T Engineer, held monthly meetings with all his senior staff covering signalling, telecommunications and maintenance. These were all-day meetings and the notes of these meetings, short statements on a long list of points, were circulated to those below the level of staff attending the meeting, for example, on the New Works side, to Mr Davies. The meeting notes in themselves would not have been sufficient to give Mr Davies a clear understanding of a task he had been recorded as having to undertake. Further discussion would have been necessary between him and Mr D Graham Brown. This should not have posed any problem as they occupied almost adjacent offices and Mr Brown had his own "works meetings" with the level of staff below him. However, as we will see later in this chapter, neither verbal nor written communication between them was wholly effective.

11.7   Mr Davies then held his own Construction Group monthly meetings with his four Senior Construction Engineers. Mr Bailey, as Regional Testing Engineer, was present at a meeting in August 1986 to discuss the role of the testing team and how that would fit in with the work of the depots. However, apart from this occasion, he did not seem to have attended Mr Davies' Construction Group Meetings on a regular basis. Indeed, the minutes of the meeting in August 1987 which discussed SL-53 and its implementation, quoted at paragraph 9.35, do not record him as being present, despite the obvious implication for the man nominally responsible for improving and training testers on the region.

11.8   There seem to have been no regular formal meetings between Mr Davies and the Regional Testing Team, the other principal area of his responsibility. Mr Deane at South Lambeth held his own briefing meetings with Mr Dine, Mr Callander and others of a similar grade within the depot. It is at this level that formal meetings stopped.

11.9   We have already seen in Chapter 8 that communication within the Wimbledon depot and previously at South Lambeth was very haphazard. For important weekend commissionings Mr Bumstead and Mr Lippett would have a brief chat on the Wednesday, to look over the weekend's workload after they had seen which staff had volunteered for overtime from the list taken down on Tuesday. Communications between the night and day shifts were also haphazard. Notes were supposed to be left if problems had been encountered. On the weekend of 27 November 1988 problems had emerged and not all the Saturday works out on the tracks had been finished, but no note was left.

S&T Departmental Instructions

11.10 We have seen in Chapters 8 and 9 that some staff in Southern Region were unaware of the full range of their responsibilities and that there was a widespread failure to observe Departmental Instructions on Testing. There were obvious weaknesses both in the adequate training of staff and in communicating to them, the force, relevance, and the importance of Departmental Instructions. Though they should have been obvious, the weaknesses were neither monitored nor corrected.

11.11 In addition to the policies of the Rule Book, the S&T Department of Southern Region had a supplementary system of Departmental Instructions which was introduced by Mr Hale in 1983. Instructions were issued, with a prefix of S for Signalling, T for Telecommunications, or A for Administration. There were sub-categories in alphabetical order for each main category. For signalling, the sub-category of L related to Testing and Commissioning. Thus, SL-53 should have proclaimed itself to all its recipients under the system as the 53rd Signalling Instruction, and one relating specifically to Testing and Commissioning.

11.12 The distribution system for Departmental Instructions within the S&T Department was based on the issue of Instructions to grades of staff identified by a code letter. Supervisors, for example, had the code E. Alongside each letter code would be the number of the last departmental instruction issued in the same main category, for instance, Signalling. This system was designed to prevent the need for each individual worker to sign for each instruction he received. Instead, each member of staff was supposed to check the last instruction listed next to his code letter against the contents of his file of instructions. If he had not received this instruction it was his duty to request a copy of the missing instruction from his manager. It was a system which as will be seen later in this chapter was more honoured in the breach than the observance and was not understood at all by some staff.

11.13 There are two main areas of instruction and training with which this Investigation is concerned: installation practices and testing. I shall deal first with the S&T Departmental Instructions and then with the training methods of the Department.

Installation Instructions 11.14 The S&T Departmental Instruction that installers should have worked to was known as SI-16 which was dated 18 November 1983. The category I is reserved for Installation of Equipment. Section 3.3.3 is the relevant section for this Investigation and reads:

> "3.3.3. Wires and crimps not terminated must have their ends insulated and secured to prevent contact with each other or with any other equipment."

11.15 Mr Hemingway had not received a copy of this instruction before the accident even though its intended circulation under the Departmental system was to technician level. He first saw it at BR's joint inquiry in December 1988 and although he described its provisions as "common sense" it is clear that the Departmental Instruction system had proved ineffective in this case. The "rogue" wire had not been "secured to prevent contact with ... ... any other equipment". Mr Hemingway had merely pushed it to one side out of the way. If he had received SI-16, been trained in its provisions and made to follow them, that wire would have been secured out of harm's way and would not have been able to get back to its former terminal on the relay. The instruction clearly existed laying down best practice in this area. A lack of supervision prevented that best practice from being implemented, as Chapter 8 has shown.

Testing Instructions 11.16 Testing had always been the prestige work for S&T staff. Experience of and skill in testing was considered valuable experience for anyone progressing through the management levels. However, there was an important distinction made between functional testing – the difficult, challenging test which involves permutating a variety of operating circumstances in an attempt to catch out the system – and other routine testing. These routine tests were often delegated to works staff, the wire count being an obvious example.

11.17 Testers in the 1970s learned their skills by watching others. The only document of any relevance to them was "New Works 128", a specification for contractors detailing how and to what standard their jobs should be installed and tested before responsibility passed to BR staff. However, this was a very different type of exercise from that of the BR tester ensuring that BR installation work had been satisfactorily completed and tested to ensure that the new or altered signalling system could safely be brought into operation.

11.18 Before the early 1980s, Southern Region had issued no written instructions to their own staff on testing or procedures to be followed. Following the London Bridge Resignalling Scheme the Project Engineer in charge of that scheme, Mr Roy Bell, was asked to prepare notes on functional testing. He reluctantly agreed, aware that these notes could not cover the whole procedure. His notes were the sole document available to testers until the issue of SL-Provisional in late 1985, although the need for such a document had been identified three years before.

11.19 Towards the end of 1982 Mr Clifford Hale, Regional S&T Engineer, asked his Signal Engineer (Works) to prepare a draft testing instruction for signalling installations. Nothing appeared to have been done to follow up this request until May 1983 when the new Signal Construction Engineer, Mr Robert Davies, was asked to prepare a draft instruction. He was given to understand that, although this was important, it should not be considered top priority.

11.20 In January 1984, when the document had still not appeared, Mr Hale is recorded as "expressing concern at the timescale for completion and requesting that efforts be made to improve". In July 1984, when the instruction was still not finalised, Mr Hale's Departmental Conference discussed whether to issue the instruction there and then with appendices following at a later date. This course was not in fact followed.

11.21 Eventually in July 1985 it was agreed that provisional copies of the draft instruction could be issued to any staff carrying out testing, but that the final issue might be different. At that stage it was decided that the final instruction should contain a section on the roles and responsibilities of those involved in testing. The Instruction was issued as SL-Provisional, and dated 1 October 1985. Those who received the draft instruction at that stage were aware that it was simply a draft document. Most felt that it simply pulled together existing practice. It emerged three years late, it still lacked the section on roles and responsibilities and its arrival was in the most halting of fashions.

11.22 In November 1985, a series of wrong-side failures including the Oxted incidents detailed in Chapter 9 had occurred which had been caused in part by failures in testing. As an immediate response to this appalling sequence, Mr Hale had a letter issued to staff down to supervisor level which stated:

"Will you please note and advise all concerned that the Departmental Instruction numbered SL-Provisional, entitled "Testing of New and Altered Signalling" and dated 1 October 1985, has the full authority of any other Departmental Instruction even though it is unsigned."

11.23 It had therefore taken three years to prepare and issue this instruction and yet the version issued was obviously still not satisfactory. Departmental Conference following the three wrong-side failures recorded that the:

"... need for a full testing procedural document was more urgent than ever, but the resource difficulty is recognised."

Mr Davies in a letter to his four senior Construction Engineers dated 10 February 1986, which accompanied his report on the Oxted accident told them:

"The Departmental Instruction on Testing is to be signed and issued shortly."

In fact it was not until May 1987 that what Departmental Conference had called a full testing procedural document, namely, SL-53 was finally issued – almost eighteen months later. Such a rate of progress was entirely out of keeping with the sense of urgency expressed in 1985. This painfully slow response to a problem which had been clearly recognised as urgent was a matter of great concern to the Court. Even while registering the urgent need for the document, management was recognising that limited resources might produce a reaction which was less than urgent. That same management failed to supply any additional resources. Matters such as the issue of the Instruction were left to drag on at their own unprompted pace.

11.24 Thus, there was no proper attention to the establishment of priorities, the provision of resources, and to the monitoring of the progress of the drafting of the document. Nothing was done by management to ensure that the document was, in fact, provided with the urgency and distributed with the speed which was known by them to be vital. Yet again the use of vigorous words belied the lack of action.

11.25 Further, even when SL-53 was eventually ready to be put to the workforce, it is still a matter of great concern to see the manner in which this document was distributed and implemented.

The introduction of SL-53 to the workforce

11.26 SL-53 should have been issued to testers and to the works staff down to supervisor level but supervisors did not receive copies. Since they did not have copies they could neither brief themselves on the Instruction, nor have any clear idea of what assistance the tester would require of them. Again the distribution system had failed, just as it had previously done for SL-Provisional: no satisfactory explanation was ever given for these failures.

11.27 When authority was given to send out copies of SL-Provisional an administrative error registered it internally with the number SL-53. This was not printed on the copies and therefore had no consequences at that stage. However, when the next instruction in the signalling series was issued it showed SL-53 as the previous instruction next to the code letter. There should have been a large number of enquiries seeking copies of the instruction SL-53, which at that stage did not exist. There were not. This should have alerted management to the fact that the system of distribution was not working: it did not.

11.28 As for the testers, they either, like Mr Callander, did not read it or they put SL-53 to one side assuming that it merely stated existing best testing practice, which they wrongly believed they were following. In fact, SL-53 contained three further elements which the workforce needed to understand. The Instruction required the observance of directions as to:

- the definition of individual roles;

- planning in accordance with laid-down procedure; and

- documenting both the planning and the implementation of the test to ensure that it had been carried out fully and properly.

11.29 SL-53 made it clear, for the first time in a written instruction, that there was to be one person in overall charge of the testing, with others in charge of internal and external testing. It then went on to describe the responsibilities of each of these three individuals. The first duty of the Person In Overall Charge of Testing (PICOT) was to draw up a testing programme and define and control detailed requirements. This should have included the number of staff needed to carry out the test and the necessary level of their experience.

11.30 There was obvious confusion caused by the long lists of tasks to be carried out by the three individuals named in the document. On large commissions three people could not carry out all those tasks, but of more specific concern, the PICOT could not hope to fulfil all the duties allocated to him.

11.31 According to SL-53 an essential element of documenting the work done was to be the checklists attached to the instruction which were to be completed after each test. These checklists were never drawn up, nor issued to staff. Management, at least up to the level of Mr Graham Brown, was aware that not only were the checklists not being completed, they were not even being issued. Further indications that SL-53 was largely being ignored were also made clear to management when works staff, at a Construction Group meeting on 21 August 1987, chaired by Mr Davies, explained that SL-53 was unworkable as drafted, because it did not provide for delegation of responsibilities.

11.32 Mr Davies undertook to raise the matter with Mr Brown to have this point clarified, which he did in a detailed minute of 8 September 1987. A conversation subsequently took place between Mr Davies and Mr Brown. Their recollections of the conversation differ:

– Mr Davies understood that Mr Brown was to raise the matter at Departmental Conference.

– Mr Brown recollected that he had told Mr Davies that delegation was implicit in the Instruction and no further clarification was necessary.

11.33 Mr Davies' next meeting recorded that they were waiting for further clarification from Departmental Conference on this point. Mr Brown did not pick this point up. No reference to this important matter appears in Departmental Conference minutes, nor did Mr Brown ever reply in writing to Mr Davies' clear questions in his minute. The document needed an answer which it never received. Mr Davies continued to record the fact that the Construction Group was waiting for an answer to the problem of the need for delegation in relation to SL-53 in Construction Group minutes, but did nothing else to break out of an intolerable situation. This was yet another example of management by inactivity and inertia to which I refer in Chapter 12.

11.34 The new instruction SL-53, was therefore issued with no accompanying explanation by management, and no seminars or training in how it should be implemented. The relevant documentation, the checklists etc., were never issued, nor even printed. Nor did management monitor the introduction of SL-53 to ensure that the workforce was complying with its provisions. It would seem that they confined themselves to a false belief that the instruction was being implemented in spirit. Such a belief had about it little more than a pious hope and had nothing to do with good management.

11.35 BR Headquarters is now in the process of producing a national testing instruction. The Court believes that this is the correct approach. The creation of a national testing team was suggested as a type of testing police force, but the Court was not attracted to the suggestion and saw disadvantages in such a system. The Board should be responsible for devising the standards to which the work is to be carried out in the Regions, while the Regional Signalling Engineers should be responsible for ensuring that the work meets those required standards. But the Board must additionally ensure that the Regional Signalling Engineers have the resources available to them and sufficient authority to ensure that standards are met. The technology of signalling is continually changing. Solid State Interlocking is now being implemented and the testing process for this form of technology is more complicated. The Board should ensure that testing instructions keep pace with new technology, that testers are properly trained and that Regional Signalling Engineers have the money and manpower to ensure standards are maintained and improved.

Training

11.36 A formalised series of training courses was introduced following the 1974 Pay and Grading Agreement which meant that those hoping to be promoted had to undertake the courses laid down in the Pay and Grading Agreement before progressing to the next grade. The basic structure was therefore highly formalised with little flexibility.

11.37 The Investigation was told that BR's efforts to maintain the national Pay and Grading courses meant that facilities and funds for additional courses were severely limited. To overcome some of these difficulties BR has focused more attention on "distance learning" allowing the individual employee to study in his own time and not at one of the BR centres. Training courses outside the Pay and Grading Agreement are run at the BR's School of Engineering at Derby: separate courses are offered in regional centres.

11.38 Until Pay and Grading courses, training within BR had been based on apprentice-type on-the-job training where new employees would learn from more experienced skilled workers. That ethos continued alongside Pay and Grading, particularly in areas such as testing which were not covered in the Pay and Grading courses.

Training for installers

11.39 Areas such as basic installation work would be covered in Pay and Grading courses. Mr Hemingway had been in the S&T Department too long to benefit from these courses. As part of the 1974 agreement, and because many workers already had long experience, assistant technicians in Mr Hemingway's position were allowed to regrade without taking the courses. No refresher courses were run for installers in the S&T Department.

Training for Testers

11.40 As part of the corrective action taken following the three incidents of wrong-side failures in November 1985, it was decided to set up a Regional Testing Team. There were to be three testers responsible for testing throughout the Southern Region, for raising standards and for developing training courses for others. The Testing Team took up their posts in August 1986, headed by Mr Bailey.

11.41 The amount of testing to be done on the Southern Region meant that the time of these three men was fully occupied so that, where they found that a competent tester existed at a construction depot, the responsibility for testing was delegated to him. It was in this fashion that testing on the WARS scheme was principally done by Mr Callander at the South Lambeth Depot. Mr Callander reported to Mr Deane at South Lambeth and was not a member of Mr Bailey's staff.

11.42 No attempts were made by the Testing Team to develop training courses in their first year of operation. In August 1987, in completing Mr Bailey's annual performance appraisal, Mr Davies noted that Mr Bailey should spend more time on this aspect of his work. Between August and Christmas 1987, Mr Bailey only managed to produce a single page of handwriting which was a draft entitled "Functional Testing" listing a number of topics that such a course should cover. No work had been done on developing a syllabus for courses, nor were either Mr Bailey or Mr Davies looking any wider than functional testing. This reflects both an overall misconception as to the requirements of proper testing and at the same time the "prestige" that was attached to functional testing while other testing aspects were relegated to lower positions.

11.43 At the end of 1987, it was announced that in the forthcoming reorganisation the Regional Testing Team was to be disbanded. No further consideration was given by the Testing Team to establishing training courses for testers. This issue was only re-opened in September 1988 and the first course was run in January 1989.

Training for Management

11.44 BR has two levels of entry into the S&T Department: the first involves entering as a junior railwayman on probation until becoming an assistant technician and from there moving up the grades to supervisor and then management levels. The second route is by joining the Department as a graduate engineer already in the management structure. Management training, unlike technical training for pay and grading groups, is not a prerequisite to promotion. Most of the key participants in the S&T Department had had no formal management training despite the scale of their responsibilities. Mr Bailey for example was moved from being the Regional Tester with a team of three, to Signal Works Engineer with over 60 staff at two different depots. The Court had no evidence that he had had any management training. In progressing its programme of Total Quality Management BR will need to consider whether it is targeting management training resources in the most effective way. Additionally, management training will need to be expanded to other groups. Mr Bumstead, a supervisor, for instance, was expected to organise his workforce, plan their work, control and motivate them without the benefit of any management training.

11.45 Deficiencies have been established in the workforce's understanding of their instructions. Training in a number of areas was defective. Those who had responsibility for organising, controlling and motivating staff below them were unaware of their staff's strengths and weaknesses. As a aid to management, the extension of the annual appraisal system down to Senior Technician level should help redress some of these problems. The formal process of writing an annual review on staff will concentrate supervisors' and managers' minds on how well staff are meeting the tasks outlined in their job descriptions.

Management Review

11.46 It is recognised that the annual appraisal system as it exists for managers needs to be simplified to be effective and relevant for more junior staff. The annual interview that goes with the appraisal system should be seen as an opportunity to assess staff's understanding of the written instructions. Every second year, staff should be asked to sign a statement to the effect that they have recently read and understood relevant Departmental Instructions. This would be an extension of the system that exists for the Rule Book at present.

Training for Drivers

11.47 This brief analysis of training in the S&T Department must not be allowed to become so compartmentalised that it omits all reference to drivers' training. In relation to the detection of signalling errors driver training has a vital role to play. Chapter 2 discussed the aspects seen by certain drivers on the morning of the accident and concluded that none of the drivers prior to Driver McClymont were obliged by the Rule Book to report any of the signal aspects they had seen.

11.48 It will be remembered that Mr Morgan's evidence as to how, in relation to the Rule Book, a driver might be expected to react when confronted with a particular sequence of signal aspects was plainly confused. This was all the more remarkable in that it was evidence coming from someone experienced in training drivers. The Court asked for and was provided with Course Notes for Driver Training Courses, and recognises the considerable extent of the information that must be inculcated into drivers. It is necessary, however, that trainee drivers receive particularly careful training in the signalling system and what constitutes an irregularity, and I shall refer to this matter in the Recommendations. Neither the training of drivers as a process, nor the daily working of the drivers themselves in practice are helped by the language used, or by the different sections of the Rule Book involved, in the telling of a driver what he should do if he sees something about the signalling which he considers unusual.

The Rule Book

11.49 We have seen in Chapter 2 that the latest edition of the Rule Book is dated June 1988. It is regrettable that the opportunity was not taken at that time to re-draft parts of the Rule Book to rationalise and clarify the action which is expected of a driver if he sees something unusual about the signal aspects.

11.50 We saw that it is Section C which is the section which deals with signals and it is understandable that this would be the first section which a driver moving down the track would think of in trying to flick through the pages in his mind to see what the Rule Book tells him to do. He would, in any event, get little or no help from this section, even if he had a photographic memory in that the only passage remotely relevant would be Rule C.6.7 which deals only with a "signal not shown or imperfectly shown". Mr Morgan in his evidence really seemed to accept that the driver would get no help from Section C.

11.51 Mr Morgan suggested that it was Section H which was really applicable and in particular Rule H.7.1.4. We have seen that the rule is headed "Observing any irregularity or obstruction" and we have seen that the whole tenor of Rule H.7 is that it is dealing with obstructions (including cattle) and irregularities affecting other trains. Passages in the Rule Book dealing with obstructions and the placing of detonators "at least 1¼ miles .... from the obstruction" are not apt to cover a situation where a driver considers there is something unusual about a signal he is travelling towards or passing.

11.52 It was suggested during the Investigation that it was the word "irregularity" which would fix a driver's mind on what he must do. Regretfully I have to say that that suggestion found no favour with the Court. The rule relied on was H.7.1.2 and if one looks at its words in full it is apparent that they are dealing with a different situation:

> "7.1.2. If he sees any irregularity affecting another train, he must immediately inform the signalman, stopping specially if necessary. If possible he must also alert the Driver of that train by sounding the horn and exhibiting a red light."

11.53 A rule which tells a driver to sound his horn and exhibit a red light to alert another driver if possible is hardly the rule which will first come to mind or appear relevant to a driver who is travelling at speed down the track puzzling about a particular signalling aspect or sequence he has just seen.

11.54 During the hearings I at one time ventured to suggest that in any event the use of the word "irregularity" was unhappy unless it was defined. It was pointed out on behalf of BR that the failure to define "irregularity" was quite deliberate and that it was intended that the word should cover as wide a range of eventualities as possible.

11.55 I understand and respect that intention to use a word which will have wide applicability. I accept also that it may be there is no significantly better word. The fact remains, however, that "irregularity" used in its context in Rule 7 of Section H has nothing whatever to do with unusual aspects of the signalling system which may be troubling a driver travelling at speed and having to make a quick decision.

11.56 A man in such a situation is entitled to be trained in and to work to a system of rules which are clear, unambiguous and helpfully presented. That cannot be said of the current Rule Book. It is of vital importance that there should be accurate and speedy reporting of what is seen by drivers as possible signalling faults. For that to be done there must be proper training of drivers on these matters and a redrafting of those passages in the Rule Book which at present only cloud the issue.

11.57 Clarity is essential, not only in any type of instruction to staff, but even more so in the Rule Book, where non-compliance can affect the safe running of the railway and can involve the member of staff concerned in disciplinary proceedings. There was no doubt in the mind of any of the BR witnesses as to the importance of obeying the Rule Book, yet the Rule Book itself is unclear in the status it accords to Departmental Instructions such as those of the Southern Region S&T Department. Rule A.1.4.1 reads:

> "Each employee must observe the Rules, Regulations and instructions applicable to him and obey the instructions of those in authority where he is required to work. He must report any infringement of the Rules and Regulations to his supervisor."

Witnesses were uncertain whether or not the word "instructions" covered such documents as SL-53 and it is therefore clear that the status of Departmental Instructions as issued by the S&T Department needs to be clarified.

Chapter 12: Waterloo area resignalling scheme: The planning of the project, its management and execution

Background

12.1   Lines into Waterloo carry thousands of passengers per day into London from the South West through Clapham Junction, the busiest railway junction, as opposed to terminus, in Great Britain. The Waterloo area extends through Clapham Junction, Wimbledon, Epsom and Leatherhead and as far as Dorking. Essential to the carrying of those passengers safely and reliably is the signalling system. It had been installed in 1936. It was in the late 1970s that the age and deteriorating condition of the system started to give cause for concern as to its reliability.

12.2   A Project Development Paper was therefore put forward by the General Manager of the Southern Region in 1978. The plan was to renew the whole of the signalling system for the Waterloo area as BR was then already doing, or planning to do, for other main approaches to London by such schemes as the London Bridge and the Victoria Area Resignalling Schemes. The objectives of the Paper included "the essential renewal of signalling equipment" and at that stage the plan envisaged work beginning in early 1982 and being completed in November 1986. It was felt that if this timetable were not followed a substantial amount of abortive work of renewal would need to take place simply to maintain the system.

12.3   However, despite the fact that renewal was said to be "essential" this project did not have a smooth passage through BR's mechanisms for approving investment on such schemes. It was discussed and deferred on a number of occasions and a submission in May 1981 recorded that the main scheme was "reduced in cost and scope". BR was advised by the Department of Transport in May 1983 that the scheme would be called in for investment approval by the Secretary of State. It continued to be discussed within BR and a detailed submission was made to the Investment Committee of BR in September 1984 in order to obtain financial approval.

12.4   The full submission was a large-scale plan to rationalise and resignal the Waterloo area and related to signalling dating back to 1936. Appendix K.5 shows the lines that were to be resignalled. These lines would then be controlled by a sole signal box at Wimbledon. A central control point was recognised as more cost-effective than a system of several signal boxes. Wimbledon was chosen because it was a virgin site with no risk of disturbing operations or having any implications for the Channel Rail link. The scheme envisaged the installation of modern colour-light signalling with 2, 3, or 4 aspects depending mainly on traffic density. Automatic Warning System equipment was also to be installed.

12.5   Staff reductions of 74 posts at an annual saving of £737,000 were anticipated. The cost of the scheme was expected to be £32.5m, including some investment not actually involved in resignalling but rather to facilitate the introduction of Driver Only Operated (DOO) trains on the lines involved. The new scheme would save the expensive maintenance costs that would be necessary to keep the old system in operation. Significantly, it was recognised that "despite increased preventative maintenance, the failure rate of the equipment is increasing and the integrity of the signalling system is at risk".

12.6   Over the six years it had taken to reach the stage of consideration by the Investment Committee, the work had moved from being merely necessary, to being vital as the signalling equipment deteriorated further. The failure rate of equipment had increased unacceptably between 1982 and 1984, and a number of essential projects had to be authorised in advance of the main scheme simply to keep the system going.

12.7   The September 1984 submission itself makes significant reading, in particular at paragraph 3.4:

> "Most of the signalling equipment in the area which was installed in 1936 is of early colour-light and track circuit block type and is now overdue for renewal, both in view of its condition and its inability to comply with current operating safety requirements. It is imperative that replacement in some form takes place within the proposed time-scale to maintain a minimum safety standard in the face of deterioration of insulation of cabling and internal wiring and corrosion of signal housings .... The signalling failure situation over the past two years shows that, despite increased surveillance and maintenance and attendant higher costs, there has been an increase of 26% over that period, including three "wrong-side" failures due to the condition of the equipment (see appendix E (i)). To permit further deterioration, unchecked, is completely unacceptable."

The problem of the wrong-side failures was recognised in that Appendix, which said:

> "However the more worrying aspect is the increasing potential for wrong-side failures. During the last two years, three wrong-side failures have occurred directly due to condition of equipment, ..."

The Appendix went on to identify three wrong-side failures, one of which resulted in a:

> "Failure to display a red signal aspect due to a technician touching a wire during routine maintenance and the wire breaking due to brittleness caused by age."

It was recognised that:

> "Clearly an increase of wrong-side failures with an inherent loss of safety cannot be tolerated and either considerable maintenance effort/cost is to be put in or equipment is to be signed out of use."

The unreliability and safety arguments were thus fully deployed in the submission considered by the Investment Committee.

12.8   On 1 October 1984, the Investment Committee endorsed the submission which then went to the Secretary of State for authorisation. That authorisation was given in a letter from the Minister for Public Transport to the Chairman of British Railways Board on 19 December 1984. The time taken on the WARS project from the first Development Paper through to ultimate authorisation by the relevant Minister was therefore a little over six years.

Planning the work

12.9 A meeting to discuss WARS commissioning strategy was held on 13 February 1985, in order to study arrangements to be adopted for commissioning New Works schemes and specifically to consider the proposals for carrying out WARS commissionings. At that meeting there was discussion of the alternative methods of bringing the works into operation by continuous recurring stages (stageworks) or of condensing changeovers from old to new systems into major commissionings. It was decided that for track circuits the stageworks system of a "rolling programme of conversions" was to be preferred to the major commissionings. For the conversion of the signals themselves, however, it was decided that there was no need to commission them in advance of the main commissioning and that therefore the signal changeover should be left until that final period.

12.10 A significant factor in the discussion, which will call for later consideration, was the extent to which commercial judgement played a part in the ultimate decision. The minutes record that:

> "It was also accepted that since the operators had become used to this department carrying out major commissionings whilst a nearly normal train service operates, there could be some resistance to a proposal that requires periods of absolute blockage, especially in busy suburban areas, the former South Western Division being particularly conservative in this respect, on the grounds that Waterloo is their only London terminus. It was however accepted that the Passenger Business Managers' commercial judgement would have a major influence."

12.11 The strategy resolved at that meeting was therefore clearly that, whatever works were to be done by stageworks, weekend by weekend as time progressed, signal changeovers should be limited to the main commissioning, and thus the old signals should remain in operation until that main commissioning.

12.12 At some time in the course of the two years between February 1985 and February 1987 that original decision not actually to commission new signals in replacement for old until the main commissioning seems effectively to have been reversed. It was on 11 February 1987, as we saw at paragraph 8.47, that a meeting was held at the South Lambeth depot in order to consider proposals for commissioning of the New Works.

12.13 The meeting was called to enable the Signals & Telecommunications Department to present its programme for staging the new signalling into works, such that the agreed main commissioning dates could be met. Under the heading "PROBLEM AREAS" the minutes record:

> "The time scale for the scheme allows a little "fall-back" time for stages 3 to 6, but none for stages 7 and 8. Commissioning work on stage 7 commences 2/3 July 1988 and from then to the commissioning of Stage 8B in August 1989, there are no "spare" weekends ...

> The times indicated on the proposed programme are the times required to complete the work. Reduction in that time would not be acceptable either to the S&T or Traffic as overruns may occur."

12.14 Attached to those minutes were the proposals put before that meeting which had been drawn up earlier by Mr Callander, who was at the time a Senior Construction Assistant at South Lambeth. He had put together those proposals in late 1986. They set out the work for the whole period and in particular for the weekend of 26/27 November 1988, on the track between Clapham Junction and Wimbledon as "track and signal conversions on up main fast". Those proposals have been mentioned in Chapter 8 and will be looked at again shortly, but they did envisage the commissioning of new signals at weekends.

12.15 It was therefore as a result of a resignalling scheme first envisaged in 1978 and later authorised in 1984, and in accordance with a timetable worked out in late 1986, that men were working on the last weekend of November 1988 to finish the installation and effect the commissioning of the new signal WF138.

Mr Callander's Proposals 12.16 Mr Callander had decided he should draw up a plan for the implementation of the WARS programme in 1986. Stages 1 and 2 should already have been completed, but 3 to 9 remained. The main commissioning dates for each stage of the scheme had already been set out (see Appendix K.5). The end date was August 1989 and he felt he should plan the work into practical sections for alterations and commissionings to ensure that the timescales could be achieved. No one had requested he should do this work, nor was anyone else addressing their mind to planning. There are two aspects of his proposals that need to be considered:

(i) his proposals to bring the signals into use in sub-stages rather than wait for the major commissioning weekend; and

(ii) the timetable he devised for the work.

The plan 12.17 Mr Callander's plan was devised over a year after the February 1985 meeting to discuss WARS commissioning strategy, at which he was not present. His overall plan reflected the spirit of the meeting in relation to all work other than signals, which was to reduce to a minimum the work to be done at a major commissioning stage. His plan, however, contradicted the meeting's decision on those signals. Mr Callander's reasoning behind bringing new signals into use on a regular basis rather than waiting for the one major commissioning weekend was to cut down on the work at the major commissionings.

12.18 The advantages of the original decision were made clear by Mr Roy Bell, BR Signal Engineer, in his expert evidence:

– until the major commissioning weekend when the new system is brought fully into use, the system runs on a mixture of old and new;

– not converting the signals until that weekend would have ensured the minimum disturbance of the old system for the temporary period;

– this would have been particularly important in the relay room where there would have been less work involved with the circuitry;

– the old signals would be carried on the new track circuits, housed in the new relay room, and these would be run from the old track circuits;

– the only new wiring work involved as an intermediary step to full commissioning would have been to change over the control circuits involving the first four terminals on the relay, but nothing else;

– broadly speaking, job 104 would have been necessary but not job 201.

12.19 This way of working would also have had disadvantages and these were the ones Mr Callander was anxious to avoid:

– extra work on major commissioning involving greater disruption to traffic;

– temporary difference in the size of the overlap section after each signal, sometimes more, sometimes less, than the standard 200 yards; and

– consequent changes to the AWS system.

12.20 Had Mr Callander's plan been put into operation correctly the system would have been safe. It can be argued, with hindsight, that the February 1985 decision would have been preferable because of the reduced work involved in the relay room and in the circuit changes necessary.

12.21 Mr Callander is not to be criticised for the plan he produced. He is to be commended in taking the initiative in preparing such a plan and the reasoning behind it was understandable and acceptable. However, his superiors did not take sufficient care or time to review his proposals. There is no evidence to suggest that Mr Davies considered them at all, much less noticed that his previous decision of "running" the old signals off the new circuits until commissioning weekend was not being implemented.

The timetable 12.22 The second area to be considered is the timetable determined by the plan. Mr Callander worked out the total number of conversions that had to be completed and looked at the number of weekends available. In consultation with the supervisors he decided that an average of 9 track circuits could be converted to new types in one shift. He then drew up his timetable of work. It was clear that there were very few "spare" weekends. He was aware that there was little room for slippage and that seven-day working would be necessary. This plan had to be drawn up in consultation with contractors to ensure they could provide the necessary equipment on time. At that point, Mr Callander requested a further three months between Stages 6 and 7 and an extra three months between Stages 7 and 8. These were never granted.

12.23 The plan was therefore based on staffing levels in late 1985 to early 1986. The situation was not kept under review despite a later loss of skilled staff. Only after reorganisation in May 1988, when asked questions on the timescale by Mr Penny, did Mr Deane and Mr Callander explain that, as long as no other senior technicians were to leave, the programme was "tight but achievable". However, this was not a carefully thought out view and was not checked against the timetable.

12.24 The timetable for introducing Stage 7B of the WARS scheme was obviously very tight. Every weekend for a period of six months was dedicated to commissioning. There was no room for slippage and the workforce available was more limited than it had been when the plan was drawn up. This situation was not being properly monitored by management. The reduced levels of skilled and experienced men now available did not cause the workload to be altered or cause the remaining workforce to be used more effectively. Chapter 8 has already shown that the amount of overtime being worked by individual workers was not monitored and that arrangements for weekend staffing levels were haphazard.

Scheduled hours 12.25 This lack of planning and mismanagement of the workload was a wholly ineffective use of resources, both human and financial. The most important, safety-critical elements of the workload were always carried out at weekends. To ensure a high standard of safety, this aspect of the workload should have been particularly well planned, to ensure adequate numbers of suitably qualified staff, aware of their responsibilities and not mentally jaded by constant seven day working. The concept of "scheduled hours" would have dealt with all these aspects. Saturdays and Sundays would be given the same status as any other day of the week and staff would be rostered to ensure that the workload was covered throughout. However, to compensate for the inconvenience of having to work a set number of weekends in a month, staff would be given a "scheduled hours payment" in addition to their basic pay. The workload could therefore be properly planned and the unhealthy reliance on high overtime levels to supplement basic rates of pay would cease. This obvious method of organisation already existed within the Civil Engineering Department of BR's Southern Region.

12.26 It was not a safe working practice to allow so many men to work excessive levels of overtime for a sustained period. The work should have been better organised to ensure that supervisors were fulfilling their proper role and not acting as senior technicians. Unless effective steps were taken on these problems the timetable should have been reviewed.

12.27 Mr David Rayner, the Joint Managing Director (Railways) explained in evidence, that if there were insufficient staff to carry out work then work would be postponed. At a minimum, that willingness on the part of senior management to adjust timetables was not communicated to more junior levels. There was a prevailing belief that the timeframe was set in stone and no individual manager wanted to be the first to suggest that targets could not be met. Mr Callander had made an initial attempt in 1986 which had failed.

Control of the project

12.28 Once an investment scheme has been given financial approval it is sponsored by one of the four business sectors. WARS was sponsored by Network SouthEast who then commissioned the Southern Region to provide the scheme. Responsibility lay with the Regional S&T Engineer to ensure that the scheme was delivered to time and within budget.

12.29 There are a number of aspects involved in ensuring that a scheme of this size is properly planned and carried through into execution. They are:

– the control of finances;

– the control of design work;

– the control of BR installation work; and

– the control of contractors' work.

12.30 In many organisations, the title "Project Manager" would cover responsibility for all four aspects. This was not the case for the WARS scheme. Financial control was carried out by a "Project Manager" who was actually a member of the General Manager's staff and outside the S&T Department. His job was to ensure that the scheme was working out within the budget. Below the Regional S&T Engineer, responsibility for the rest of the project was diffuse. The design work was done within the Region's Drawing Office, which prior to the May 1988 reorganisation reported to the Regional S&T Engineer through Mr D Graham Brown. Control of BR installation work and day-to-day management was carried out by the individual local depot managers reporting to the Signal Works Engineer. Control of contractors was organised under a "Project Engineer". It can therefore be seen that below the Regional S&T Engineer no one person was responsible for all aspects of project management.

12.31 After reorganisation the situation was complicated further when Design Office work and project control became the responsibility of the Director of S&T, Mr Hodgson, but with the same staff and the same location at Southern House, Croydon, Surrey.

12.32 In an ideal situation there should be a strong "Project Engineer/Manager" responsible directly for all four aspects of the project. If these cannot all come within his chain of command then they should be established in a clear contractual relationship with those who will provide those other functions, without diminishing the Project Engineer/Manager's role or responsibility.

12.33 On predominantly signalling projects, the ultimate responsibility would lie with the Regional S&T Engineer who would nominate a project manager from within his own staff. The Project Manager should, however, not have line management responsibility for the Testing & Commissioning Engineer. This will preserve the independent role of the Testing Engineer, who would also ultimately report to the Regional S&T Engineer.

12.34 If this had been the situation on the WARS scheme, one person could have reviewed the overall plan of works to ensure it met with strategic decisions already taken. This strengthened role of Project Engineer/Manager could have ensured that deadlines were realistic and that they were regularly reviewed. In addition he could have considered and reduced the competing claims of the drawing office which was under pressure with insufficient time to produce modified drawings, and the requirements of the installation staff to have accurate drawings of the work to be done.

The role of the Railway Inspectorate

12.35 Section 41 of the Road and Rail Traffic Act 1933 requires that, before being taken into use, certain specific classes of new work on the railway have to have the approval of the Secretary of State for Transport who may ask for an inspection to be carried out before giving his approval. That inspection is in fact carried out by the Railway Inspectorate (RI). These provisions are essentially a restatement, with additions, of section 5 of the Regulation of Railways Act 1871. Even in 1933 the provisions as enacted were almost unworkable on the everyday existing railway.

12.36 As a result, an administrative letter was sent to the railway companies explaining in more detail those schemes which had to be submitted for approval and how such approval was to be obtained. This letter was revised and reissued in 1958 ("the 1958 letter") but even this letter is ambiguous.

12.37 The RI has therefore been placed in an extremely difficult position. Although RI were aware that WARS was being carried out, it was notified of only two parts of the work. These had been given prior approval and were inspected after they were commissioned. The RI would therefore seem to have condoned the non-submission for approval of the remainder of the scheme. If that is so, the reason is likely to be the interpretation placed both by the Inspectorate and by BR upon the "stageworks" clauses in the 1958 letter.

12.38 Even if the RI has not condoned the failure to submit WARS for approval and on the assumption that the Inspectorate is equipped to deal with such a submission, it has no mechanism under the present arrangements for forcing the timely submission by BR Southern Region of the whole scheme. This is an unsatisfactory state of affairs for which the present members of the Inspectorate are only partially responsible. I am of the view that there is merit in having a scheme for the approval of New Works on the railway and that such a scheme should be properly designed to discharge this function.

Conclusions

12.39 A number of criticisms of the WARS scheme have clearly to be made:

(i) it took six years to push the scheme through BR's investment authorisation machinery;

(ii) there was no one individual responsible for the scheme as a whole;

(iii) the planning of the work was not reviewed initially at a sufficiently senior level, nor was it subsequently reviewed on a regular basis;

(iv) the organisation of the work on a day-to-day level was inefficient; and

(v) the timescale was perceived as inflexible and was running very tight. No-one had the power or the will to introduce more efficient arrangements and/or to demand that the main commissioning dates be delayed.

12.40 Thus it was that a smaller workforce than envisaged was attempting to keep to a programme based on the previously larger workforce. Keeping to the programme meant excessive amounts of overtime for many of the staff. The reason for the same workers attending every weekend was BR's complete lack of method and organisation of weekend working within the S&T Department. In short, too few staff meant too many hours of overtime. The reason that there were too few staff was BR's inability to recruit and keep sufficient workers.

PART FOUR: THE CONCEPT OF SAFETY

Chapter 13: The Management of Safety

Introduction   13.1 Concern for safety in relation to the product of any industry must by necessity be driven by a number of factors: some will be humanitarian, some commercial and some a combination of both. Where the activity of the particular industry is the creation, for example, of consumer durables, that concern can usually be met by the institution of adequate quality control programmes. These should satisfy both the human and the commercial needs. In the case of the railway industry, however, where the function of the industry is to transport people and freight in trains at high speed and in close proximity to other trains, both the human and commercial requirements of safety demand much more: they require that the concept of safety must be at the forefront of all thinking at all times. The reasons are all too obvious: there is so great a potential for disaster if attention to that concept is permitted to drift.

13.2 Management systems must ensure that there is in being a regime which will preserve the first place of safety in the running of the railway. It is not enough to talk in terms of "absolute safety" and of "zero accidents". There must also be proper organisation and management to ensure that actions live up to words.

13.3 Sadly, although the sincerity of the beliefs of those in BR at the time of the Clapham Junction accident who uttered such words cannot for a moment be doubted, there was a distressing lack of organisation and management on the part of some whose duty it was to put those words into practice. The result was that the true position in relation to safety lagged frighteningly far behind the idealism of the words.

13.4 Such a finding would be distressing enough in relation to any part of the structure of the railway's organisation. When it is found to be true of the Signals & Telecommunications Department, the very nerve centre of the railway system, it is all the more alarming. It is upon the accurate and timely dissemination of signalling information that the safety of the modern railway depends. As speeds get higher and traffic density greater, so the demands upon that signalling system become more urgent and complex. In a modern railway system these demands bring with them not only a need for modern technology, but also a complementary need for an attitude receptive to change. There has to be a willingness, not just to accept change grudgingly, but to welcome it with enthusiasm. The challenge has to be met and change effectively managed if the cause of safety is not to fail.

The change of culture   13.5 In the early part of this century the railway industry had built for itself and was justifiably proud of a culture of work where pride in one's work and high morale went hand in hand. The acquisition of skills was sought after and was achieved mainly by on-the-job training. There was a proper realisation of the vital importance in the field of safety of the careful installation and the proper and detailed testing of any new or altered signalling. There was a proper respect for the special expertise of those whose knowledge of the intricacies of signalling installations had progressed to skill in the testing field.

13.6 That culture is now going through a process of change, not merely by reason of factors within the railway but also from those without. The dedicated workforce who regarded the railway as a way of life and a job for life have also been affected by change. The growth of the electrical communications industry has seen an increase in the number of potential employers for that workforce. Competition for that workforce in the form of the offering of higher rates of pay and more sociable working hours has made it more difficult for the railways to attract, train and retain appropriate staff.

13.7 Advances in modern technology, too, have necessitated the training and retraining of staff in further skills. A modern S&T Department of BR Southern Region in the 1990s is bound to be a very different place from that of 20 years ago. BR is competing more fiercely with other employers to recruit and retain staff in an area which is not only continually expanding but also demanding an increasing level of technical skill. Wastage rates for skilled staff have increased over the last few years. In addition, BR has conducted a number of reorganisations to reduce staff and improve efficiency. Reducing staff does not necessarily mean reducing safety provided that compensatory improvements in efficiency and effectiveness can be achieved by the remaining workforce.

13.8 It is essential, therefore, that in paying proper attention to the needs of change and of training for that change, management must not lose sight of what the words "absolute safety" mean in practice. Otherwise the lessons of safety that were taught in the old culture of on-the-job training may become lost.

13.9 The last twenty years have seen vast works of resignalling on Southern Region among them those at three London termini, first London Bridge, then Victoria and finally Waterloo. The massive scale of such resignalling work meant that in order that the concept of "absolute safety" be followed, there had to be strict and total adherence to the maintenance of proper working standards, both in the installation and in the testing of all this new work. It was management that had the duty to ensure that such a regime existed. Sadly, that regime did not exist and management at all levels within the S&T Department of BR's Southern Region failed abysmally, irrespective of any good intentions, to see that such a regime was developed, cultivated and enforced without fail throughout their areas of responsibility.

13.10 That failure can be simply described. In the management of an organisation which is dedicated to ensuring a safe signalling system it is essential that day-to-day functions are properly planned, organised, implemented and regularly reviewed. Management systems must be sufficiently robust to ensure that human error does not go unchecked. The systems were not robust enough and they failed.

13.11 I shall consider towards the end of Chapter 16 whether long standing BRB policies created the correct environment and framework to allow the target of "absolute safety" to be achieved.

The Board's systems

13.12 Sir Robert Reid, Chairman of BR, assured the Court that BRB was committed to "absolute safety" and that no accident was acceptable. He explained that all BR employees are committed to running a safe railway and that no railwayman or woman would do anything other than put safety first. The Court respects the sincerity of that statement.

13.13 In this case the target of absolute safety was not met. The causes were a combination of bad practice and mismanagement. Having heard the evidence of more than 60 witnesses from BR, I am satisfied that the errors which were made did not result from any deliberate decision to cut corners on safety. The important issue remains the priority accorded to safety.

13.14 Within BR, the Board maintains responsibility for policy on safety. It is quite correctly not delegated. The Board's sub-committee on safety meets every quarter and additionally if necessary. In the wake of the Investigation into the King's Cross Fire, BRB reviewed its management structure to ensure that safety was being taken into account at all levels. As a result the post of Director Safety was established to report to the Joint Managing Director (Railways), Mr David Rayner. The first Director Safety was appointed in November 1988 and is Mr Maurice Holmes. His previous position had been Director of Operations, in which capacity he had been responsible for preparing an annual report on safety within the field of Operations. The Board made it clear that this new appointment was not intended to reduce the responsibilities of the Director of Operations in ensuring the safe running of the railway, but was to be an extra safeguard.

The concept of "Total Quality Management"

13.15 In January 1988 BR had also adopted a policy of Total Quality Management (TQM). It should be stressed that work on developing this policy had been going on for some time and this was not therefore resorted to as a reaction to the King's Cross fire on 18 November 1987. TQM is a formal system designed to improve the quality of the work produced, the procedures used and the working practices involved. It is estimated that the systems involved would take five years to implement in full, starting from the top of the organisation down. At the time of the accident a "quality plan" for the S&T Department had been developed but not yet put into effect. BR's policy of TQM is discussed in detail later in this chapter.

13.16 TQM was not specifically designed as a safety initiative, but with the implementation of improving standards, procedure and training there would inevitably be safety benefits. If fully implemented TQM will eventually form an important tool in the range of options available to management in ensuring safety on the railways. However, the two important advances of the appointment of a Director Safety and the intended implementation of TQM, cannot be a substitute for good management, safe working practices, continual review and formal auditing.

13.17 Previous chapters have set out the management weaknesses within the S&T Department from 1983 onwards and the bad working practices which were allowed to go unchecked. Before looking to the future of TQM and formal safety audits it is necessary to look at the past and at S&T's own monitoring system for signalling failures before the accident. Only in this way can the question be answered whether safety levels were being properly monitored.

13.18 It is necessary to examine:

(i) whether the system of monitoring was sufficiently robust to ensure that sufficient information was available;

(ii) whether a proper analysis was made of the causes for and lessons to be learned from any failure; and

(iii) whether this information was acted upon, thus reducing any risk of the same mistake being repeated and safety being further compromised.

Previous monitoring of signal failures

13.19 The S&T Department is responsible for the integrity of the signalling system, an essential element in running a safe railway. As we saw in Chapter 1, signalling failures fall into two categories - right-side and wrong-side failures (WSFs). WSFs are sub-divided further into protected and unprotected failures. A protected wrong-side failure is a failure which has occurred in the signalling system on the wrong side of safety, but which another part of the system will protect from having dangerous consequences. An unprotected WSF does not have that secondary protection. How WSFs were monitored within the S&T Department before the accident provides a valuable insight into how management systems lacked the ability to see the dangers of bad working practices and to prevent them.

Wrong-side failures – the mishandling of a problem

13.20 The whole safety of railway signalling depends for its effectiveness on one cardinal principle: that a train can be prohibited entry to a given section of track when that entry would be unsafe. But there are two main ways of breaching that cardinal principle and it is vital that both ways are kept at the forefront of the mind and that the one does not claim so much attention as to drive out the other:

(i) the first is that an error in the control of the train can cause it to enter the prohibited section of the track;

(ii) the second is that there is an error of the signalling of that train which can have the same effect.

Both these two breaches can be caused either by equipment failure or by human failure on the part of the driver or signalman respectively if there is no automatic system to prevent human error.

13.21 Looked at carefully from this viewpoint, both ways are in fact but two halves of the same coin. The former, as we saw in Chapter 2, would be described in railway jargon as a SPAD, a signal passed at danger. An equipment failure causing the latter would be a WSF. Both have the potential to cause untold loss of life and damage, both should have received the same degree of attention from those involved in the management of safety in BR: they did not. A signalman's error causing the latter did not fall to be considered in this Investigation.

13.22 The monitoring and investigation of SPADs in BR received a great deal of attention. SPADs were rightly seen as the potentially dangerous occurrences they were. Full reporting of each incident was required. There followed a thorough investigation of the incident and the appropriate learning and teaching of the lessons which could be drawn from the specific incident. The Royal Holloway College was asked to carry out an independent study. None of this, however, followed after a WSF.

13.23 In contrast to what happened following a SPAD, there was a blurring of distinctions in relation to an incident described as a wrong-side failure. Part of the reason for the blurring of distinctions was that this was a "catch-all" title which covered the whole spectrum of occurrences varying in gravity from the potentially disastrous to the least significant. An example of the latter would be the failure of an indicator light for points or signals in a signalman's panel. Had such a bulb on the signalman's panel been out on the morning of 12 December 1988, both the situation there and that at WF138 would equally correctly have been classified as WSFs. The former would have been of little significance, the latter was to be completely disastrous.

13.24 Whether or not it was a confusion of thought produced by such a broad categorisation which led to the difference in attitude towards and treatment of SPADs and WSFs, it is certain that the monitoring of wrong-side failures and the realisation of their true importance became something of a poor relation compared with that of SPADs.

13.25 The monitoring of wrong-side signalling failures often begins with a driver's report to the signalman of something amiss. The Court heard that normally a driver would hear nothing more about the report he makes. He therefore will not find out the explanation for the apparent fault nor will he know whether he was mistaken in what he thought he had seen. This can only encourage guesswork on the driver's part as to the nature of the fault and the belief that the signal aspect seen could be put down to action by the signalman. It would be helpful, I believe, for the drivers always to receive feedback on the reports they had made explaining the outcome of any investigation.

13.26 The failure is investigated by the Maintenance Department and a report is made. Only failures which actually cause an accident must be reported to the Railway Inspectorate under the Railways (Notification of Accidents) Order 1986. The reporting chain is through the Regional General Manager's staff and is recorded in BR HQ's control log. This ensures that the Director of Signal and Telecommunications is aware of the accident. Thus, in the more usual case where happily the failure has not caused a reportable accident the incident is dealt with entirely within the Signal and Telecommunications Department in the Region. All too often the investigation ends in a result which again has a three letter acronym, "NFF" standing for "No Fault Found". In respect of serious failures the system was changed after the Oxted incidents. After investigation and report, such failures were discussed at the Departmental Conference, monthly meetings of senior managers in the S&T Department, chaired by the Regional Engineer.

13.27 After an alarming number of signal failures in 1985, both right and wrong-side, a computer system known as FRAME (Fault Reporting and Maintenance Evaluation) was introduced to act as a check on the reliability of the system. It was not introduced specifically to monitor the level of safety. FRAME is however the starting point for monitoring the safety of the signalling system in the S&T Department, but is by no means a comprehensive data base on which to draw. Wrong-side failures are recorded as a single category and are not subdivided in any way according to the potential for danger of the incident. While it is true that any wrong-side failure is a serious cause for concern, a defective light bulb on a signal indication in a signalman's panel plainly produces less potential for danger than a faulty track circuit which permits trains to proceed although the track ahead is occupied. As a minimum, WSFs should at least have been categorised into protected and unprotected failures to allow some analysis of the more dangerous failures. There were large numbers of WSFs reported as paragraph 13.29 below shows. Without proper categorisation it would be over simplistic to look at all WSFs as of equal significance.

13.28 FRAME also has limitations because it shows the definition of the fault as originally reported and not as subsequently investigated. The trend in signalling failures as a whole was being monitored by the Regional S&T Engineer on a regular basis, but only by reference to data with these in-built imperfections.

The statistics 13.29 The Court asked for figures outlining the total number of wrong-side failures in 1985-88 on the WARS scheme and in addition any failures within Southern Region relevant to the accident. The figures are shown at Appendix H. It must be stressed that a large number of wrong-side failures have little potential for danger. There were 114 WSFs on the WARS scheme in 1985-88, two of which had relevance to the Clapham Junction accident in that they were caused by S&T staff or contractors where checking or testing was inadequate. Another two had relevance in that as a result of a track circuit failure the signal gave a false clear or proceed aspect. One further incident at Waterloo on 19 November 1987 had occurred because the points had not been correctly set as a result of a cable fault during installation work.

13.30 A total of 15 WSFs which were a result of inadequate testing had occurred on the Southern Region for 1985 to 1987. These incidents were spread evenly over the period with five failures each year in 1985, 1986 and 1987, but from 1985 to the start of 1988 there was no downward trend.

13.31 This information became available in that it was partially extracted from FRAME, and partially retrieved by going to the source documents. It was clear that it was not a simple process for BR to discover how many wrong-side failures had occurred in recent years and the type of problem which had caused them.

13.32 One of the problems with which this Investigation is concerned is inadequate testing. Between 1985-87 there were fifteen WSFs caused by inadequate testing, two on WARS and thirteen elsewhere in the Region. If these figures had been considered by senior managers in 1987, those managers must have became aware of the continuing state of unacceptable standards of testing. They were certainly made aware of the problem in 1985, but it is now necessary to look at how closely they monitored the situation thereafter to see whether there was any improvement.

The response 13.33 Following a number of wrong-side failures which had occurred in November 1985 at Northfleet, Oxted and East Croydon, Mr Hale had asked that a list of serious failures be presented each month to the Departmental Conference. Most of the November failures including the Oxted incidents were discovered before they were able to cause an accident. That at East Croydon had resulted in a side-on collision between passenger trains. Fortunately, there were no injuries to passengers. The distinction between these incidents is important.

13.34 Since there had been no accident at either Oxted or Northfleet, there was no requirement to report them to the Railway Inspectorate under the Railways (Notice of Accidents) Order 1980 (subsequently revoked by the 1986 Order). They were therefore considered only within the S&T Department itself. The East Croydon collision, on the other hand, as an accident was reportable to the Railway Inspectorate and was therefore dealt with in the General Manager's office and drawn to the attention of the Director of S&T. Investigations therefore followed different routes and the vital information went through different channels. Immediately following these incidents on 15 November 1985 a letter was issued by Mr Hale to inform staff that the draft testing instruction, recently issued under the title SL-Provisional, was to have the full authority of any other Departmental Instruction.

13.35 One of the Oxted incidents is most relevant to the Clapham Junction accident, since the fault could have been discovered by an independent wire count and adequate testing. Mr Davies, Signal Works Engineer, prepared reports of the three Oxted incidents which were considered at Departmental Conference. The minutes record the outcome of the discussion:

> **"Signalling Incidents**
>
> A (Mr Hale) expressed great concern, shared by G (Mr Thompson), at number of signalling wrong side failures and incidents occurring apparently due to design defects and lack of effective testing.
>
> M (Mr Penny) will produce list of incidents for each Departmental Conference and an aide memoire for departmental enquiry officers covering factors to be considered at enquiries.
>
> Discussion on problems with testing procedures on SR. Good testing relies on:
>
> 1. Organising and planning testing work and documenting the plan.
>
> 2. Definition of roles and responsibilities in testing.
>
> 3. Allocation of trained and competent staff to specific testing tasks.
>
> 4. Soundly based procedures.
>
> 5. Well documented testing records, particularly for multistaged conversions.
>
> 6. Analysis of subsidiary testing activities by functional tester, so that his testing is soundly based.
>
> 7. System for identifying poor performance in testing.

On SR, procedures seem to be faulty or non-existent at key points in the procedure of safe signalling installations; the biggest loophole is the tying together all the individual bits of conversion and staging at functional testing stage.

The need for a full testing procedural document is now more urgent than ever, but the resource difficulty is recognised. Consultancy to be pursued with J Fadden, recently ex LM Commissioning Engineer. W (Mr Wilkinson) will contact and arrange."

13.36 A full testing procedural document and consideration of it at Departmental Conference were, therefore, to be the urgent response to the defects clearly identified as a result of these three WSFs. Chapter 11 has already shown that:

(i) it took 18 months before the testing document was introduced;

(ii) even then it was not considered to be in force; and

(iii) SL-Provisional its predecessor which should have both been in force and known to be so, was considered by most staff still to be a draft.

13.37 A Regional Testing Team was appointed on Southern Region in August 1986 with the express task of raising the standard of testing and providing training to others so that a cadre of testers would be established who would be qualified and available for further testing work. Chapter 11 has already shown that the Regional Testing Team was so heavily involved in carrying out testing that almost nothing had been done by way of training before the team was disbanded in May 1988.

13.38 It is surprising that all of the managers above the Regional Testing Team were of the firm view that the team had contributed to an improvement in the failure rate. In a safe system, unprotected wrong-side failures should be zero. It may be true that the failure rate overall was declining, but the number of wrong-side failures in fact caused by inadequate testing remained steady throughout 1985, 1986 and 1987. Mr Hale seemed to continue in that mistaken belief that all was well until this Investigation.

13.39 When asked whether there was any systematic monitoring of wrong-side failures, he explained how he monitored the information:

"*First of all, I received every month from the reporting computer system, a detailed list of every failure classified as wrong side. The level of information that gave me, enabled me to follow up those I felt were of significance. In addition to that I was fed at the Departmental Conference each month, details of the more significant failures again from the Maintenance Engineer. The number of failures arising from new works activities - design installation and testing - in fact steadily declined throughout that period.*"

The data available from FRAME, which Mr Hale used to monitor WSFs, could not give him the level of detail he needed to review the testing situation. He was content simply to look at broad totals to establish trends. No one was asked to monitor the situation in more detail because Mr Hale felt that he was being fed enough information.

13.40 Raw data require proper analysis and the action taken as a result needs proper review. It is clear that senior management within the S&T Department, having correctly identified a problem in the standard of testing, did not adequately monitor that standard, or review that standard regularly. The figures produced to the Court which appear at Appendix H, also show that of the twenty-five WSFs from 1985 to 1988, where checking or testing was inadequate, fifteen occurred on the Southern Region. While the Court heard no evidence as to whether there were any differences in the stringency of reporting WSFs between Regions, and while the density of signalling equipment on Southern Region is recognised, had those figures been requested from the computer records, the comparison should have provided searching questions.

13.41 At more senior levels within BR, WSFs were only considered if they had caused an accident which was reportable to the Railway Inspectorate. The RI were concerned with overall accident trends. To the Inspectorate the most worrying trend was the rapid increase in signals passed at danger (SPADs). Each signal passed at danger meant the possibility of an accident, and the figures had increased to 800 incidents in a year. While BR was obviously right to accord high priority to establishing the causes of the incidents and reasons for the upward trend, there were other dangers to be dealt with.

13.42 Nobody in management seemed to recognise that an unprotected wrong-side failure would cause exactly the same risk of an accident. Nobody in management it seems grasped the nettle of the potential of the wrong-side failure to cause an accident at least as disastrous as a SPAD. If they ever did grasp that nettle, it never occurred to them to give the reporting and investigation of WSFs the priority and the monitoring that was needed.

Total quality management

13.43 In January 1988, BRB committed itself to a policy of Total Quality Management. This concept was best defined by Mr David Maidment, BR's Reliability Manager, in his statement to the inquiry:

> "Typical Total Quality Management policies include two main strands of activity. The first involves company wide training of all staff in quality awareness and commitment to a philosophy of allowing no acceptable deviation from the laid down standards and specifications of quality which must be properly measured. These programmes concentrate on a responsible commitment of all staff to improving quality and a shared communication between management and staff towards the ultimate goals. The second main strand of such a policy involves a systematic overhaul of processes and procedures which contribute to the delivery of a quality product. Procedures need to be laid down in writing to identify what quality is required, who is responsible for producing it and how the product quality is to be designed, built and maintained."

13.44 The philosophy behind Total Quality Management is that the prevention of error is more effective in saving time and cost compared with those involved in correcting the consequences of error after the event. It thus balances the humanitarian and the commercial approach to the concept of safety with which this Chapter began. The theory appears as a simple statement of the essence of good management. This should not be considered as criticism since it takes great skill to set out "common sense" in a way which is acceptable and practicable as a guide for such a large organisation as BR.

13.45 It takes even more commitment and dedication to ensure that these lessons are put into practice. This commitment and dedication have to stem from the top downwards and not in the opposite direction. I am encouraged by the commitment of the Chairman of BR to this route towards the establishment of the concept of "absolute safety".

13.46 Mr Maidment's description of TQM encapsulates several major aspects of this Investigation in relation to:

(i) the training of staff;

(ii) the strict accordance with laid down standards, procedures and instructions;

(iii) the importance of shared communication between management and staff towards defined goals;

(iv) the systematic review of processes and procedures; and

(v) The establishment of written procedures setting out what quality is required, who is responsible for that quality, and how the work is to be carried out.

13.47 Again, in fairness to BR, it must be stressed that work had already begun on the quality initiative before the Clapham Junction accident. Policy documents had been produced in June and July 1988 on the provision of signalling, signalling maintenance and the implementation of a Total Quality Campaign throughout the S&T section. Mr Hale had been appointed to the post of Quality Manager and took up his new duties on the day of the accident.

13.48 BR's aim is to introduce its Quality Initiative at all levels within five years. This task will need a major commitment by senior management. The difference between the recognition of the need for training and the implementation of that recognition by the actual programme of relevant training courses has already been stressed in this Report. It remains an area of concern. The implementation of the policy will centre on training for managers and workers and the application of British Standard BS5750: Quality Systems. Such courses would deal with organisation of work, working practices, clarity of responsibilities, and auditing procedures.

13.49 Before applying for certification under the standard, BR management would have to be certain that procedures were effective and an internal audit system was in place. Those courses would need to be better conceived, planned, organised and monitored than any so far run on BR Southern Region. I do not for a moment under-estimate the difficulty of introducing what will for many years be a stark change in culture for the BR workforce. Great drive will be needed to do so in five years.

13.50 Had the quality initiative been in place and work within the S&T Department been certified as meeting British Standard BS5750, the major weaknesses which allowed circumstances to combine in such a way as to cause the Clapham Junction accident might well have been eradicated. Instructions should have been more clearly drafted. Staff should have been better aware of their own responsibilities and those of others, staff should have been trained to work to laid down standards, fully and at all times and the quality of the installation work and the testing process should have been regularly reviewed.

13.51 I therefore welcome BR's quality initiative and will recommend later that it be implemented with the greatest possible speed, particularly within the S&T Department of Southern Region.

13.52 Management consultants have been appointed to review BR's management systems and how they match up to BR's target of "absolute safety". The scope of their review is wide and I am encouraged by the points they have been specifically asked to cover. At Appendix J is reproduced the specification for the consultants. I am convinced that this work should be progressed as quickly as possible and that their eventual recommendations should be implemented with all speed.

Safety Audit 13.53 In addition, the question of formal safety audits must not be forgotten. There are a number of internationally accepted methods of safety auditing appropriate to operations such as BR. A safety audit was recently carried out under Major King of the Railway Inspectorate into London Underground under one such system known as the International Safety Rating System. Formal safety audits could play an important part in reviewing the quality of the work and procedures employed. Weaknesses would be identified more speedily and action properly targeted.

13.54 I have noted elsewhere that both SPADs and WSFs which lead to accidents are reportable to the RI as such under the Railways (Notice of Accidents) Order 1986. However, for RI to be able to monitor all those events which bear directly on public safety, those occurrences which do not lead to accidents should also be reportable. A recommendation to this effect would however cause a number of problems in practice. Firstly, precise legal definitions will be essential in order to confine reportable incidents to those which are significant. Secondly, it may be necessary to amend the primary legislation as well as the 1986 Order. This is not something which should be allowed to be a deterrent since the updating of the Road and Rail Traffic Act 1933 also involves primary legislation and will also be necessary for other recommendations which I note elsewhere.

13.55 Lastly, in the case of both SPADs and WSFs, where at present there is often no tangible evidence, reporting of the event will frequently be self-incriminating. This obviously may lead to a degree of under-reporting which could only be overcome by having tachographs (or data-recorders) on both signalling equipment and trains. Despite the acknowledged problems, the benefits of a proper continuous review of both SPADs and WSFs by an independent body seem to me to be overriding.

Chapter 14: The Funding of Safety

The Constraints

14.1   Before considering the funding of safety, it is necessary to set out the various statutory and financial constraints which are imposed on the British Railways Board (BRB) in the running of the railway system. These can effectively be summarised as:

(i) Basic requirements of principle.

(ii) Requirements to maintain a fixed historic standard.

(iii) Requirements as to revenue generation.

(iv) Requirements limiting external financing.

(v) Requirement for the obtaining of investment approval.

(i) Basic requirements of principle

14.2   The basic requirements of principle stem from section 3 (1) of the Transport Act, 1962. This section enacts that:

> "It shall be the duty of the Railways Board . . . to provide railway services in Great Britain . . . and to have due regard, as respects . . . those railway . . . services . . . to efficiency, economy, and safety of operation."

(ii) Requirement to maintain a fixed historic standard

14.3   The requirement to maintain a fixed historic standard comes from powers given to the Secretary of State by Section 3(1) of the Railways Act 1974. BRB is made answerable to the Secretary of State's authority by Section 3(1) of the Railways Act 1974 which provides that:

> "The Secretary of State shall be the competent authority of Great Britain in relation to the Railways Board for the purposes of the relevant transport regulations and, as that authority, may give directions to the Board imposing on them obligations of a general nature with respect to the operation of the whole or any part of their railway passenger system."

The Secretary of State has from time to time made such directions. The financial consequences of such directions have to be considered and provided for and accordingly provision for payment to BRB by central government is enacted in the following sub-section, section 3(2) of the 1974 Act:

> "It shall fall to the Secretary of State to make any payments which are required to be made to the Board by any provision of those regulations and he may, subject to and in accordance with the provisions of those regulations, determine the manner of calculating, and the conditions applicable to, those payments."

It is in this way that Government makes compensatory payments to the Board for any obligations imposed upon it by Government in order to ensure that the public service of the railway is maintained. Those obligations are known as the Public Service Obligations (PSO).

14.4   The obligations are defined in Article 2 of EEC Regulation 1191/69 as being:

> "Obligations which the transport undertaking [in question] if it were considering its own commercial interests would not assume or would not assume to the same extent or under the same conditions."

Article 1 paragraph 4 provides that:

> Financial <u>burdens</u> devolving on transport undertakings by reason of the maintenance of the obligations referred to in paragraph 2 ... shall be subject to compensation made in accordance with common procedure laid down in this Regulation."

14.5   In December 1974 the Secretary of State exercised his powers to direct the Board to continue to operate its railway passenger systems so as to provide a public service comparable generally with that provided by the Board at that time. A later direction by the Government dated 30 March 1988 revoked that direction and ordered the Board to maintain its passenger system at a level comparable to that on 1 April 1988. The payment by Government of the relevant compensation for the net cost of carrying out these obligations is usually known as the Public Service Obligation (PSO) Grant.

(iii) Requirements as to revenue generation

14.6   The Board is under a statutory financial obligation to break even on its revenue account in the provision of its services. This arises under the provisions of section 41 (2) of the Transport Act 1968 which enacts that:

> "It shall be the duty of each of the authorities to whom this section applies so to perform their functions under the Act of 1962 or this Act as to secure that the combined revenues of the authority and of their subsidiaries taken together are not less than sufficient to meet their combined charges properly chargeable to revenue account, taking one year with another."

(iv) Requirements limiting external financing

14.7   In common with all other nationalised industries the Board has to operate to an External Financing Limit (EFL) placed upon it by the Government. That limit relates to external sources of finance in the form of:

–   PSO grants

–   level crossing grants

–   borrowings; and

–   the capital value of assets leased.

The effect of these first four requirements

14.8   BRB is set objectives for achievement by the Government over a three year period. For the three years 1987-88, 1988-89 and 1989-90 these objectives were set by the Secretary of State in a letter dated 21 October 1986. The objectives directed the Board to develop proposals both to improve the service to the customer and to reduce operating costs through improved efficiency. There were specific objectives directed to the PSO grant which required a significant reduction in grant requirement for Network SouthEast to be achieved by 1989-90.

128

14.9   BRB determine their annual budget in relation to a five year rail plan, the budget for the current year forming the first year of the five year plan. BRB's five year plan is referred to as the Corporate Plan and relates to the whole of BRB's organisation, both railway and ancillary businesses. In working out its needs for external financing BRB bases the figure for its request to the Government on its Corporate Plan. When as in the years 1986-87 and 1987-88, the Government set an EFL below BRB's request, it is clear that problems can arise. To avoid overshooting the EFL, BRB has to reduce the planned requirement and this can only be done in a number of ways:

(i) by reducing working capital, trading loss or capital investment; and/or by

(ii) increasing internal resources i.e. by means of asset sales.

14.10 BRB gave evidence to the Monopolies and Mergers Commission (MMC) in 1987 that this form of constraint can cause additional pressure on the achievement of future objectives by deferring capital investment and thus delaying income generation or cost reduction.

14.11 The Report of the Monopolies and Mergers Commission "British Railways Board: Network SouthEast" [NSE] (Command 204) in September 1987 found that:

> "Across BRB as a whole rail investment fell in the early 1980s to well below the level of the late 1970s but investment excluding continuous welded rail had recovered by 1985-86. An increase in NSE investment is now planned after a steady decline since 1980. It will not be possible to implement BRB's plans for increased or accelerated investment set out in the 1986 Rail Plan unless they can be accommodated within the EFL."

The MMC report noted at paragraph 2.19 that:

> "Despite the planned increase in investment, we are not convinced that BRB have considered a wide enough range of investment projects to be confident that its investment programme is adequate."

It also found (at paragraph 2.21) that:

> "The method of including investment projects in the planning process does not include rigorous ranking of projects because capital at present is said by BRB not to be a constraint. We are concerned that if a constraint does arise BRB does not have a system for comparing projects with each other or with newly introduced projects to decide how best to ration resources available to it."

14.12 In considering in this chapter the funding of safety, it is impossible to look at specific proposals for the expenditure of capital on identifiable projects, such as those for Automatic Train Protection (ATP), without bearing in mind the potential for delay in their progression by reason of cost constraints caused by the deferment of capital investment.

14.13 It is worth noting that before the formal hearings of the Investigation opened, BRB sent a letter to the Investigation dated 3 February 1989, in which it sought to assure the Court that the Board had adequate funds to ensure the safe running of the railways. The letter said:

> "I am advised by Counsel that it may assist the Court in respect of the ambit of the Inquiry, to indicate the stance which British Railways Board will take upon the question of finance: It is accepted by the Board that it considered, and considers, that at all material times sufficient funds were available to British Rail to discharge its statutory obligations with regard to safety of operations."

14.14 A further significant matter arose much later, during the last few days of the hearing of evidence by the Court. On Day 51 the Chairman of BRB, Sir Robert Reid, at the very beginning of his evidence was at pains to say:

> "A: ... While both I and my Board are anxious to give all necessary assurances to the Court about the Board's intentions, there are certain matters which in some cases preclude the giving of irrevocable guarantees. In particular, there is the requirement of the Department of Transport, which reserves to itself the right to authorise (or reject) major investment expenditure."

> "Q: If I could interrupt you there, I think you spoke to the Secretary of State yesterday. Is that right?"

> "A: Yes. I spoke to the Secretary of State and he assures me that he will give sympathetic attention to any proposals for authority for major investment to enhance safety."

14.15 While the reporting by Sir Robert of that assurance had the effect of placing it in evidence before the Court, any ostensible comfort which might be derived from those words is countered:

(i) by the limited nature of their ambit;

(ii) by the effect of financial constraints referred to earlier in this chapter; and

(iii) by the pertinent example of the protracted delays imposed upon the implementation of the WARS project by the six-year process of obtaining investment approval.

14.16 It is necessary at this stage to look at those procedures, through which any projects involving the expenditure of capital sums have to pass, in order to see both:

(i) their historic effect upon such projects as WARS; and

(ii) their potential for future deferment of projects essential to safety.

(v) Requirements for the obtaining of investment approval

14.17 Authorisation of investment proposals occurs at a variety of levels within BR management according to the cost of the scheme proposed. Additionally, the Secretary of State for Transport has power to call schemes in for his authorisation. Any scheme over £1m must be approved by BRB's Investment Committee. A list of schemes over £5m (raised in July this year to £10m) is submitted to the Department of Transport and is categorised by the Department into the following groups:

A – projects of which the Secretary of State wishes only to be informed, once they have been authorised by BR;

B – projects where, following authorisation by BRB, the Secretary of State wishes to see the appraisal and submission;

C – projects called in for authorisation by the Secretary of State.

14.18 BRB's structure involves the division of the organisation into five business sectors and six operating regions. The business sectors are Network SouthEast, InterCity, Provincial, Freight and Parcels. The regions are Scottish, Southern, Eastern, London Midland, Western and Anglia.

14.19 On the business side of BR the Sector Managers are responsible for the financial performance of their sector. The operational side of BR provides services for the business sectors. Any investment proposal must be sponsored by one of the business sectors as part of the authorisation process.

14.20 All nationalised industries are expected to show a positive required rate of return on their capital investment programme which is set by government. (It has recently been raised from 5% to 8%). Each nationalised industry then negotiates with its sponsor department, a test discount rate for individual investment schemes: in BR's case, it negotiates with the Department of Transport. At the time of the hearings that figure for BR was 8%. In the subsidised sectors (Network SouthEast and Provincial) the 8% rate is used as a means of ensuring the best value for money when making investment decisions. Non-commercial schemes carried out for purely safety reasons are not expected to make a direct financial return. Examples given to the inquiry were the completion of the Advance Warning System installation programme, first begun in the 1950's and the £12m fire safety investment made following the King's Cross fire.

14.21 The fact that each investment proposal has to be sponsored by one of the business sectors has the potential to raise difficulties for safety investment proposals because it is conceivable that business managers might be reluctant to take on a non-commercial proposal not totally relevant to their business. This organisational disincentive within BR against safety investment was recognised by Mr Maurice Holmes, then Director of Operations, in January 1988. He wrote to the joint Managing Director (Railways), warning that:

> "A further concern is that there are signs that the past high safety standards at local level achieved by giving a high priority to a "safe railway" above other issues are starting to be eroded by the change in railway culture. If continued, this will strike at the root of our structure. I would not like a major disaster with loss of life to be the reason that forced British Rail to invest in modern safety aids."

14.22 He had referred in that letter to "the change in railway culture". He explained to the Investigation that the new business culture was ensuring that investment proposals were, in his view quite rightly, being subjected to more rigorous scrutiny before being authorised. However, this meant that investment into safety-related projects, such as ATP, was not being progressed. At that point Mr Holmes believed that BR was still within the margins of safety but he was firing a warning shot to ensure that this potential problem was recognised.

WARS

14.23 The WARS project was first proposed in 1978 and the content of the scheme is considered in greater detail in Chapter 12. BR was informed in May 1983 by the Department of Transport that WARS would be called in for authorisation by the Secretary of State. This was because the Department had categorised the project as falling into Group C of the groups listed earlier at paragraph 14.17. Discussions were then held between BR and DTp at official level. On 5 November 1984, the Chairman of BRB wrote to the Secretary of State seeking approval for the WARS scheme which was granted in a letter dated 19 December 1984.

14.24 WARS is an example of a scheme which would have been carried out for commercial reasons. The substantial time delay between the first proposal of the project in 1978 and its eventual authorisation in 1984 is of great concern. WARS was put forward as a scheme to replace and to rationalise the system, to reduce staffing and to prepare the system for the introduction of Driver Only Operated (DOO) trains. After three WSFs had occurred, as a result of the age of the equipment, this project was pushed through with a greater emphasis on safety. Initially, the potential for danger had not been sufficiently recognised nor accorded high enough priority. The six years WARS took to progress through the investment procedure caused alarming and protracted delays to this project, so vital to the safe running of a railway.

14.25 In the early eighties, a period when the MMC reported that investment was falling, the WARS programme would therefore have been competing for more restricted resources. The Court did not inquire into the early years of the project and therefore sought no evidence upon which it would be possible to make a finding as to whether or not the WARS project was deferred because it had to compete for limited funds until the safety situation was so grave that the investment had to be authorised. However, the possibility that such may have been the case is enough to make the point for the future. The Court recognises that the present investment constraints on BR are not as rigid as in the late seventies and early eighties. However, the progress of the WARS project presents us with a clear lesson to be learned for future investment projects with very significant safety benefits.

14.26 Having looked to the past in relation to WARS and its progress, it is necessary to consider projects planned for the future and their progress, actual and intended. It is interesting to see how two purely safety proposals, Automatic Train Protection and cab radios fared under this investment regime. Both systems are now being developed by BR.

Automatic train protection

14.27 As will be seen in the next Chapter, the Chief Inspecting Officer of Railways in his Annual Report for 1985, called on BR to consider a system of ATP. In previous reports he had pointed out that while great improvements had been made in the signalling system the driver had been left without any additional technical aids. Despite this, the development of ATP did not become BR policy until a paper prepared by the Director of Operations and the Director of Signals & Telecommunications was considered by the Railway Executive in November 1988.

14.28 Until then it had been thought that the safety advantages of ATP could not justify the investment. This was the main reason behind the concerns which Mr Holmes expressed in his letter of January 1988 which are outlined in paragraph 14.21. At the November 1988 meeting, it was agreed that a version of ATP should be introduced at a cost of £140m over a ten year period and the Director Network SouthEast (NSE) was tasked with carrying the project forward.

14.29 This project would not have met the 7% rate of return then required by the Department of Transport. BR therefore attempted to calculate the theoretical annual savings in the cost of accidents, if ATP had been in existence between 1970-86 in order to see if the investment case could be strengthened. By using the £500,000 figure the Department of Transport applies in assessing the cost to society of a road fatality BR estimated that the *annual* offsetting savings produced by investing in ATP would be around £6-10m. These were very rough figures and BR felt at the time not worth considering further.

14.30 Ironically, BR announced trials for ATP two days after the Purley accident on 4 March 1989. The Investment Committee authorised on 6 March 1989 both development expenditure of £1m and provision for £17.4m to be made in BR's 5 year investment plan. It has to be recognised that development expenditure does not mean authorisation of funds for the full scheme. Once the type of scheme has been chosen and BR has approved the investment, it is likely that such a large scheme will require approval by the Secretary of State.

14.31 The October 1988 paper concluded that if given high enough priority this project could be completed in 5 years. However BR has now adopted a policy of implementation over a 10 year period. BR believes that it might be possible to move more quickly, although it points out that a very large part of the benefits will accrue in the first few years of implementation. More will need to be said on this topic in Chapter 15.

Cab radios

14.32 In opening for BR on 21 February 1989, Mr Roger Henderson Q.C, stated that:

> "... Continuous radio communication from train to shore, as it is called, is recognised by BR to be beneficial. It is the Board's policy to extend that facility consistent with other demands for safety enhancing features .... If the Court asks the question, should cab radios be in place on all trains, then there would need to be evidence which we would suggest would go beyond the Secretary of State's remit relating to this accident. If limited to Southern Region and then to passenger trains, then the question leads to a comparative analysis of investment priorities."

14.33 In the early stage of the hearings it was clear that BR's approach to cab radios and signal-post telephones was to look at them as alternatives and compare and contrast their relative merits and demerits. Much emphasis was properly placed by Mr Alan Gore, Counsel for ASLEF, on the essential importance of the provision of cab radios to the driver and to safety. By 13 April, BR's Director of Operations was recommending the extension of the national radio plan and its implementation over a shorter time period. Completion was due in 1992. The Investment Committee approved the extra £5.5m necessary in June of this year.

Safeguards for the future

14.34 A number of safeguards exist within BR to ensure that safety investment is not overlooked or overruled. One such important safeguard is the position of Director Safety, created in the wake of the King's Cross fire. Mr Holmes had been appointed to that post in November 1988. He quoted a number of examples where his intervention had ensured that a specific safety proposal was adopted by a business sector. One example was that the Railway Inspectorate had recommended that hammers should be installed in certain specific rolling stock, but this had not been accepted by the relevant business sector director, whose decision was duly overruled. While an encouraging indication, it was hardly the most wide-ranging or major application of the safeguard. It may be that Mr Holmes picked on this relatively minor example to illustrate further his point that the margin of safety had not yet been breached, but that the situation could arise if nothing further were done.

14.35 The Joint Managing Director (Railways), Mr David Rayner, was also content that the organisational framework was strong enough to resolve any potential difficulties. He quoted the Business Resources Group as having a responsibility for choosing a sponsor and said that if a business director absolutely refused to put a safety project into a financial programme he would overrule him.

14.36 Further, in a written Parliamentary answer in March of this year, given by the Minister of State for Public Transport, Mr Michael Portillo, it was stated that all investment proposals submitted to the Department of Transport should in future contain a specific section on safety implications.

14.37 These are important safeguards but more could and should be done to ensure that safety is not compromised by permitting commercial considerations to delay investment in safety-related projects.

14.38 Mr Rayner was asked about a recommendation in the MMC Report into Network SouthEast which had suggested that BR develop a system of ranking investment projects according to priorities. Mr Rayner explained that since that recommendation BRB had attempted to rank projects: there was "quite strict sector ranking" within each sector. However, it had proved very much more difficult to establish priorities for Corporate ranking across the sectors. There is still a clear need for BRB to review the system of allocating priority to investment proposals to discover whether safety projects receive a high enough ranking.

14.39 After Mr Portillo's Parliamentary answer in March, any proposal which goes forward to the Department of Transport will contain a specific section dealing with the safety implications: safety benefits will, however, still prove difficult to quantify. It is interesting to note that BR in appraising ATP considered the annual saving against the cost of installation over 10 years. It did not compare annual savings against the total period of time that the ATP system would be in operation, on the basis of the concept of "whole life costing".

14.40 In an attempt to justify a scheme on the basis of the accidents it would save, BR had no firm basis on which to assess either the costs to itself or the cost to society of a fatal rail accident. It looked only at the DTp's figure for a road fatality which is hardly a direct comparison since the factors involved in the calculation must be quite different. Having arrived at a figure for total investment BR did not pursue the concept of "whole-life costing": that involves assessing the benefits over the total period of time the scheme would be in operation and not simply looking at initial capital investment costs. It is clear that if sensible decisions are to be made by BR and by Government on the most effective use of funds for saving the lives and reducing the injuries of staff and passengers, then it must establish a way of assessing in financial terms the effect on safety of investment schemes. Both the Government and BR need to conduct a thorough review of its investment appraisal procedures so that a financial value can be put on safety.

The funding of safety through the workforce

14.41 The acquisition and retention of a high quality workforce which is imbued with a respect for proper working practices, trained to carry them out on all occasions, and motivated by a desire to do the best job possible to attain the objective of "zero accidents" has clear funding implications. Basic wage rates, overtime payments, and training costs are obvious examples.

14.42 BR has recognised the importance of its staff in achieving quality workmanship in its "Quality Through People" initiative. Chapter 8 considered the working arrangements that existed within the S&T Department and their effect on the safe running of the railway. Chapter 12 made the case for the introduction of "scheduled hours" to ensure proper planning and organisation of weekend working. Scheduled hours could also contribute to reducing the problems of recruitment and retention of staff in the S&T Department.

14.43 There were two areas of difficulty in recruiting and retaining staff:

(i) the differentials in basic pay between BR and other employers, such as British Telecom; and

(ii) the unsociable hours factor derived from the large amounts of overtime which needed to be worked to bring basic pay up to the market level being offered in other industries without overtime.

14.44 The Court's task is not to direct any party on the conduct of pay negotiations. I have pointed to scheduled hours as a formula to ensure that important safety work can be carried out at weekends with a full and properly structured complement of staff. It is a formula which would give all staff an additional scheduled hours payment and so improve rates of pay for all workers in the S&T Department while ensuring that the previously unhealthy reliance on overtime to supplement (and in some cases double) income would not continue.

14.45 Equally it is not the task of the Court to determine what that level of pay should be. That is properly a matter for management and unions to consider. However, I would point out that for BR to attempt to match the basic rates of pay of companies in the private sector such as British Telecom would only start an unnecessary spiral of wage increases for both sectors since British Telecom would be in a position immediately to offer staff a more attractive remuneration package than BR. With the greater financial freedom of the private sector, British Telecom's levels would be unlikely to be matched. Retention of staff, however, is more complex than mere comparisons of basic rates: recruiting, training and conditions of service all come into the equation.

14.46 The commitment to the railways among many of the older BR staff was clear. We heard from one technician who had joined another industry, but had returned to BR. His son had made the same move but had not returned. BR cannot afford to rely on the old commitment to the railways to resolve recruitment and retention problems. Both unions and management will need to adopt a flexible attitude to ensure that pay and conditions within BR are such that the railway can be run safely, maintained safely and renewed safely, by sufficient numbers of qualified staff.

The funding of training

14.47 The Court was told by Counsel for BR in his opening submissions of a figure of £5.5m for the annual expenditure incurred on training in the S&T Department and it was submitted that that figure expressed as a percentage of the Supervising and Wages Staff pay bills was 7.4%. It was suggested that this was a remarkably high percentage when compared with other industries. No comparable figures were put in evidence before the Court and no valid conclusions can therefore be drawn as to the statistical position. It would, in any event be inevitable as a result of BRB policy on recruitment and promotion that large sums would be spent on training. The Court was told that BR, in agreement with the NUR, does not recruit Assistant Technicians, Technicians, Leading Technicians, Senior Technicians and Technician Officers, but relies on an internal promotion system for such staff. The same policy holds true also for promotion to fill supervisory, clerical and managerial vacancies, which are advertised internally.

14.48 Since British Telecom, Mercury and other competitors of BR do recruit externally and in particular from BR staff, it follows that there must be a continual demand for training of those who fill the gap created by such recruitment either by joining BR or rising within its ranks to a higher grade.

14.49 It is a matter of some concern to the Court that the problems BR face in recruiting a workforce of sufficient numbers and of sufficient quality do not appear to be being surmounted. BR's policy of not recruiting higher levels of staff, whether of conciliation grades (the workforce) or of management (other than graduate engineers) does not fall within the terms of reference of this Investigation. The size and quality of the available workforce within the S&T Department, however, clearly does, and the Court was concerned at the effect the former could have on the latter. It is a matter which is too complex to be dismissed in a single sentence, and it is one to which BR is no doubt giving consideration.

14.50 It therefore follows that the bald figure of £5.5m as annual sum spent on training, neither establishes the adequacy nor the inadequacy of the funds devoted to training.

14.51 The Court is unable to say whether or not the financial resources provided for training within the S&T Department of BR Southern Region are or are not sufficient. What it does say and indeed has already said in Chapter 10, is that the attention given to training within the S&T Department was inadequate and wholly ineffective in relation to staff levels:

- up to and including senior technicians, such as Mr Hemingway

- in relation to the supervisory levels such as Mr Bumstead

- in relation to testers, such as Mr Callander and

- in relation to management at junior and middle levels.

14.52 It is essential that resources, both human and financial, are provided at an appropriate level to ensure that in an industry which properly has as its objective "absolute safety", the vital first step along that route provided by thorough and effective training should not be missed. The evidence the Court heard demonstrated beyond contradiction that the provision of proper training within the S&T Department was woefully inadequate. It may well be that this is an example where "sufficient funds were available to British Rail" in the words of BRB's letter of 3 February 1989 to the Investigation quoted at paragraph 14.13. Whether or not they were available, however, manifestly they were not used in an effective manner or to an effective extent.

14.53 The funding of safety in relation to training in an industry where the requirements of safety are paramount must be part of the review BRB must make of training on the railways and that funding must be demand-led.

Chapter 15: The Future of Safety

15.1   The link between the funding of safety and the future of safety is an obvious one. The provision of radically new safety equipment costs money and the use of that money has to be justified in accordance with the procedures that we have looked at in the previous chapter. In this way the future of safety at any one point of time already depends upon decisions that have been taken in the past. It is therefore not as illogical as it might seem to begin a chapter entitled "The Future of Safety" with some words from the past.

15.2   In his annual report on railway safety for the year 1985, the then Chief Inspecting Officer of Railways, Major C.F. Rose, wrote in his foreword and summary:

> "It could be argued that the number of serious accidents today is so low that investment in radically new safety equipment is unjustified. But if accidents such as the collision at Wembley, or the high-speed derailment at Morpeth, are to be avoided in future some form of automatic train protection will have to come. Continental railways, not only those looking towards higher speeds, are installing or planning such systems and I cannot believe that BR will allow itself to fall behind. The question is going to be what system, and at what cost?
>
> Pending any decision on automatic train protection, a welcome move has been BR's decision to speed up and extend the provision of radio throughout the network, both train-borne and ground equipment. This should bring significant benefits for safety, not least the provision of an instant link between train drivers and signalmen or controllers when emergencies arise."

Those words were written on the 8 August 1986.

15.3   A year before in his report on railway safety for the year 1984, he had written that:

> "... The human factors behind some of the more serious train accidents suggest that improvements should be sought in the training and supervision of train drivers and in the equipment provided to assist them in their duties."

In the previous year he had concluded his report for 1983 by saying:

> "For the rest, the task in the coming years would be to maintain present levels of safety, and if possible to improve them, but to find ways to achieve this at less cost – in the interests of the Railways' customers, the taxpayer, and the Railways' own future."

15.4   By drawing attention to these words from successive annual reports on railway safety, in particular in relation to such radically new safety equipment as

Automatic Train Protection (ATP) and train-borne radio (hereafter called cab radio), I have sought to show that a movement into the future of safety inevitably takes time for consideration, evaluation and financial approval for the particular project. But time as a resource is not infinite and what there is of it should be spent wisely. The 1986 report referred both to ATP and to cab radios. Neither device was fitted to the trains involved in the Clapham Junction accident. We shall see later in this Chapter whether either of these devices could by themselves have prevented that accident from happening. However, in any event both are devices vital to the future of safety on BR, whose introduction must not be the subject of any unnecessary delays. It is because of the Court's concern at the potential for delay that I begin this chapter with this emphasis.

15.5 This chapter therefore considers the additional benefits of ATP, cab radios, tachographs, improved rolling stock, and the role of the Railway Inspectorate in monitoring their introduction. It will be necessary to consider whether any of these additional safety benefits, had they been in place on 12 December 1988, would have prevented the accident.

The need for automatic train protection

15.6 At present the only aid which a driver is given to help him with the visual instructions passed to him by the signals is the BR standard Automatic Warning System (AWS). This provides an audible warning of the aspect of the signal ahead, the sound depending on whether that signal is at green or not. If the signal is not at green, a visual reminder in the cab changes from an all-black disc to a "sunflower" (black and yellow) when the driver cancels the automatic brake application which would otherwise occur. (The sunflower appearance of the AWS indicator in the cab can be seen at Figure 4). Such a system was fitted to the trains and the signals involved at Clapham Junction. Because the information given to the warning system is derived from the signalling system, the AWS itself was affected by the same faults in the controls for signal WF138.

15.7 Ordinary AWS does not distinguish between double yellow, yellow, or red aspects. The Court was told of an earlier experimental development, the Signal Repeating AWS (SRAWS), where instead of just the two alternative visual indications in the cab (black or black and yellow), the full range of aspects is displayed. This system, whilst providing marginally more information about the signal which had just been passed, gives no additional information about the state of the line ahead. It too would have had no effect upon the course of events on 12 December 1988. Both systems are, as their names imply, warning systems which the train driver can ignore (either wittingly or perhaps unwittingly) by cancelling the warning of a caution or stop aspect without taking the necessary action to control the train.

Automatic Train Protection 15.8 Automatic Train Protection (ATP) is a term used to cover a wide range of systems in use on the Continent which are provided to stop a driver passing a signal at danger and in most recent applications exceeding a safe speed for the line and if he does so the train is automatically brought to a stop.

15.9 The main pieces of information needed for a speed monitoring system of ATP are, the train length, speed, weight and braking characteristics, characteristics of the route such as gradients, maximum permitted track speed and track occupancy ahead.

15.10 During the Investigation the Electrical Sub-Committee met to examine BR's proposals for the introduction of ATP to determine whether such a system would, or could in the future, have prevented the accident at Clapham. BR has considered two possible kinds of ATP system;

(i) a continuous system, where the required information is conveyed to the train by superimposing coded messages onto the track circuit carried either in the rails or in wire loops near the running rails; and

(ii) an intermittent system where information comes from individual beacons mounted at intervals along the track.

In both systems the messages are detected by equipment mounted on the trains.

15.11 The principal advantage of the continuous system is that data is constantly fed to the train and so drivers can respond instantly should conditions ahead change. Its disadvantages are that it is costly and is not easily grafted onto the existing signalling system which would need to be retained for parts of the railway system, including trains, which were not fitted with ATP. Intermittent systems are easier to adapt to the existing signalling system and are less expensive but are less responsive to changes in the state of the line ahead.

15.12 Whichever system is chosen a decision can be taken either to implement it over all railway lines or selectively. French experience suggests that the selective use of an ATP system on 30% of route miles can cover 80% of traffic because of its use on high density routes. BR has chosen a selective, intermittent system to provide protection for some 80% of passenger miles. The cost of such a system would be around £140m as compared to £380m for a comprehensive continuous system.

BR's proposal

15.13 The exact type of intermittent system to be introduced has not yet been decided. BR has approved expenditure on two pilot schemes to cover two different technical systems. One is to run on the high-speed Great Western Main line and the other on the Chiltern line.

15.14 On the latter line the advent of resignalling and of new trains has presented an ideal opportunity for such trials. Concern has been expressed that the Chiltern line was not truly representative of the modern high-density urban railway and the Court acknowledged that a trial on such a railway could have disadvantages. However, there were other particular advantages in choosing the Chiltern line on this occasion.

15.15 All the current types of ATP systems are run using existing signalling equipment. If there is a fault in the signalling system that will be replicated in the ATP system. It therefore follows that only an ATP system run totally independently of the signalling system could have prevented the accident. However, the Court is satisfied that at this stage that type of system is not a feasible option. BR could not have been expected to have such a system in place. The Court believes that the important issue is to perfect the existing signalling system, rather than run ATP from a parallel system which itself could be subject to errors.

15.16 The Court is also content with BR's decision to implement a selective intermittent system. It understands the reasons behind that choice. However, I am concerned at the timescale for introduction of ATP. It may be that in 1991, rather than make a decision then on which system should be implemented, further developmental work will be planned. If, as is fervently to be hoped, there has been no further serious accident which ATP could have prevented before then, the urgency may be lost. At a minimum BR must stick to its present timetable. In addition the Railway Inspectorate must review its progress and ensure commitment is not allowed to wane.

15.17 The basis for that concern that the timetable might slip is the example of the AWS. The system was first introduced 30 years ago, but has not yet been installed throughout the network. Within a few days of the dreadful accident at Harrow in 1952 when over 112 lives were lost, BR announced the widespread introduction of AWS. Thirty years is a long time. It is easily understandable how this happens. A gradual programme of installation can take a large number of years, particularly when it is to be introduced in rolling stock which has a life span of over twenty-five years. If a decision were taken to implement ATP only in new rolling stock the timescale could be equally long.

15.18 However, putting that aside, the Court believes that if accorded high enough priority the ATP system could be introduced within five years from the 1991 date of selection of the specific system. The Court agrees with BR that the developmental process cannot be reduced much further. It is important that full trials take place. There seems to be no technical reason why ATP, once a system is chosen in 1991, should not be fully implemented by 1996/1997.

15.19 Before coming to these conclusions the Court considered whether a better level of protection could be afforded whilst the ATP system was being developed by resurrecting the SRAWS in a more modern form. They accepted that there was no justification for going up what would effectively be the blind alley of redeveloping SRAWS because:

(i) considerable resources, which would be the same as those used for ATP, would be needed so to do; and

(ii) the development time-frame would be only marginally less for SRAWS than for ATP.

Cab radios

15.20 BR has moved forward in its policy on cab radios during the course of this Investigation. As Chapter 14 shows BR was initially resistant to the idea of speeding up its gradual introduction of cab radios. It felt it was not the purpose of this Investigation to recommend cab radios for all trains. If, at that stage, it had been recommended that they should be introduced on Southern Region passenger trains, then it would have been a question of cab radios taking their place in a list of other safety enhancing projects, competing with them for funds. I was concerned at this suggestion, not borne out fortunately by the rest of the evidence, that BR's individual safety projects compete against each other for funds.

15.21 I am glad to say that BR has since, in evidence to the Investigation, given a commitment to extend its plan for the introduction of cab radios and to quicken the timescale to ensure that all units are fitted by 1992.

15.22 Cab radios, or driver-to-shore radios as they are often called, can be implemented either as a secure radio between driver and signalman only, or as part of a railway radio network which would have an override emergency link to the signalman. BR prefers the driver to signalman secure version and the Court endorses this approach.

15.23 The question has to be asked: Why have radios not been introduced in all cabs before now? Plans were originally introduced in the 1970s and some channels were authorised, two for a pilot scheme on King's Cross suburban lines and a further two in 1978 for the Bedford/St.Pancras lines. The impetus for the introduction of cab radios has been driver only operated trains. The Railway Inspectorate has supported BRB's decision to equip all passenger Driver Only Operator (DOO) traction units with a cab radio.

15.24 BR has had difficulties, first with the Home Office and subsequently with the Department of Trade & Industry in securing a sufficient allocation of frequency channels for cab radios. Until recently the safety arguments had not been strongly pressed. Cab radios are an important safety feature which could help prevent accidents and could save lives in an accident by promptly alerting the signalman and electrical control who could then prevent other trains from travelling towards the accident site. The DTI must ensure that sufficient frequencies are given to BR to ensure that this important safety function can be implemented with the greatest speed.

Could cab radios have prevented the accident?

15.25 This hypothetical question can only be answered on two hypotheses, the first obvious one being that cab radios were installed on the relevant trains, and the second less obvious one that the Rule Book had certain consequential amendments made to it. When Driver McClymont saw signal WF138 turn to red when he was only one and a half coach lengths away, he would still have brought his train to a stop. But in doing so, he could simultaneously have contacted the signalman on his cab radio. The signalman could have told him the line ahead was clear and could have allowed him to continue. Mr McClymont could then have proceeded, without stopping, past signal WF47, provided it was showing a proceed signal. With the fault in the system the same situation could have occurred for Driver Rolls. He would have seen signal WF138 turn to red in front of him. He too could have radioed and been allowed to proceed. This should have alerted the signalman to the problem at WF138, but I bear in mind the evidence of Mr Warburton quoted at paragraph 2.39 that "the danger was unlikely to be realised immediately . . .".

15.26 From these hypothetical situations it can only be further speculation to suggest that Signalman Cotter might, as a next step, have been able to radio Driver Pike to alert him to a possible problem at signal WF138 and to tell him to proceed with caution. Constant contact between signalman and successive trains might have prevented an accident happening until the precise nature of the fault and its seriousness was discovered, but it would have depended on many other factors. It would have needed swift reactions on the part of the drivers and the signalman. It would have needed quick appreciation of the likely fault on the part of that signalman. It would have needed that signalman not to have been busy talking to another train. Finally, it would have needed a willingness on the part of the signalman to stop the traffic on a busy Monday morning while the fault was found.

15.27 The results of the consideration of all these hypotheses is that it is impossible to exclude the chance that the accident could have been prevented. It is impossible to say whether such a chance is likely or unlikely. In a situation where there exists, therefore, a possibility that the Clapham Junction accident might have been prevented, it is clear that in the interests of safety all traction units should be installed with radios as soon as possible and that the DTI accord high priority in providing frequencies to ensure that safety is enhanced.

15.28 In addition, as recommended by ASLEF, all radio communications should be recorded both to ensure that the system is not abused and to provide an accurate record of communication in case of any incident.

On-Train data recorders (tachographs)

15.29 On-train data recorders, also known as tachographs or "black boxes" can record a variety of information which will ensure that in the event of an incident the facts can be clearly and indisputably established. These bring clear benefits for accident investigation.

15.30 BR's current policy is to introduce on-train data recorders into all new units and progressively to introduce them on traction units expected to have a long life. BR is also currently considering whether to introduce a more basic form of recorder on units of medium to short life.

15.31 The full data recorder records information over eight hours or one thousand miles, whichever is the greater. The approximate cost of such equipment is £10,000 per cab. The more basic "incident recorder" only has a capacity for recording ten inputs of information for a period of approximately ten miles before it is over-written. This option clearly has limitations when compared to the full tachograph recording unit, although its costs are considerably less at £2,000 per cab. Both ASLEF and BR are agreed that tachographs should be introduced in all cabs, although ASLEF would want them introduced more quickly than BR is currently proposing. The Court endorses ASLEF's proposal that BR should accelerate the introduction of on-train data recorders.

15.32 BR will also have to consider the use to which the information recorded by the tachograph could be put. It clearly has the important role already mentioned of assisting accident investigation, and it provides an additional discipline for drivers. The presence of the tachograph will, to their knowledge, provide an independent record of, for instance, the aspect shown by a particular signal, or the speed of the trains. However, BR will be reviewing its management of safety and particularly safety audits and, as part of that review, it would be worthwhile considering the use of on-train data recorded information as part of the safety audit process.

Rolling stock

15.33 All thirty-two coaches of the three trains involved in the Clapham Junction accident were of the traditional slam-door Mark I stock. Their structural performance in the conditions involved in the Clapham Junction accident is analysed in the technical report at Appendix G. In that report references are also made to valuable information gleaned from the Purley and Bellgrove accidents which also involved Mark I stock. No attempt will be made in this chapter to summarise the detailed engineering analysis of the way in which the stock behaved. It is clear, however, that there are lessons to be learned in relation to the rolling stock from these accidents and indeed the last part of that Appendix is devoted to the lessons to be learned.

15.34 Those lessons must be learned in the light of the fatalities and injuries which those accidents produced. In the Clapham Junction accident no-one who had been travelling in the first third of the leading carriage survived: compression of the passenger space was the cause of most of the fatal injuries. In the remaining two-thirds of the coach there were fatalities along the near-side, mostly but not exclusively among those who were sitting next to the carriage wall which was stripped off. The same area in the second carriage, the buffet car, was the scene of similar devastation. Further back in the buffet car the loose seating coupled with the hard edges of tables caused fatalities and serious injuries. Other injuries were caused by direct contact with internal fittings such as luggage racks or with the luggage expelled from them. There is a clear need to minimise the risk of deaths and injuries in railway accidents by the improvement of collision resistance in rolling stock and more particularly in passenger stock on intensely worked routes as is put forward in the Appendix. Such improvements include greater resistance to diagonal loading, additional structural strengthening at unit ends, and the strengthening of the components which unite the bogie and the coach. Improved internal fittings would be an additional benefit in saving lives and reducing injuries in the event of an accident.

15.35 In the light of the accident BR has set in motion a programme of further research into the Mark I coach which is expected to cost £1.0m and to be completed by April 1991. The research will cover six principal areas: couplers, override protection, combined coupler/override protection, structural developments, bogies, and enhanced passenger safety. Each area has its own timetable and their completion dates range from September 1989 to April 1991. That programme will introduce for the first time dynamic testing as an addition to the traditional approach of static testing. It may be that the use of structural models will be found to be feasible in providing data to permit the comparative study of structural details involved at an early stage of collision.

15.36 Such research is vital and is to be welcomed. It is the more important in view of the fact that Mark I coaching stock continues to form a large part of BR's fleet of rolling stock and will continue to do so for many years to come. In view of the length of time during which that stock will continue to provide for passenger services on BR the future of safety and public confidence demand that such research is fully and expeditiously carried out.

Overcrowding

15.37 The question was raised during the course of the Investigation as to whether overcrowding was a significant factor in increasing the tragic effects of the accident. Criteria in relation to overcrowding are used by BR and have been agreed with the Secretary of State and the Transport Users' Consultative Committees. For the type of stock involved in the accident there should be no standing for journeys over 20 minutes (except by choice) and the load factor should not exceed 110%.

15.38 The two passenger trains involved in the collision were often described as "busy". However, despite the strenuous efforts of the British Transport Police to establish the numbers on board, the results were bound to be approximate. I can, therefore, make no finding as to whether or not the passenger trains were overloaded that morning which is based on any firm evidence. Such evidence as there was came from the guards and passengers on the Basingstoke and Poole trains. On that evidence it would seem that the Basingstoke train probably would have been overcrowded, but that the Poole train probably was not.

15.39 It was of greater importance to establish how standing and seated passengers were affected by the collision. Wing Commander Hill, an eminent pathologist, and an expert in fatal accident investigations prepared a report for the Investigation. His unchallenged evidence was that the severity of injury, or the risk of fatality, was no greater for standing than seated passengers.

15.40 Had the trains been overloaded, those passengers having to stand as a result would not have been placed at any greater risk than those seated. However, the fact is inescapable that the higher the number of passengers on a train, the higher the number of casualties is likely to be in absolute terms. I will therefore recommend that BR continue to monitor overall levels of passengers carried to ensure that the present criteria are met and that the Department of Transport and BR continue to keep these criteria under review.

The role of the Railway Inspectorate

15.41 There is a further matter which clearly needs attention, and that relates to a vital ingredient in the safe running of a railway, namely the rolling stock. It is a surprising omission from the scheme of the Acts that, apart from one specific exception, railway rolling stock is not subject to the scrutiny or the approval of the Secretary of State after inspection by the Railway Inspectorate. It is a clear lacuna in section 41 of the Road and Rail Traffic Act, 1933. Since it is in my view essential that there be legislation to strengthen and clarify the position of the RI, such legislation should also widen the ambit of the Secretary of State's powers to include the approval of railway rolling stock.

15.42 I have mentioned earlier that the powers available under the railway legislation to the RI for enforcing the submission of new works for approval are almost non-existent. This arises out of the very limited number of instances covered expressly by section 41 of the 1933 Act, contravention of which, in any event, carries a penalty of only £20 per day. By virtue of the Agency Agreement with the Health and Safety Commission, RI has powers under the Health and Safety at Work etc. Act 1974. Successful prosecutions have been undertaken in relation to accidents to staff and notices have been issued in relation to required improvements or to prohibitions, again almost exclusively in the realm of staff safety.

15.43 However, the application of section 3 of the Act, as a means of requiring a railway to instal specific items affecting passenger safety, has not been tested and it may be doubtful whether a test case would succeed. I consider therefore that the Regulation of Railway Acts need strengthening in this respect and the opportunity should be taken, when dealing with the lacunae in section 41 of the 1933 Act tó cover this aspect as well.

15.44 It will fall to the Railway Inspectorate to monitor BR's commitment to introducing the important safety enhancement features discussed in this chapter. I recommend that BR report to the Railway Inspectorate every six months on its progress in implementing ATP, cab radios, tachographs and its rolling stock research programme. Under existing legislation the Secretary of State through the Railway Inspectorate has no power to require that he approve the types of rolling stock before their introduction by BR. This is clearly a point which will need amending legislation and the Court is of the view that the Secretary of State's powers of approval should be extended to include rolling stock.

PART FIVE: THE CONCLUSIONS

Chapter 16: Where Responsibility Lies

16.1   An inquiry under the Regulation of Railways Act 1871 is not a trial: it is not a test of legal liability, whether civil or criminal. Its procedures are not accusatorial: no one is put in the dock, or made the object of a civil suit for damages. Its procedures are instead inquisitorial, it is an investigation with the object of discovering the truth.

16.2   It is important to make this restatement at this stage, since the reader will already be aware that this is to be the last section of the Report and it is to contain conclusions. It is therefore inevitable that this chapter will deal with specific names of persons and what I find to be their responsibilities for the events which culminated in the accident at Clapham Junction on 12 December 1988.

16.3   It would be an abdication of duty if at the end of a long and detailed Investigation I did not indicate what my findings were in relation to specific matters of criticism. It follows that this chapter is bound to contain both observations of a general nature and criticisms of individuals and that such criticisms will vary in their degree of gravity. In fairness to those who are to be criticised, two important factors must be stressed at the outset:

(i) Almost without exception, those who gave their evidence to the Investigation did so with conscientiousness, care, dignity and with a measure of frankness which was wholly to be admired. Those qualities are all the more commendable in that they co-existed with a realisation that the evidence they were giving had the potential to expose them to that very criticism.

(ii) There is almost no human action or decision that cannot be made to look more flawed and less sensible in the misleading light of hindsight. It is essential that the critic should keep himself constantly aware of that fact.

16.4   As a final introduction to the task of reviewing the responsibility of those involved in the causes and the circumstances surrounding the accident I should indicate that I propose to follow the pattern already adopted in this Report and to move from the ground upwards, starting with the wiring errors in Clapham Junction "A" relay room. As a result of this approach there will inevitably follow a list of names with critical comment on the individuals concerned. I wish to state quite categorically that this is not in any way intended to be a charge sheet, or a particularisation of pleadings in a civil suit. It is solely and exclusively the result of an investigation under section 7 of the Regulation of Railways Act 1871.

Mr Hemingway

16.5   The direct cause of the Clapham Junction accident was undoubtedly the wiring errors which were made by Mr Hemingway in his work in the Clapham Junction "A" relay room. Those errors were made on Sunday, 27 November 1988 when he was working on the circuit between track repeater relay DM and fuse 107 on row 12. Those errors lay dormant and might still have lain dormant but for the fact that, two weeks later on Sunday, 11 December 1988, totally unrelated work of changing a different relay top had to be done in that relay room. By mischance the particular relay top was next to TRR DM, whose wiring was disturbed by the physical effort involved in moving out the adjoining relay top. By coincidence it was Mr Hemingway who was responsible for carrying out that task. There was no error of practice in the carrying out of that task that December Sunday afternoon and no one could have realised the tragic consequences which were to follow next morning.

16.6   The errors Mr Hemingway committed while working in that relay room on 27 November, could be divided into those that were characteristic of him and those that were uncharacteristic of him. He was a man who was methodical in his practices, whether good or bad, and among the bad were his habits of failing to shorten wires and in particular to cut off eyes and failing to secure such wires by tying them back out of harm's way. (He also re-used insulating tape, but this practice was not involved in the accident). The uncharacteristic errors were:

(i)   at the fuse end, to place a new wire on top of the old wire so that there was a double connection when there should have been a single; and

(ii)   at the relay end, to fail to insulate the old wire at all.

16.7   It is to be stressed that, in the welter of criticism which is justifiably laid at Mr Hemingway's door, he has never for one moment sought to evade his responsibility for the appalling consequences of his errors. From first to last he has sought to accept the burden of the consequences of his mistakes and has not sought to blame other people or other factors. Not one word of excuse came from Mr Hemingway, rather was there complete acceptance of responsibility.

16.8   For Mr Hemingway's characteristic errors, since they were so and were his normal working practice, the blame must clearly be a shared one. For those bad practices Mr Henderson for British Rail was entirely correct to say that:

> "The blame for that does not lie with you, it lies with British Rail. Either it should never have been allowed in the first place, or once it had happened and the practice had become your practice and was indeed commonplace, it should have been stopped because the matter should have been monitored."

It is a collective liability which lies on British Rail.

16.9   So far as individuals are concerned, therefore, the blame also lies with those who should have been doing the monitoring. Mr Bumstead's name clearly heads that list, but his is only one name upon it. Mr Bumstead was principally responsible for the supervision Mr Hemingway received over a twelve-year period before the accident, but the blame for the development and maintenance of Mr Hemingway's bad practices lies also on the shoulders of all others who had supervised him in the years leading up to the accident.

16.10   So far as his uncharacteristic errors are concerned, in failing to see that the old wire was detached from the fuse end and was insulated at the relay end, Mr Hemingway again is not alone in his responsibility for those actions. They are so uncharacteristic, so much a contradiction of his methodical working life that there has to be a further cause.

16.11   I find that cause to be the constant repetition of weekend work in addition to work throughout the week which had blunted his working edge, his freshness and his concentration. Because he enjoyed being involved in the end product of the work he had been doing during the week and also in order to achieve the lifestyle which he required he, like many others, accepted every opportunity he was given to do overtime with the result that in the three months before the accident he had had one sole day off in the entire 13 weeks. I find this to be totally unacceptable and to be conducive to the staleness and lack of concentration which has been manifested in the evidence. It was a practice which had in fact been going on for years in British Rail and was one which was well known to management. It should not have been countenanced and it was a contributory cause to the accident. It was a direct result of the demands made by the WARS tight timescale.

16.12 It meant that, whereas in different circumstances Mr Hemingway would have taken in his stride an interruption such as I find broke his concentration that day and gone straight back to the task in hand, on this occasion his staleness and the dulling of the edge of his thought processes misled him into thinking he had finished the particular job before he was interrupted.

16.13 I specifically do not find that Mr Hemingway or any of the workforce were physically tired by the actual work involved, either during the week or at the weekend. Though such suggestions were put before the Investigation, no such evidence was ever produced and the evidence I heard contradicted the suggestions. It was not a question of exhaustion which was the culprit, but rather the mental and emotional blunting and flattening which was produced by protracted periods of working every day of the week without the refreshment of time off with family and friends. I do not believe (and Mr Hemingway expressly rejected the idea) that he was suffering from the effects of tiredness that day.

Mr Bumstead

16.14 Mr Bumstead's responsibility for failing adequately or at all to monitor Mr Hemingway's working practices, so as to detect and correct the manifestly bad ones amongst them, has already been sufficiently identified. In addition, for the weekend in question, he failed to conduct any satisfactory planning for the work involved and failed to ensure that the work was ready for testing thereafter. He knew what workforce he had available and his choice of method of employing that workforce inevitably meant that he was removing from himself the ability properly to supervise the whole of the work to be done on that Sunday, 27 November. Although he worked hard with his gang out on the tracks he was not working in the role which it was his duty to discharge that day, namely that of supervisor. The result was that he was never in Clapham "A" relay room that day and to his knowledge Mr Hemingway's work was bound to go unsupervised.

16.15 Further, he failed to make any plan with Mr Dray, the Testing & Commissioning Engineer, as to which of them would carry out which responsibilities in relation to the preparation for the actual testing of the work done. Between them, Mr Bumstead's and Mr Dray's lack of forethought, coordination and planning meant that they effectively ensured that there would be no independent wire count of Mr Hemingway's work. Neither Mr Bumstead, nor Mr Dray turned their minds to what each of them should have been doing, separately and together, that day.

16.16 In addition the work on that Sunday involved a combining of two jobs, numbers 104 and 201, both outside on the tracks and in the relay room. While Mr Bumstead adequately directed his mind to the effects of that combination of jobs on the outside work, he did not trouble to see if there were any problems or any potential confusion in relation to the work in the relay room: he just left it to Mr Hemingway as was his style. Proper supervision would have involved enquiring whether the combination of the two jobs had produced any problems and checking whether it had. That quality of supervision was never the level of performance that Mr Bumstead attained.

Mr Dray

16.17 Mr Dray manifested all the problems that are produced by the BR system of reorganisation. It requires staff to re-apply for posts in circumstances where if their application is not successful they become what is described in Railway jargon as "unallocated". He was less than happy with his job and with its distance from his home and his performance in the days preceding and including Sunday, 27 November exemplifies this. He had taken no trouble to try to master SL-53. He made no proper preparation for the work of testing, instituted no plan and had no discussion with Mr Bumstead on their respective roles in testing. Although he was present in the box from soon after 9 o'clock on the morning of that Sunday, he used his time ineffectively. He had the facilities, the time and the available assistance for the carrying out of an independent wire count of Mr Hemingway's work which was required by SL-53 and was, in any event, good practice: despite that he did not carry out the wire count which could have prevented the Clapham Junction accident or see that it was carried out. The way in which he performed his duties as Testing & Commissioning Engineer on the day in question meant that the testing process, far from being "the last defence" was no defence at all.

Mr Lippett

16.18 Mr Lippett was Mr Bumstead's immediate superior and had been since reorganisation in May 1988. He was another of the casualties of reorganisation in that, although he was within the last eighteen months of his service after 42 faithful and hard-working years, he had spent almost all of his working life on the maintenance side rather than New Works. Thus he was pitched in the twilight of his career into work that was foreign to him. Not only that but it was work being conducted on the WARS project by a workforce which was strange to him and at a stage in that project which was the most intensive yet. Since, as he was perfectly entitled to, he chose not to work at weekends, he never saw the work being done immediately before commissioning or the testing of that work. He did, however, see the quality of work being done during the week. He actually saw and identified bad practices in Clapham Junction "A" relay room on a visit in June 1988, when he saw wires hanging down that, although they were insulated, were not cut back and were not tied. He chose not to raise the subject with the supervisors or with the workforce. Although he thought that what he saw "failed to conform to good practice" he did not take any steps to correct their bad practices because he "believed it was their way of doing things". He, as did so many other people in the S&T Department, left others to get on with their own tasks when he should have been carrying out the duties of management. Effectively, he turned his back on the bad working practices he saw and made no attempt to stamp them out.

Mr Callander

16.19 It has to be stressed that there is much to be admired in Mr Callander's attitude to his work up to the time of reorganisation in May 1988. He had about him a quality of enthusiasm and eagerness which meant that, when nobody seemed to be getting on with a particular job, he would willingly take it on and tackle it himself. It was in this way that, when nobody seemed to be getting on with the planning of the stageworks involved in WARS, he took up the task of planning it himself. He was, in fact, at much too junior a level to have the responsibility for such a task, which, whilst it was certainly not thrust upon him, slipped down the levels of authority until it came to rest on his desk.

16.20 When it did, he set to with a will working out suitable packages of weekend work to be done for the whole of the WARS timetable to the end of Stage 9 expected in August 1989, using as his base line the working force existing in 1986. It is not his fault that nobody more senior in BR than he, either through 1986, 1987 or particularly before reorganisation in 1988 and at the start of Stage 7B shortly after that, ever reviewed, or adequately monitored, the plan which he had set out in early 1987 in handwriting on a few sheets of paper. He was a willing horse. He did his very best to devise a first draft of a future programme which should not have been left to him in the first place.

16.21 It is incidentally a matter of interest as to whether the plan would ever have been left in that informal handwritten state if it had been thought necessary for the scheme as a whole to be referred to the RI for approval. The Court considers that the level of management at which the plan would have been constructed and approved would have been significantly higher if such a requirement for the scheme itself had been involved.

16.22 It was the same good qualities of Mr Callander that took him into the world of testing. Nobody else seemed to be taking up the problems when he was at South Lambeth and so he took them on himself. He built up a reputation on the region of being a competent and knowledgable tester. The problem was that the reputation was not the complete picture: yet again the appearance was not the reality.

16.23 As a tester, Mr Callander was neither working to good practice nor to SL-53. When SL-53 arrived on his desk he never even read it. He had no concept of the importance of an independent wire count. When, on reorganisation in May 1988, he moved to the Wimbledon depot as Testing & Commissioning Engineer, he took with him his own bad practices and working attitudes and in particular his failure to observe SL-53.

16.24 He too was disenchanted with reorganisation and the post that it had given him and was anxious to get away as soon as he could: this he achieved shortly before the accident. Before he left he gave no thought to the way in which Mr Dray had been carrying out his duties as his assistant, or was about to carry them out as his stand-in successor. There was very little communication between them, and the subject of SL-53 was never even mentioned. This was another example of the failures of communication and management which were widespread in the S&T Department.

16.25 Although he was fully aware that SL-53 was not being implemented and worked to in BR Southern Region he nonetheless devised and drafted a Certificate of Test which purported to show that it was. I am satisfied that this was not done with any intention to deceive but was merely an expedient which he lit upon in order to fill a vacuum. It was probably thought of by him as a first gentle step, gingerly taken, towards the implementation of SL-53. The fact remains that he knew that SL-53 was not being implemented, but drafted a Certificate of Test which to anyone who read it would have suggested quite the contrary. Any direct communication on the subject between him and his superiors, any proper monitoring of his work would have disclosed the reality behind the appearance: that however did not happen.

16.26 The problem, yet again, was that Mr Callander was left to his own devices by higher management and his devices were neither adequate nor safe.

Mr Bailey

16.27 Mr Bailey came to Southern Region to head the Regional Testing Team in August 1986. He came from a testing position on the Western Region, but his actual experience in testing was much more limited than might have appeared. The concept of the Regional Testing Team had been devised by Mr Hale in the wake of the Oxted and East Croydon incidents in November 1985. Mr Bailey's appointment was intended to be part of a three-pronged attack devised by Mr Hale on the problems he had directly identified of post-commissioning wrong-side failures. That attack involved:

(i) the urgent drafting and distribution of a new and complete Departmental Instruction on testing;

(ii) the setting up of the Regional Testing Team; and

(iii) the training of members of staff in order to form a specialised cadre of testers.

16.28 Within a few days of his arrival on the Region, Mr Bailey was briefed by Mr Hale on what was expected of him in his new post. He was clearly told that the primary function of his position was to raise the standard of testing throughout the Region, to carry out testing training for that purpose, and particularly to attempt to avoid some of the failures that had occurred at or just after commissioning. In that task he utterly and completely failed. In his time in post of just under two years no cadre of testers was set up and in fact not a single tester was trained. Not only were no training courses ever run, but the nearest approach to the discharge of this function was a single hand-written sheet for a possible syllabus for a course. Although he knew of the importance attached to SL-53 and had some input into its drafting, when it emerged as a document in mid-1987 he neither implemented it himself, nor saw that it was implemented throughout the Region. He said in evidence that if he was to implement it he should have had an instruction to that effect from Mr Davies, the Signal Works Engineer. That was, to say the least, a surprising explanation for his failure to obey a Departmental Instruction.

16.29 He considered that SL-53 was not to be implemented until the Forest Hill relay room work had to be done. In fact the Forest Hill work had not been done by the time of the accident, or indeed by the time the Investigation's hearings ended. It has still not been done. Effectively, although his was the responsibility for spreading the gospel of good practice in testing enshrined in SL-53, his attitude and actions ensured that quite the contrary result was achieved.

16.30 He did not even have a clear idea himself of what good testing practices involved. He had no concept of the vital importance to proper testing of an independent wire count. It was a "blind spot" to which he admitted in his evidence to the Investigation.

16.31 Although I accept that he worked energetically and well in carrying out all the testing that he did on the region, and that his testing team was under-resourced so that the demands on his time were great, the fact remains that he effectively turned his back on the very responsibilities for which he had been appointed. Sadly, not only did that happen but it was allowed by his superiors to happen because of a total failure to monitor his performance.

16.32 When he moved to Wimbledon on reorganisation he, of course, took with him the same attitudes. Again in his favour he was energetic in getting out to the depots. He perfectly correctly spent a large part of his time attending to his duties at Eastleigh and he was always ready to do weekend work: he was, as we know, present in the Clapham Junction "A" signal box on Sunday 27 November. It has also to be said on his behalf that this was his first job in management. He was given the appointment on 14 April 1988, but in the time before he took up his new post he had no interview with anyone senior to himself, no lead into the new organisation and no training for management. But even allowing for all that, there are still serious criticisms to be made of Mr Bailey's performance in his new post.

16.33 First, in the six or so months leading up to the accident he was the manager of the workforce which, because of the pressure of WARS, was working the excessive overtime which we have seen. It was his job, with the help of Mr Lippett his junior manager, and Mr Deane his superior to manage that workforce effectively and this both he and they failed to do.

16.34 No real determined attempt was made by anyone to relieve the pressure on that workforce by insisting on the stopping of some of the weekend work, the curtailing of that overtime, and the slowing down of WARS. The effect of the evidence of Mr Rayner, the Joint Managing Director (Railways) was that if such a request had been made it would have been granted. He was asked:

> "Q: One question which might be asked is the extent to which financial constraints have affected your ability to provide pay, which is sufficient to attract sufficient people into the railway. That is one question which undoubtedly has been asked and will be asked, I suspect by the public, whether we ask it of you today or not.
>
> A: I think it is still a long jump from there to say that the individuals that we still do employ working in the area of safety work unsafely. I don't believe it.
>
> Q: But if there aren't enough of them to do the job ---?
>
> A: Then we curtail the work. We slow it down."

16.35 While that was the attitude of someone as senior as Mr Rayner in management, it was certainly not the attitude of those at the other end of the scale in seniority. Mr Bumstead was asked what he thought would have happened on Sunday 27 November, if an additional seven men had not been available to be drafted in from Eastleigh:

> "Q: Can you say what would have happened if there had not been seven further staff available?
>
> A: Well, I can assure you the job wouldn't have got cancelled, we should have had to cope with the staff that we had available that day."

16.36 That attitude was clearly the one which was the widely held view which prevailed at all levels in the S&T Department. Nobody wanted to be the one who took the step of actually cancelling weekend work: the philosophy of "the show must go on" meant that there was a reluctance to be the one who stopped it. Mr Rayner genuinely believed that, if there were not enough people to do the job, BR curtailed the work or slowed it down. The evidence points the other way. In those circumstances it is a cause for grave concern that nobody in the S&T Department had the will to make the request in sufficiently strident terms that it was acted on and granted. Mr Bailey was at the first level of management which could have expressed that concern. The fault again was not that of Mr Bailey alone, it is one which also lay with his superiors in management.

16.37 The last area of criticism relates to Mr Bailey's reaction to the Queenstown Road incident. He investigated the matter and put his report to Mr Deane. He therefore discovered that the tester involved had prepared no plan for testing, had not functionally tested the work and had left part of the testing to another supervisor. He actually identified in respect of the Design Office a need for a tightening of managerial control and yet took no action whatsoever to have managerial control tightened in relation to testing staff. He failed to take the elementary step of investigating why Mr Callander had selected this particular tester to do the work and what was the state of testing in the area. Effectively he wrote the incident off as an isolated incident and did not concern himself with what it showed about the management of testing after re-organisation. He was no longer Regional Testing Engineer and he left the matter at that. A further blind spot in relation to testing had developed in Mr Bailey. It is fair to point out, however, that Mr Bailey's report went to Mr Deane to whom both Mr Bailey and Mr Callander reported, and as we shall see, Mr Deane showed the same lack of reaction.

Mr Deane

16.38 Although Mr Callander had drafted his programme for the WARS stagework commissioning proposals in late 1986, it was not until a meeting on 11 February 1987 that they received formal approval. That approval came in a meeting which was chaired by Mr Deane, while SCE at South Lambeth. The minutes of that meeting contained the passage:

"Commission work on Stage 7 commences 2/3 July 88 and from then on to the commissioning of Stage 8B in August 89 there are no "spare" weekends."

That passage comes in a section of the minutes entitled "Problem Areas". The last paragraph of that section reads:

"The times indicated on the proposed programme are the times required to complete the work. Reduction in that time will not be acceptable either to the S&T or Traffic as overruns may occur."

Mr Deane was identifying the problem that the proposed timescale was the minimum acceptable, both to his department and to Traffic.

16.39 Mr Deane was clearly totally aware of the tightness of the timescale for the carrying out of the WARS project and the particular constraints in relation to Stage 7B and was obviously concerned that further time pressure might be applied: there simply were "no spare weekends". That was knowledge he had as Signal Construction Engineer at South Lambeth and knowledge which he took with him on moving to a similar post at Wimbledon in the reorganisation of May 1988.

16.40 He was in that position directly responsible for the labour force which, in accordance with Mr Callander's programme was to work through from July 1988 to August 1989 week in week out without a spare weekend for a break.

16.41 He knew the amount of overtime which would be necessitated by the programme and should have closely monitored the way in which that overtime was being worked so that he was in a position to make professional management decisions on whether the programme and the overtime could be allowed to continue unchanged. Had he carried out that monitoring, he should as a logical consequence have sought an extension of the programme.

16.42 He also knew from Mr Callander that, although testing was being done on these weekends, it was being done without the preparation of any plans beforehand. Mr Callander had told him that no plans were necessary and he accepted that. This is somewhat surprising in itself in that he had the responsibility for overseeing the report into the Queenstown Road incident and he read Mr Bailey's report before sending it on with his comments to Mr Penny. Mr Bailey had said that he was most concerned to note that the tester "appears to have come on to the job without any preparation" and further "had not carried out any "functional" testing". This was the clearest possible indication of the need for proper planning of testing work and the need for the proper selection of testers who had sufficient expertise to do the testing. Instead of taking appropriate managerial action to remedy the situation Mr Deane accepted the explanation that it was just the "sloppy methods" on the part of the tester and left the matter there.

16.43 There was a further reason why he should have looked at the question of testing in his area once he assumed his new job on reorganisation. No job specifications had been issued at that time and therefore very sensibly Mr Deane arranged a meeting with four members of his staff, Mr Bailey, Mr Hunter, Mr Callander and Mr Dine in an attempt to sort out their respective roles. That meeting produced a rough piece of paper divided into four quarters. Mr Callander's duties were set out as Testing & Commissioning on that piece of paper which was described at the bottom as "Checklist of "Who is doing what"". Against the words "Testing & Commissioning" Mr Deane had added in his own writing:

"Testing – programmes
– resources
– C.O.T's
– Testing Copies"

154

16.44 The fact that Mr Deane wrote these words demonstrates that he was aware of the need for them to be attended to in the testing on his area. Despite that fact, he told the Court frankly in his evidence that he did not believe he discussed those matters with Mr Callander before he left. Although he knew from two different sources namely, from Mr Callander himself and from the Queenstown Road incident, that there was no planning of testing being conducted in his area, he did nothing about it. In this he failed in his management duties. He should have been particularly aware of the importance of planning in testing, since he had received a copy of Mr Davies's report into the Oxted Signalling Failures in February 1986, when he was Senior Construction Engineer at Ashford, and had discussed the report in detail at a Construction Group Meeting a month later. That report had said that the lessons to be learned from Oxted were fundamental and that they would be noted by all staff. Queenstown Road should have reminded Mr Deane that the lessons of Oxted had not been learned. Once again in the S&T Department a problem existed and was known about, but a back was turned to it: it was never faced.

Mr Penny

16.45 Mr Deane's immediate superior was the Area S&T Engineer (SW), Mr Penny. Mr Penny did not have an easy task when he came to that post on reorganisation. His main experience was in telecommunications. He had come straight from a period of six years on the maintenance side into an area which was just about to start its most intensive period of work on WARS Stage 7. Almost as soon as he was in post there came the investigation of the Queenstown Road incident. His part in this matter was to recommend to Mr Porter that disciplinary action be pursued against the two key people responsible. It may be that it was his recognition that he had only limited testing experience himself that caused him not to take wider action. What would have been more appropriate would have been to have taken up with Mr Deane and with Mr Callander what light the incident threw on the overall state of testing in his area. Had he done so, it is at least possible that the question of SL-53 and its lack of implementation by Mr Callander might have emerged. Since, however, there is no reference to SL-53 in the reports on the Queenstown Road incident of Mr Bailey, Mr Deane or indeed Mr Penny, no firm assessment can be made.

16.46 Mr Penny's position was that his responsibilities in his new post were great and the staff resources available to assist him were very small. In June 1988 at an early walk-through along the track from Vauxhall to Clapham Junction to familiarise himself with the WARS scheme he had been assured that the schedule was tight but that as long as no more senior technicians were lost it could be implemented on time. He had accepted what he was told and to his credit followed the proper management practice of thereafter monitoring the ranks of senior technician to see that no more were lost. The Court saw the document he used for that purpose.

16.47 In his evidence he accepted that he did not make enquiries to ensure SL-53 was being carried out. He accepted also that he knew there was a considerable amount of seven-day working in general terms in the S&T Department, but he was not aware that individual people were working seven days for weeks and weeks at a time. I have already indicated that others should have been making him aware of the situation by seeking an extension. He said that by late November 1988 he had become aware that he was getting out of touch with what was going on on the track in that he had only been out on the track three or four times since August.

16.48 Mr Penny frankly accepted a degree of personal responsibility of the events that led to the disaster. In that, it may be that he himself was applying a degree of hindsight to his own activities and was in a sense doing himself an injustice. There are criticisms to be made of his management of his area and these have been summarised. In the final analysis, however, the Court considers that such responsibility as Mr Penny has for the accident is the least of any of those employed within the S&T Department who were given leave to be represented before the Investigation.

Mr Davies

16.49 In the five years before reorganisation from May 1983 onwards, Mr Davies had had a single job, although its title changed from Construction Engineer to Signal Works Engineer. He it was to whom Mr Hale gave the task of implementing a new Testing Instruction which was to be first SL-Provisional and later SL-53. Despite a long passage of time he failed completely to get on with the Testing Instruction. SL-Provisional only emerged (and even then in an incomplete form) in October 1985, the month before the Oxted incidents. Even with the warnings that those incidents should then have given, the pace did not quicken towards the introduction of SL-53 which only arrived in May 1987.

16.50 By that time Mr Bailey had had nine months in his post as Regional Testing Engineer. Mr Bailey had provided Mr Davies with written comments and checklist to assist in the drafting of the new testing instruction. In those comments and checklist, by reason of his "blind spot" about the need for an independent wire count, Mr Bailey left the wire count out completely. Mr Davies merely put it back in again without for a moment considering with Mr Bailey the important question of why it had been omitted. Had there been any proper communication by Mr Davies with Mr Bailey on this vital topic the "blind spot" might have been revealed.

16.51 Mr Davies must bear the brunt also of a further serious management failure in relation to the monitoring of Mr Bailey's performance as Regional Testing Engineer from August 1986 to May 1988. It was to Mr Davies that Mr Bailey reported, and it was Mr Davies who left Mr Bailey totally to his own devices and did not at any stage detect and correct the deficiencies in Mr Bailey's performance which should have been apparent.

16.52 Hardly had SL-53 emerged in May 1987 than questions began to be asked in the S&T Department as to how, if at all, it could be implemented. The Construction Group meeting of 21 August 1987 discussed it in detail, concluded that SL-53 had a lack of flexibility about it, resolved that full implementation should be delayed until the Forest Hill relay room work was completed and finally made detailed proposals for a redrafting of paragraphs 1.1 to 1.4. The purpose of the redrafting was in order to cover the delegation of tasks which they thought inevitable for the proper working of SL-53.

16.53 On 8 September 1987, Mr Davies sent a detailed memorandum to Mr D Graham Brown, the Signal Engineer (Works) his immediate superior. That memorandum set out for the consideration of Departmental Conference the detailed proposals for the redraft of Section 1 of SL-53 which the Construction Group was requesting. Thereafter Mr Davies and Mr Brown had a conversation: their individual recollections of that conversation differ sharply on an important matter. Mr Davies believed Mr Brown had said he would raise the matter at Departmental Conference, whereas Mr Brown said that he had told Mr Davies that the delegation was implicit in the Instruction and there was no need for any further clarification. The two accounts cannot live together.

16.54 Although Mr Brown said in evidence to the Investigation that he had in fact raised the matter at Departmental Conference, no reference to such an important matter appears in the minutes. Mr Brown sought to explain this point by suggesting that the matter had been raised by him right at the end of a Departmental Conference and therefore not minuted. The Court is satisfied that Mr Brown did not in fact ever raise the matter at Departmental Conference whether early or late. I will refer to this matter later in this chapter.

16.55 So far as Mr Davies is concerned, he had asked of his superior detailed questions in a perfectly proper written minute which needed a written answer: that written answer was never forthcoming. Successive minutes of Mr Davies's Construction Group recorded the fact that an answer was still awaited to the questions on delegation in relation to SL-53, but apart from making that record in the minutes, Mr Davies did nothing else to solve the problem.

16.56 This was not only an example of the failure of communication within the S&T Department, it was also an example of Mr Davies turning his back upon the vital problem of the proper implementation of SL-53. This failure was a vital factor in the causation of the accident in that, had the testing on 27 November 1988 been conducted in accordance with SL-53 and an independent wire count been properly conducted, then the accident would not have happened.

16.57 Mr Davies was the Signal Works Engineer who chaired the meeting on WARS Commissioning Strategy on 13 February 1985, which made the decision differentiating between the method of work to be followed in relation to track circuits and the signals themselves. Track circuit changeovers were to be commissioned by stageworks at weekends, but signal changeovers were said to be "the least problematic area" because there was no need to commission them in advance and that stage could be reserved until the main commissioning. By the time the work necessary for Stage 7B of WARS was due to commence in July 1988, Mr Davies was in the post of Signal Engineer Projects. At no stage between the 1985 meeting and July 1988 did he become aware of the change of policy in relation to the commissioning of signals.

Mr D Graham Brown

16.58 Mr Brown was Mr Davies's superior as Signal Engineer (Works). He was the other party to Mr Davies in the conversation they had about the memorandum of 8 September 1987. He was also the other party with Mr Davies to the failure of communication which followed thereafter. I am satisfied that he did tell Mr Davies that he would raise the matter at Departmental Conference. I have indicated that I am equally satisfied that he did not do so. However, these findings merely serve to aggravate a situation which would already have been bad enough without them.

16.59 Even were the situation as Mr Brown now remembers it, it would follow that, despite full knowledge on Mr Brown's part that the Construction Group felt that SL-53 lacked flexibility and required detailed amendments to allow for the delegation of tasks which were essential to make it work, Mr Brown had brushed the matter aside. In a short word-of-mouth comment to Mr Davies he had dismissed the matter by saying that delegation was implicit in the Instruction anyway. That would mean that, in the full knowledge that there was concern and uncertainty about SL-53 in the Construction Group who wanted a redrafting of the Instruction, Mr Brown did nothing at all to clear away that concern and uncertainty, or to check that it had been cleared away. Such conduct, in any event, would be the clearest breach of his duties as a manager. It is an example of management by inactivity and inertia which we have seen earlier.

16.60 In the event I accept Mr Hale's evidence as to the way in which Mr Brown mentioned the matter to him and conclude that there was no raising of the matter at Departmental Conference. A matter as important as this should, in any event, have led to the subject being tabled as an agenda item for Departmental Conference at which the minute itself should have been considered and a decision arrived at as to how it should be dealt with. That decision should thereafter have been communicated to the Construction Group through Mr Davies. None of that happened and the responsibility for that fact lies squarely with Mr Brown.

16.61 Not only would it have been good practice to have followed that course, it was in fact the laid down procedure within the S&T Department. At the Departmental Conference on 2 August 1984 it was:

"Agreed that once an instruction has been agreed and issued any complaints must be channelled via the appropriate Senior Manager for discussion at Conference."

16.62 Mr Brown was not in post at that time but the Court found it surprising and disturbing that someone in as senior position as he was could handle a matter so vital to safety in such a cavalier way.

16.63 Finally, Mr D Graham Brown had overall responsibility for the performance of the Design Office. There were Design Office deficiencies involved in the failures of testing at Oxted and at Queenstown Road. The Design Office was clearly working under extreme pressure with a reduced level of staffing following the 1984 and 1986 reorganisations. Though Mr Brown came to his post after the Oxted signalling failures, it should have been clear to him by the time of the Queenstown Road incident that the Design Office needed tighter managerial control and greater resources.

Mr Hale

16.64 Mr Hale gave his evidence in a careful, clear and considered way and dealt with matters with total frankness. That he is a man devoted to the service of the railway and serving his employers loyally and with the fixed intention of doing his utmost to see that the railway philosophy of absolute safety is maintained cannot be doubted. The problem, in relation to Mr Hale's case, is that loyalty, application and good intentions were not enough.

16.65 Mr Hale's skills lay in identifying problems and these skills are nowhere better demonstrated than in his initial approach to the problem demonstrated by the Oxted incidents. He was as completely correct in identifying the problem as he was in arriving at correct initial solutions. Mr Hale identified the urgent need for a completely new Departmental Instruction on testing, the need for the creation of a new cadre of testers and the need for the appointment of a new Regional Testing Engineer to raise the overall standard of testing on the region and to train that cadre.

16.66 The difficulty was that having identified the problem and arrived at solutions, he then turned his attention to other things and made the dangerous assumption that the solution would work and the problem would go away. In fact it did not. No cadre of testers ever came into being up to the time of the accident three years later. No training course was ever run. Mr Bailey did not raise the overall standard of testing throughout the region. The urgently-needed full new testing instruction did not even appear for a year-and-a-half and was then virtually ignored by those doing the WARS testing.

16.67 Save for the last factor, these were all matters that were known to Mr Hale. The one which must have been most obvious of all was the complete lack of training that was going on in the region. In 1985 Mr Hale had requested 64 places on testing courses at BR's Railway Engineering School, Derby for the following year. His request had been refused on the basis that the BR school did not have the resources and that the Region would have to do its own training. Since Mr Hale had identified the extent of the Region's requirement for testing training for the year 1986 as being 64 course places, he must have been aware that such a need could not be met within the region without further resources. He was fully aware of the limits imposed upon his own resources and had indeed had to seek the assistance of the General Manager, Mr Pettitt, in obtaining two assistants for Mr Bailey in the form of Mr Blain and Mr Bassett.

16.68 Effectively Mr Hale had identified an urgent need for the training of testers, but had failed so to organise his management of the S&T Department to ensure that that need would be met. His failure was the failure to see to it that what he had put in place as the answer to the problem was in fact working to that end: it was a failure to monitor the effect of his actions. It is a failure he frankly accepted in his evidence. Had Mr Hale seen that the good intentions properly expressed immediately after the Oxted incidents had been put into practice, proper testing on 27 November 1988 should have revealed the wiring errors.

16.69 The Queenstown Road incident in June 1988 should have alerted Mr Hale to the fact that the errors of Oxted were still being perpetrated thirty months on. The Queenstown Road incident called for far stronger, more decisive and more widespread action than the mere disciplinary proceedings which ensued. It produced a reaction which was totally insufficient in relation to the dangers it demonstrated. It should have demonstrated to Mr Hale the need to look more carefully at the whole question of testing and of the monitoring of wrong-side failures. Although Mr Hale was looking each month at the figures produced by FRAME, such data was not specific enough to give him a correct and complete picture. Though the figures might show that the total number of WSFs on BR Southern Region were going down, they masked the seriousness of the WSFs they included, and had no national comparison which would have revealed a significant weakness on the Southern Region.

16.70 As to the 1988 reorganisation, it was not the type of reorganisation Mr Hale wanted. He had worked out his own "matrix" method which did not find favour with the Board and he was told of its rejection on 22 December 1987. It is to Mr Hale's credit that he nonetheless buckled down and put all his enthusiasm and undoubted skills into seeking to make a success of the form of reorganis-ation which had been preferred. He attempted to get further resources to assist in reorganisation and obtained some but not enough. That was not his fault. Before the 1988 reorganisation he was already a veteran of three previous such moves since he was in post for those of 1982, 1984 and 1986. He would have been fully aware therefore of all the problems they create, and, had he been able to do so, I find he would have done his utmost to alleviate them.

16.71 The problem about Mr Hale's management was that it demonstrated the lack of communication which pervaded the S&T Department. A good illust-ration exists in the way in which Mr Brown merely mentioned in passing to Mr Hale the vital problem of the workforce's attitude to, and difficulties with, SL-53 on the question of delegation. Mr Hale described the incident in these words:

> *"I do recall that an informal discussion took place in my office with Graham Brown at which he said that Bob Davies had raised with him the question of delegation within section 1. Graham Brown said that he believed it was implicit in the instruction, that the instruction covered the situation adequately and there was no need to change it. I did not immediately look at my copy of the instruction. On his assurance that it was properly covered by the instruction, I agreed certainly that delegation was inevitable and was a part of what was intended. He assured me that he would advise Bob Davies accordingly and I agreed at that point in time that that was the correct action to take."*

16.72 Good management involves creating an atmosphere in which things happen. Nothing was to happen to resolve the problem of the failure to implement SL-53. The reason lay fairly and squarely in a lack of management.

16.73 Mr Hale was the Regional S&T Engineer until the day before the Clapham Junction accident. As such he was the "Captain of the ship" and accepted in his evidence that the position carried with it responsibilities. He is the most senior of the BR employees who have been criticised in earlier parts of this chapter. However the fact that the criticisms there so far stopped at the top of the S&T Department should not for a moment be taken to mean that there were no other failings.

Other factors: The failings of the system

16.74 There were other factors causative of the Clapham Junction accident which are not so much faults which can be attributed to any individual as faults of the system and the way in which it is run. They are faults which have a historic character about them in that they go back a long time in the running of the railway. They are faults which do not stem, from any of the employees in the Southern Region S&T Department. They are faults that are inherent in the way the railway has been run for a number of years. They are many and they must be pointed out.

 16.75 At the centre of the problems which caused the Clapham Junction accident were the bad wiring practices followed by the workforce in the S&T Department and allowed to continue unchecked by its management. BR allowed its operations, its business to be conducted in reliance on a workforce recruited, trained and promoted in a historical way and controlled by management, which was itself recruited, trained and promoted in the same way. The result was that the workforce was neither adequate in size, nor adequate in skills. The questions asked by Counsel to the inquiry, Mr David Latham Q.C, of Mr Rayner bear repetition at this stage of the Report:

> "*Q: One question which might be asked is the extent to which financial constraints have affected your ability to provide pay, which is sufficient to attract sufficient people into the railway. That is one question which undoubtedly has been asked and will be asked, I suspect by the public, whether we ask it of you today or not.*
>
> *A: I think it is still a long jump from there to say that the individuals that we still do employ working in the area of safety work unsafely. I don't believe it.*
>
> *Q: But if there aren't enough of them to do the job ---?*
>
> *A: Then we curtail the work. We slow it down.*"

16.76 Over the years BR has recruited its workforce and trained it. It has promoted only from within its own numbers. This may in times past have been a proper and sufficient way to run its affairs. Times have changed, however, and there is in the industrial world outside the railway a growing need for staff skilled in the electrical and communications fields. BR has hungrier and fiercer competition for its workforce than it has ever had. It is, however, still relying on its old culture and its old methods to try to maintain its staffing levels. The only route, for instance, to the rank of senior technician is by way of internal promotion starting from the bottom and not from external recruitment. It must break the mould in relation to this recruitment, the training of its staff and their promotion. It is out of date and damaging to BR.

16.77 The situation is not the fault of BR alone. The unions too must bear their share of responsibility for attitudes of entrenched resistance to change which are out of place in a modern world. It was a matter of regret to the Court to see during the evidence how obvious and how deep was the mistrust and suspicion employer had for union and union had for employer. This was particularly evident during the cross-examination, on behalf of BR, of Mr James Knapp, the General Secretary of the NUR. This Report is not the place to debate these matters, nor to seek to determine where and to what extent fault lies for the situation. It would, however, be turning a blind eye to the problem not to state it. The internal promotion system which is an inevitable handicap to BR in satisfactorily filling the higher posts in its wages grade staff in the S&T Department, is the result of a formal agreement between BR and the NUR. It is a fetter upon the acquisition of skilled staff and it is long overdue for reconsideration.

16.78 Likewise the question of what is the proper payment for any level of staff is not one for this Investigation. It is, however, abundantly clear that the present arrangements are failing and have failed to provide BR with the overall size, structure and quality of workforce it needs. The question of payment again involves formal agreement with the unions. The Court recognises the difficulties that exist and that have existed in this area and cannot comment further, other than to express the hope that there may yet be a movement away from entrenched positions on both sides and towards a new beginning in the interests of the railway, the workforce and not least, the public.

16.79 The comments I have made on recruitment and promotion and on payment of wages apply with equal force to the level of overtime working tolerated in BR. It is an outdated and wasteful system which, by reason of the unsociable hours involved inevitably has a resultant adverse affect on recruiting. Constraints on recruiting are constraints on safety and have to be removed.

16.80 All these matters are not the fault or responsibility of any one person. They are historic to the railway culture and method of organisation. Three other matters need to be mentioned as circumstances relevant to the Clapham Junction accident and circumstances which were not the fault of any individual. They are:

(i) deferment of projects involving large capital expenditure;

(ii) the method and frequency of reorganisation within BR; and

(iii) the control of the execution of major projects.

The problems which all three factors have caused stem not from any one person's individual decision but from the way in which the railway has come to do things.

16.81 I have said enough about the deferment of the WARS project for it to be clear that the necessary resignalling of the Waterloo area was deferred until a time far later than it should have been. It look no less than six years from the original project paper in 1978 until 1984 for the project to obtain approval. It hardly needs to be said that this was too long and too long by a large measure.

16.82 There were four reorganisations in the S&T Department in the seven years from 1982 to 1988, and the inevitable upheaval, disruption and harm to morale they caused by reason of the way in which they were carried out must be obvious. There must be a better way of doing things and that better way must be urgently sought and found before the next reorganisation of any kind.

16.83 Finally, there must also be a better way of organising the running of a large project such as WARS than the system which was in fact employed. Reliance on lateral management is bound to produce a lack of teeth in getting to grips with problems and getting them sorted out. Large schemes need firm, positive and sufficiently senior control in order that they are carried through properly, which means safely, efficiently and economically.

16.84 Safety, efficiency and economy are the three duties placed upon BRB by the statute. No distinction is made between them in the statute but efficiency and economy must be employed in order to establish and maintain the concept of safety.

Chapter 17: Where things went wrong – The Lessons to be learned

Appearance and reality

17.1   BRB is responsible for an industry where concern for safety should be at the forefront of the minds of everyone, from the Board itself at the top to the newest beginner at the bottom. The concept of absolute safety must be a gospel spread across the whole workforce and paramount in the minds of management. The vital importance of this concept of absolute safety was acknowledged time and again in the evidence which the Court heard. This was perfectly understandable because it is so self-evident.

17.2   The problem with such expressions of concern for safety was that the remainder of the evidence demonstrated beyond dispute two things:

(i) there was total sincerity on the part of all who spoke of safety in this way but nevertheless

(ii) there was failure to carry those beliefs through from thought into deed.

17.3   The appearance was not the reality. The concern for safety was permitted to co-exist with working practices which we had seen from Chapters 7 and 8 were positively dangerous. This unhappy co-existence was never detected by management and so the bad practices were never eradicated. The best of intentions regarding safe working practices was permitted to go hand in hand with the worst of inaction in ensuring that such practices were put into effect.

17.4   The evidence therefore showed the sincerity of the concern for safety. Sadly, however, it also showed the reality of the failure to carry that concern through into action. It has to be said that a concern for safety which is sincerely held and repeatedly expressed but, nevertheless, is not carried through into action, is as much protection from danger as no concern at all.

17.5   On a superficial level, in the month before the accident, an outsider looking at the documentation which set the standards for the working practices of the S&T Department might well have thought that all was well in the Department so far as safety was concerned. More particularly would this have been the case in the specific examples of the installing and testing of new works which are central to this Investigation. So far as installation work was concerned, there was after all a clear direction in Departmental Instruction SI-16 dated 18 November 1983 at paragraph 3.3.3 that:

> "Wires and crimps not terminated must have their ends insulated and secured to prevent contact with each other, or with any other equipment."

Further so far as testing was concerned there was a Departmental Instruction as recent as 3 April 1987, SL-53, which required at paragraph 4.4 the person in charge of external testing to:

> "Carry out a wire count on all free wired safety relays and terminations and record on the contact/terminal analysis sheets."

It was a detailed instruction and at paragraph 1.2 it required the person in charge of internal testing:

> "To carry out all internal testing requirements and coordinate with person I/C external testing ..."

17.6   That outsider might have been forgiven for thinking that, with those two Departmental Instructions in place, a safe working system had been evolved for the installation and testing of new signalling works. He would have been wrong if he had come to that conclusion. As to installers, he would have been wrong because he would not have known that some installers were not in fact following those safe practices, but were following dangerous working practices of their own.

17.7   The outsider would not have known that, as to SI-16, for instance, Mr Hemingway had never received it and Mr Bumstead thought it only referred to new works. He would also not have known that, though the testing instruction SL-53 was intended by management to be in force, many of those in vital testing positions did not believe it to be in force, were not following its instructions and did not for a moment appreciate the vital importance of an independent wire count.

17.8   Even the system for distributing Departmental Instructions had the same characteristics. An outsider might have looked at Departmental Instruction AG-1 entitled: "DEPARTMENTAL INSTRUCTIONS - POLICY" dated 29 November 1983 and concluded that there was a safe and workable system for their issue which was in fact working satisfactorily. The truth was the opposite. As an example, Mr Hemingway said of the system:

> *"I remember when these type of documentations came out first. We were explained how the lettering worked but I never did grasp it, for some reason. I just couldn't get hold of how the lettering and coding worked."*

17.9   The appearance to that outsider would not have been the reality. What might have looked on the surface to be perfectly safe was, in fact, quite the opposite. While the outsider could be forgiven for his mistaken belief, it is the task of management to be aware of the working practices to which its workforce works and to ensure that those standards are of the highest. It is the task of management to ensure that its instructions to its workforce on how work is to be done are clear and that they are in fact being obeyed. It is the duty of management to see that its workforce is properly trained and that such training is renewed from time to time. It is the duty of management to ensure that the efforts of the workforce are properly monitored and supervised so that the quality of the work may be maintained at the proper levels.

17.10 There were failures in the discharge of each of these responsibilities of management. These failures meant that the appearance to an outsider which would have been presented by the working practices set out in SI-16 and SL-53 was one thing. The reality of the work which was actually being carried out in the installing, testing and commissioning of new signalling for WARS Stage 7B was another. Whilst it may have looked on the surface as though things were going well, things were in fact far from well. They had been going wrong for some time and that fact was about to receive the worst sort of confirmation in the Clapham Junction accident.

17.11 We have already seen the parts played in the causes of the accident by the particular bad practices of individuals, such, for example as Mr Hemingway in installing, Mr Bumstead in supervising and Mr Dray in testing. But it was not merely the errors and omissions of those who were engaged in the work on the day in question which caused the accident. The errors go much wider and higher in the organisation than merely to remain at the hands of those who were working that day.

17.12 In the rest of this Chapter I shall look at the lessons that are to be learned from a terrible tragedy. It is convenient, as a first step to identifying those lessons, to look first at and to list the principal areas where things went wrong. The very size of the list and the importance of its individual components is its own indictment of the systems that were in operation before the Clapham Junction accident.

17.13 The relevant errors include the facts that:

(i) working practices were permitted to slip to unacceptable and dangerous standards;

(ii) the quality of supervision was permitted to slip to an equivalent degree, so that those unacceptable and dangerous working practices were allowed to continue;

(iii) the quality of testing did not meet standards set by BR and testers were allowed to believe that their role was limited to functional testing only;

(iv) there was no proper system of training of installation and testing staff, nor was there any proper system of refresher training;

(v) there was no proper system of allocating meaningful job descriptions to particular staff, so that they were clear as to their duties and as to what was expected of them;

(vi) there was no effective system of communicating to the workforce the proper standards required of installation and testing work;

(vii) there was no vetting of the weekend workforce in order to prevent individuals working excessive overtime;

(viii) there was no review of the WARS timetable to ensure that the constant pressure of weekend work was not blunting the edge of the skills of the workforce;

(ix) there was no effective planning of the weekend work to ensure sufficient numbers of appropriately qualified staff were available to match that particular weekend's workload;

(x) in fact, there was no effective project control of WARS at all, so that no overall view of the WARS workload and timetable was taken;

(xi) there was no effective control over the Design Office to ensure that the workforce were supplied with drawings which accurately reflected the work to be done;

(xii) there was no proper realisation of the potential danger of unprotected wrong-side failures, and as a result there was no effective monitoring of such wrong-side failures;

(xiii) there was total failure to ensure that lessons were learnt from such failures and taught to the relevant staff;

(xiv) the reorganisation of 1988 was under-resourced and therefore badly implemented;

(xv) there was a total failure to consider and deal with the effects that that reorganisation might have on WARS Stage 7B;

(xvi) finally, there was a total failure to communicate effectively both up and down the lines of management.

Lessons to be learned

17.14 It was the task of this Investigation, declared at the outset, to inquire into and to establish two things. First, exactly how the accident happened and, second, exactly what must be done to reduce the risk of a recurrence to the lowest level humanly possible, if not to zero then as near to zero as can be reached.

17.15 In order to achieve the second objective, the prime factor and vital need is for BR to ensure that installation and testing work is carried out to a much higher standard. That higher standard must exist, not only in theory but in practice. It will not be sufficient merely to lay down new or amended written instructions. Improved communication must exist between all levels of the organisation to ensure that instructions reach and are understood by those who have to carry them out. Management must monitor progress to ensure that new safety objectives are met. Supervisors must play an active part in greatly improving standards of workmanship: a small improvement will not be enough. The role of independent auditing both internally and externally must be a major one.

17.16 These lessons cannot be implemented without better technical training for those carrying out the work and proper management training for those responsible for ensuring that it is carried out safely. Better planning of the workload and organisation of the workforce should ensure that a new and better climate is created where work can be carried out without undue and unnecessary pressures.

17.17 This accident need not have happened if previous WSFs had been thoroughly investigated in order to establish the lessons to be learned and if those lessons had been effectively taught to all relevant staff. The lessons from the Oxted incidents in November 1985 and the Queenstown Road incident in June 1988, should have prevented the tragic combination of circumstances which led to the Clapham Junction accident. BR must therefore take every possible lesson from this accident and ensure that appropriate action is taken and regularly monitored and audited.

17.18 BR's commitment to safety is unequivocal. The accident and its causes have shown that bad workmanship, poor supervision and poor management combined to undermine that commitment. The appearance of a proper regard for safety was not the reality. Working practices, supervision of staff, the testing of new works in the S&T Department of Southern Region failed to live up to the concept of safety. They were not safe, they were the opposite.

17.19 Management, staff and unions must all work together for the future to ensure that the appearance becomes the reality, that actual practice lives up to the concept. Only by constant vigilance can they seek to ensure that the needless deaths, injuries and mental suffering caused by this accident will not be repeated.

166

RECOMMENDATIONS

The Investigation into the causes of and circumstances attending this accident has established a large number of lessons that must be learned and actions that need to be taken as a result. These can be subdivided into three categories:

(i) most importantly, to seek to prevent another such accident happening by addressing both the immediate and underlying causes;

(ii) to promote a better safety culture within British Rail; and

(iii) to mitigate the effects of any future accident.

A long list of recommendations is included below which cover all those three categories. Action must be taken on all these recommendations and, where it appeared necessary to include a timescale, I have done so. I am encouraged by the fact that much has already been done towards meeting some of these recommendations: in BR's case this, in part, is as a result of the conclusions of its own internal inquiry. However, I believe it is important to set out in this document a complete list of recommendations consequent upon the accident in order to ensure that the results can be monitored both by the public and by those responsible for the safety of passengers and staff.

Recommendation to address the immediate causes of the accident

The wiring errors   1.   BR shall ensure that there is rigorous implementation of the practice of cutting back redundant wires, insulating, and securing them, so that there is no risk of wires coming into contact with working circuitry. Cutting back must be done before commissioning.

(Paragraph 8.3)

2.   BR at national level shall be responsible for updating and creating new standards of installation.

(Paragraph 11.35)

3.   BR shall enforce tighter control on Design Office procedures for the production, issue and amendment of documents to ensure that all working drawings are complete and are an accurate representation of the system to be worked on and of the work to be done to that system.

(Paragraphs 7.6 – 7.11)

Specific Testing   4.   BR shall urgently ensure that an independent wire count is carried out as a matter of practice during testing. It shall be the responsibility of the person in overall charge of testing to ensure and to document that an independent wire count has been done. This function may be delegated to works staff who did not do the work.

(Paragraphs 8.27 – 8.33 and 9.1)

5.   BR shall ensure that one individual is always identified as the person in overall charge of testing.

(Paragraphs 11.29 – 11.30)

6. BR shall ensure that a testing plan is drawn up for every commissioning.

(Paragraph 11.30)

7. BR shall ensure that sufficient numbers of suitably qualified staff are included in the testing plan.

(Paragraph 11.30)

8. BR shall ensure that full documentation is provided and later monitored in order that proper testing is carried out.

(Paragraph 11.31)

Testing General 9. BR shall introduce a national testing instruction with all speed. Such introduction shall be accompanied by a full explanation to the workforce, including workshops or seminars as necessary. Implementation must be monitored and audited.

(Paragraph 11.35)

10. BR shall ensure through its system of audit that the necessary resources and authority are available to Regional Signal Engineers to implement the national testing instruction.

(Paragraph 11.35)

11. BR shall ensure that the Testing & Commissioning Engineer must be independent of the line of command between Area Signalling Engineer and new works staff, but able to call on new works staff to assist him in his testing duties.

(Paragraph 11.35)

Instructions 12. BR shall ensure that there are effective systems for distributing Departmental Instructions on a personal basis to all relevant employees and that provision is made for the situation where an employee moves to a new post.

(Paragraphs 11.11 – 11.15)

13. BR shall ensure, as a matter of practice, that all staff understand and regularly re-read the Departmental Instructions relevant to their posts. In addition, every two years, those staff involved in an annual appraisal interview, shall sign a statement to the effect that such Instructions have been recently read and understood.

(Paragraphs 11.45 – 11.46)

Training 14. BR shall give technical training as necessary to ensure that efficient and safe practices are carried out by all technical staff.

(Paragraphs 11.36 – 11.39)

15. BR shall provide refresher courses for installers at intervals of not more than five years.

(Paragraphs 8.9 and 11.39)

16. BR shall urgently progress and monitor training and certification of testers. Refresher courses shall be evolved.

(Paragraphs 11.40 – 11.43)

17. BR shall ensure that the structure and content of courses are regularly reviewed.

Recommendations to address the underlying causes within Management

Effective Organisation 18. BR shall ensure that overtime is monitored so that no individual is working excessive levels of overtime.

(Paragraphs 8.54 – 8.56)

19. BR, in conjunction with the Unions, shall introduce the concept of scheduled hours within the Signals and Telecommunications Department in order to make better provision for work which has to be carried out at weekends.

(Paragraphs 12.25 and 12.26)

Recruitment and retention 20. BR shall monitor and forecast wastage and recruitment of skilled S&T staff and take urgent steps to ensure that sufficient numbers of skilled staff are retained and recruited to match work requirements safely.

(Paragraphs 8.48 and 8.49)

21. BR, in reviewing recruitment and retention levels, shall also consider recruiting staff at levels at and above assistant technician.

(Paragraphs 11.44 and 14.48)

Management of staff 22. BR shall provide all grades with job descriptions for their particular post so that staff know what is expected of them

(Paragraph 10.25)

23. The annual appraisal system, albeit in a simplified form, shall be extended to senior technician level.

(Paragraphs 11.45 and 11.46)

24. BR shall ensure that there is an effective system in place on a continuous basis to identify which employees would benefit from additional training.

(Paragraph 11.36 – 11.46)

Safety monitoring 25. BR shall introduce, within S&T Departments, a system of reporting and reviewing all WSFs and shall ensure that they are classified according to potential for danger, and that they are monitored up to and including Board level.

(Paragraphs 13.26 – 13.41)

26. BR shall ensure that any unprotected WSF with potential for danger shall be thoroughly investigated with a view to learning and acting upon wider lessons.

(Paragraphs 13.33 – 13.41)

27. Unprotected WSFs shall be reportable to the Railway Inspectorate as a "dangerous occurrence" and reported on by the Chief Inspecting Officer in his annual report.

(Paragraph 13.54)

28. Government shall seek to give legislative effect to recommendation 27.

Project Management 29. BR shall ensure that new works schemes in future shall have one clearly identified person in overall charge of all aspects of the project who would nominate a Project Manager from within his chain of command. For predominantly signalling schemes that individual would, in the present BR structure, report to the Regional S&T Engineer.

(Paragraphs 12.28 – 12.34)

30. The Project Manager nominated in 29 above shall be responsible for the execution within budget and timescale of the whole project from the original estimate preparation to the project completion. He shall report to the person in overall charge as necessary for approval.

(Paragraphs 12.28 – 12.34)

31. BR shall ensure that where work is required from areas outside the command of the person in overall charge, that work should be carried out on a contractual basis to a specification provided by the Project Manager.

(Paragraphs 12.28 – 12.34)

32. BR shall ensure that the Testing Engineer shall be ultimately responsible to the person in overall charge of the scheme, but not through the Project Manager.

(Paragraphs 12.28 – 12.34)

Quality Management

33. BR shall make available necessary training resources for wider management training down to supervisor level.

(Paragraph 11.44)

34. BR shall require that any future reorganisation shall be properly planned, effectively resourced and implemented to an agreed timetable which takes account of all relevant problems.

(Paragraphs 10.12 – 10.33)

35. BR shall implement improved procedures to replace the cumbersome arrangements on reorganisations which allow staff to be displaced and to remain unallocated.

(Paragraphs 10.24 and 10.25)

Recommendations to improve BR's safety culture

Total Quality Management

36. BR shall continue to press ahead with its Total Quality Management Initiative and the application of British Standard BS5750: Quality systems.

(Paragraphs 13.43 – 13.51)

37. S&T Departments shall implement the Board's existing quality plan with the greatest urgency.

(Paragraphs 13.43 – 13.51)

External Review and Audit

38. The Court endorses the use of outside consultants to review safety management issues within BR and recommends that the consultants proceed with their programme with the greatest urgency looking particularly at problems of communication up and down the organisation.

(Paragraph 13.52)

39. BR shall introduce monitoring and independent auditing systems in all safety-related aspects of work, in particular the S&T Departments, with the greatest urgency, in advance of Total Quality Management as an aid to good management.

(Paragraph 13.53)

40. BR shall give a higher priority to the introduction of on-train data recorders to assist investigation of any future incident.

(Paragraphs 15.29 – 15.32)

41. BR shall consider the use of information from on-train data recorders as part of a systematic safety monitoring procedure.

(Paragraphs 15.29 – 15.32)

42. BR shall report at 6 monthly intervals to the Railway Inspectorate on its follow-up to the Clapham Junction accident and implementation of its own and this Report's recommendations.

Cab Radios   43. BR shall implement as a priority its programme to install a system of radio communication between driver and signalman on all traction units. The introduction of this system shall be in addition to signal-post telephones and not automatically entail their removal.

(Paragraphs 14.32, 14.33, 15.20 – 15.28)

44. BR shall instal voice recorders for the purpose of providing a record of all radio messages relayed.

(Paragraphs 15.28)

45. Government, in discussion with BR, shall allocate a sufficient number of frequencies for this important safety function

(Paragraphs 15.20 – 15.28)

Automatic Train Protection   46. The Court welcomes BR's commitment to introduce Automatic Train Protection on a large percentage of its network, but is concerned at the timetable proposed. After the specific type of ATP system has been selected, ATP shall be fully implemented within 5 years, with a high priority given to densely trafficked lines.

(Paragraphs 14.27 – 14.31, 15.8 – 15.19)

47. BR shall report at 6 monthly intervals to the Railway Inspectorate on its progress in implementing ATP.

(Paragraphs 15.13 – 15.19)

Funding   48. The Department of Transport and BRB shall make a thorough study of appraisal procedure for safety elements of investment proposals so that the cost-effectiveness of safe operation of the railway occupies its proper place in a business-led operation.

(Paragraphs 14.38 – 14.40)

49. BR shall develop an adequate system of allocating priority to projects to ensure that safety standards are not compromised by delay.

(Paragraphs 14.38 – 14.40)

50. BR shall ensure that the organisational framework exists to prevent commercial considerations of a business-led railway from compromising safety.

(Paragraphs 14.34 – 14.41)

Reporting of signal failures   51. BR shall ensure that during driver training the definition of a signalling irregularity and situations which are reportable are given greater emphasis.

(Paragraph 11.47 – 11.56)

52. BR shall ensure that drivers, reporting on signalling irregularities, are given appropriate feedback on the outcome.

(Paragraph 13.25)

Installation Procedures   53. BR shall ensure that the practice of the re-use of insulation tape is eliminated and the method of insulation is secure.

(Paragraph 8.14)

Recommendations to mitigate the effects of any future accident

Structures   54. BR shall carry out its stated programme of research into the structural integrity of its rolling stock within its planned timescale of completion by April 1991.

(Paragraphs 15.33 – 15.36)

55. On completion of the programme BR shall discuss its conclusions with the Railway Inspectorate and obtain their agreement to the structural changes necessary to strengthen all relevant rolling stock with a subsequent life span of eight years and over.

(Paragraphs 15.33 – 15.36)

56. BR shall extend its programme of research to include dynamic testing of full-scale simulations of collision retardations in order to improve the design of internal furniture under conditions of passenger impact.

(Paragraphs 15.33 – 15.36)

57. BR shall, as an alternative to full-scale testing, seek economic and practical methods of dynamic modelling during development stages when researching the structural resistance of coaches to collision conditions.

(Paragraphs 15.33 – 15.36)

58. BR shall continue and expand its involvement in collaborative European railway studies of performance of passenger stock, including collision resistance.

(Paragraphs 15.33)

59. Government shall seek to amend S.41 of the Road and Rail Traffic Act 1933 to clarify what work has to be approved by the Secretary of State after inspection, if necessary, and to include rolling stock within the terms of the statute.

(Paragraph 15.41)

Overcrowding 60. BR shall ensure that overall train loading criteria are achieved. The Department of Transport and BR shall keep the criteria under review.

(Paragraph 15.40)

Recommendations to improve the response of the Emergency Services

Communications 61. The Emergency Services shall improve communication between them to ensure, in particular, that the declaration of a Major Incident by any service is immediately passed by a dedicated phone line to all other services and acted on by them . Systems shall be checked daily and logged.

(Paragraphs 5.72 – 5.75)

62. Emergency services shall carry out exercises simulating a Major Incident on a regular basis to test specifically their communication systems in the light of the shortcomings identified in Chapter 5.

(Paragraphs 5.70 – 5.82)

63. Ambulance services shall review procedures to ensure that the designated and supporting hospitals are given a major incident warning as early as possible.

(Paragraph 5.75)

64. Hospitals shall ensure that emergency alert telephone lines receive incoming calls only and are tested weekly. Switchboard operators shall be fully trained in their use and procedure.

(Paragraph 5.80)

65. The LAS shall implement its proposal to train prospective Medical Incident Officers in the use of radio communications.

(Paragraph 5.87)

66. Hospitals shall provide training in the duties of Medical Incident Officer for staff who could be called upon to act as such in the event of an accident.

(Paragraph 5.87)

67. Emergency services shall provide local radio communication at the accident site to facilitate liaison between the control units and experts on site.

(Paragraph 5.87)

68. The Ambulance Service shall provide aerials at all designated hospitals for radio telephone communication in an emergency. The transmitter/receiver should be provided on declaration of a Major Incident.

(Paragraphs 5.84 – 5.87)

Arrangements on site 69. All emergency services shall ensure that personnel are provided with and wear protective clothing, including protective headgear.

(Paragraph 5.91)

70. All emergency services, hospitals, BR and local authorities shall provide their personnel with coloured high visibility vests with the name of the service printed on it. Each service shall be easily identified by the colour of its emergency clothing.

(Paragraph 5.92)

71. Ambulance services shall require staff properly qualified in intubation and infusion to wear "Millar trained" badges prominently displayed, including on protective clothing.

(Paragraph 5.31)

Casualty bureaux 72. Police forces shall arrange that all casualty bureaux be equipped with a telephone queuing system with a recorded message.

(Paragraphs 5.43 – 5.50)

73. The Association of Chief Police Officers shall continue their efforts to establish an effective system for extending the number of calls which can be dealt with simultaneously by a casualty bureau.

(Paragraph 5.49)

Command and control 74. The emergency services shall recognise the primacy of the Civil Police authority in accidents of this kind where there is no fire. This recognition does not preclude delegation to the LFB of control at trackside.

(Paragraphs 5.94 – 5.96)

75. Police Forces shall study and follow the excellent arrangements made by the Metropolitan Police for the bereaved and relatives of the seriously injured.

(Paragraph 5.47)

76. In the exercise of command and control at accident sites BR and the emergency services shall maintain their policy of joint planning supported by table-top exercises.

(Paragraph 5.93)

77. The ambulance service and designated hospitals shall require that all medical personnel report to the forward control unit of the ambulance service on site.

(Paragraph 5.88)

78. Each service shall additionally maintain on site an up-to-date list of staff within the inner cordon in case evacuation is necessary.

(Paragraph 5.88)

Emergency planning 79. The Department of Health shall review DHSS Circular 71 in consultation with emergency and medical services to reflect all lessons learned but in particular in relation to procedures for declaring a Major Incident. The Department of Health shall specifically require that the terms used to warn hospitals of a possible Major Incident, and subsequently to declare an actual Major Incident are sufficiently distinct to prevent any confusion between the two. The terms used shall exclude any colour.

(Chapter 5 in general, 5.70 – 5.82 in particular)

80. In revising the Circular the Department of Health shall consider the role of BASICS in emergency planning and review BASICS' funding arrangements.

(Paragraphs 5.56 – 5.63)

Recommendations to improve BR's response

Communications

81. BR shall complete its programme of equipping major signal boxes with direct lines to the appropriate electrical control and equipping other signal boxes with priority emergency dialling systems. Those direct lines and emergency dialling systems shall be logged and tested daily. The purpose of this programme shall be to ensure that:

(i) the signalman is able to take full responsibility for ensuring that the area surrounding the accident site is electrically isolated;

(ii) the action is confirmed to the signalman, the emergency services, and to BR officials at site; and

(iii) the boundaries of isolation are similarly confirmed.

(Paragraphs 4.10 – 4.17, 4.26 – 4.27)

82. BR shall review its communication systems with the emergency services to ensure that efficient methods exist to provide and disseminate early information requiring immediate action. In the course of the review BR shall look particularly at communication between signal boxes and the emergency services. Systems shall be tested weekly and logged.

(Paragraphs 4.14 and 4.30, 5.2 – 5.4)

83. BR shall ensure that those likely to use such systems in recommendations 81 and 82 above shall be properly trained in their use. Instructions in the use of these systems must be clearly drafted, prominently displayed and regularly checked for relevance and accuracy.

84. BR shall ensure that efficient arrangements exist to rectify as a matter of high priority any deficiencies in the communication systems involved in recommendations 81 and 82 and in signal-post telephones.

(Paragraphs 3.9 and 4.14)

85. BR shall extend its programme of installing public address systems in all new trains and those with a life of over 5 years to allow the driver and/or guard to speak to passengers.

(Paragraph 4.27)

BR's emergency planning

86. BR shall produce an up-to-date manual on Accident Procedure to replace such incomplete and out-of-date documents as the Southern Region Accident Procedure booklet of November 1984. BR shall ensure that all staff are given appropriate training in such procedures.

(Paragraphs 6.1 – 6.14)

87. BR shall ensure that each area manager, station manager and all senior station staff have an effective emergency plan for their area that is understood by all their staff and is the subject of regular exercises.

(Paragraphs 4.32, 4.33, 6.1 – 6.13)

88. BR shall introduce into all signal boxes the facility to switch all automatic signals to red in an emergency, and BR shall review and update where necessary its procedures to protect rail traffic in the vicinity of immobilised trains.

(Paragraphs 4.2, 4.19 – 4.25)

89. BR shall examine the possibility of introducing short-circuiting bars which achieve a positive clamp on the running rail.

(Paragraph 4.17)

BR's post-accident investigation 90. BR shall set out in its manual on Accident Procedure the procedures that should be followed to ensure the proper recording and preservation of evidence.

(Paragraphs 6.22 – 6.34)

91. BR fault finding teams shall report to the Railway Incident Officer who, in consultation with the Police Incident Officer, shall ensure, in all but the most exceptional circumstances, that the team is accompanied by a police officer and a photographer to provide for the proper recording and retention of evidence.

(Paragraphs 6.22 – 6.34)

Consequent Recommendations

92. The Rule Book and Books of Instruction of a similar status shall be promptly updated and observations made in this Report taken into account.

(Chapter 11)

93. Government shall ensure that the Railway Inspectorate is adequately staffed and resourced to match the increased responsibilities incurred as a result of recommendations made in this Report.

(Chapters 13 and 15)

RECOMMENDATIONS AS TO COSTS

1.   At the preliminary hearing of the Investigation I indicated that the position as to costs was that I had no power under the Regulation of Railways Act, 1871, to direct that any person's costs be paid to him, and that I therefore had the limited role of making recommendations on the question of costs to the Secretary of State. I said that:

> "The Secretary of State has indicated to me that he would consider favourably any recommendation of mine that the costs of the bereaved and injured, and those of individuals subject to criticisms and granted individual representation by me, should be met from public funds to the extent that these would not be paid by British Rail."

2.   As to the bereaved and injured, I indicated that I did not consider that it would be right to make a recommendation involving duplicate representation. They very sensibly and helpfully formed a consortium of solicitors to arrange joint representation. Because of her special position as the widow of Driver John Rolls, the driver of the Poole train, I gave leave for Mrs Rolls to be separately represented.

3.   As to those subject to criticism, I gave leave for the eleven persons who have been sent the letters referred to in paragraph 9 of the Procedural History to be represented. For the avoidance of doubt, those eleven included the three parties represented by Mr Gavin Millar of Counsel, who also appeared for their Union, the Transport Salaried Staffs' Association.

4.   Having now heard all the evidence and come to my conclusions, I consider that it is right that I make such a recommendation in relation to the costs of the bereaved, the injured, and those individuals subject to criticism to whom I granted individual representation.

5.   Accordingly, in respect of the bereaved and injured represented by the consortium of solicitors, of Mrs Rolls, and of all eleven represented parties subject to such criticism, I recommend the payment of their standard scale costs, to the extent that such costs are not paid by British Rail, in a sum to be agreed with the Treasury Solicitor, or failing such agreement, to be taxed.

6.   Arrangements were very properly made during the course of the Investigation by British Rail with certain of the represented parties in relation to the costs of those parties.

7.   I have no power to recommend that one party pay the costs of another party, and so the decision as to which party's costs British Rail make themselves responsible for must be a matter for British Rail.

8.   I do not think it appropriate to make any recommendations in relation to a public authority such as the London Fire and Civil Defence Authority, which is, by its, nature publicly funded through the medium of the ratepayer. I have considered the arguments properly put before me, but I make no recommendation in respect of these costs. This is in no sense to derogate from the helpful part the Authority played in the proceedings.

9.   As to the Trade Unions who were represented, the Association of Locomotive Engineers and Firemen, the National Union of Railwaymen and the Transport Salaried Staffs' Association, I consider it right to recommend that they each receive a proportion of their costs. It will be remembered that the last two named, the NUR and TSSA, had members of their Unions who were among those subject to criticism, but the former, ASLEF, did not. My recommendation

is that the National Union of Railwaymen and the Transport Salaried Staffs' Association should each receive one-half, and the Associated Society of Locomotive Engineers and Firemen should receive three-quarters of their standard scale costs out of public funds, to be agreed with the Treasury Solicitor, or, failing such agreement, to be taxed.

10. That completes my recommendations.

Appendix A

List of those who died

Gillian ALLEN

Clive William ATTFIELD

Jane Melanie AUBIN

John Felmingham BARRETT

James Robert BEASANT

Michelle BOYCE

Timothy Charles BURGESS

Glenn Ashley Allen CLARK

Arthur George CREECH

Norman Edward DALRYMPLE

Brian Richard Gerald DENNISON

Stephen Michael DYER

Romano FALCINI

Paul Derek George HADFIELD

Edna Rosa HANNIBAL

Geoffrey Ralph HARTWELL

Stephen Griffiths HOPKINS

Everett William Parks LINDSAY

Stephen John LOADER

Joseph MARTIN

Alison McGREGOR

Christopher Roger MOLESWORTH

David John MOORE

Teresa MOORE

Michael NEWMAN

Beverlie NIVEN

Austin Paul PERRY-LEWIS

Alan PHILIPSON

John Philip ROLLS

Alma SMITH

Tracey STEVENS

Erroll Derek TAYLOR

David Arthur George THOMAS

William Joseph WEBB

Alan WREN

Appendix B

List of Parties and their Representation

The Inquiry

Mr David Latham Q.C, Mr Philip Havers and Mr John Gimlette of Counsel, instructed by the Treasury Solicitor.

The Association of Locomotive Engineers and Firemen

Mr Allan Gore and Mr Simon Walton of Counsel, instructed by Messrs. Robin Thompson & Partners.

The Bereaved and Injured

Mr Michael Spencer Q.C. of Counsel, instructed by Messrs Pannone Napier for a consortium of solicitors.

The British Railways Board

Mr Roger Henderson Q.C, Mr Adrian Brunner and Mr Andrew Prynne of Counsel, instructed by the British Railways Board.

The Central Transport Consultative Committee, the London Regional Passengers Committee and the Transport Users Consultative Committee for Southern England

Mr John Cartledge

The London Fire & Civil Defence Authority

Sir John Drinkwater Q.C. and Mr Charles Gibson of Counsel, instructed by the Legal Services of the London Fire & Civil Defence Authority.

ML Holdings plc

Mr Roger Toulson Q.C. and Mr Ian Burnett of Counsel, instructed by Messrs. Simmons & Simmons.

The National Union of Railwaymen

Mr Jeremy McMullen and Mr Barry Cotter of Counsel, instructed by Messrs. Pattinson & Brewer.

The Transport Salaried Staffs' Association (including members: Mr Lippett, Mr Dray and Mr Callander)

Mr Gavin Millar of Counsel, instructed by Messrs. Russell Jones & Walker.

Mr G D Bailey

Mr Alan Cooper of Counsel, instructed by Messrs. Lawford & Co.

Mr D G Brown

Mr Stephen Irwin of Counsel, instructed by Messrs. Russell Jones & Walker.

Mr D Bumstead

Mr Barry Cotter of Counsel, instructed by Messrs. Pattinson & Brewer.

Mr R A Davies

Mr Christopher Goddard, of Counsel instructed by Messrs. Steggles Palmer.

Mr J G Deane

Mr F.J. Marr-Johnson of Counsel, instructed by Messrs. Evill and Coleman.

Mr C Hale

Originally represented by Mr Roger Henderson Q.C. and subsequently by Mr Conrad Griffiths of Counsel, instructed by Messrs. Hamlin Slowe.

Mr B K Hemingway

Mr Jeremy McMullen of Counsel, instructed by Messrs. Pattinson & Brewer.

Mr R W Penny

Mr Mark Bishop of Counsel, instructed by Messrs. Bindman & Partners.

Mrs S Rolls

Mr Benjamin Browne and Miss Catherine Rabey of Counsel, instructed by Messrs. Joynson-Hicks.

Appendix C

ALPHABETICAL LIST OF WITNESS

ADAMS Trevor*   BR Operating Manager
ALSTON Joseph   BR Driver
ASH Brian   LFCDA, Deputy Assistant Chief Officer
ATKINS Bernard   BR Driver
BADERMAN Dr Howard   Accident and Emergency Consultant, University College Hospital, London

BAILEY Geoffrey   BR Signal Works Engineer
BAKER Richard   BR Guard
BEAUCHAMP Charles   LFCDA, Station Officer
BELL Roy   BR Signal Engineer
BONE Richard   LFCDA, Area Controller
BOOTH Dr Stephen   St.Stephen's Hospital, Senior Registrar
BRADLEY Robert   BR S&T Signal Maintenance Assistant
BRANDON Bill*   Home Office
BRIANT Helen   Basingstoke passenger
BROWN D. Graham   BR Signal Engineer
BUMSTEAD Derek   BR S&T Supervisor
BURRAGE Kenneth   BR Director Signal & Telecommunications (from 1.4.89)
BUSHELL Lorraine*   LFCDA Control Officer
CALLANDER Gordon   BR S&T Testing & Commissioning Engineer (from 1.4.88)

CALVERT Paul   St.George's Hospital, Consultant Orthopaedic Surgeon
CANNON George   Emanuel School Teacher
CHAMBERS Hugh   LAS, Assistant Chief Ambulance Officer
CHILVER Christopher   Basingstoke passenger
CHIVERS Christopher   BR S&T Training and Safety Engineer
CHRISTIE Peter   BR S&T Signal Maintenance Supervisor
CHRISTY George   BR Driver
CLARKSON Gerald   LFCDA, Chief Officer
CLYRO Andrew   London Borough of Wandsworth Borough Engineer
COATES Lester*   BR Relief Signalman
CORNALL David   BR Project Engineer
COTTER Patrick   BR Signalman
COURT Alfred   BR S&T Supervisor
CRAWFORD Edward   BR S&T Supervisor
CROSBY Thomas   LAS, Deputy Chief Ambulance Officer
CROSS Andrew   BR Assistant Systems Engineer
DAVIES Gary   Basingstoke passenger
DAVIES Robert   BR S&T Signal Engineer (Projects)
DEANE John   BR S&T Area Signal Engineer (Works)
DOWD Patrick   BR S&T Technician
DRAY Peter   BR S&T Testing & Commissioning Engineer
EDISS Peter   Department of Health
EVANS Frederick   BR Guard
FISHER Dr Judith   BASICS Chairman
FLOOD Robert   Basingstoke passenger (BR Driver)
FORSEY David   BR Mechanical Engineer
FOSTER Michael   Basingstoke passenger (BTP Inspector)
FRITSCHE Simon   BR Guard
GIDDINGS Peter   BR Guard

* = Statements read out in Court

GILBERT Geoffrey	LAS, Divisional Officer/Control
GOODYEAR Anthony	BR Project Assistant
GUY Peter	BR Driver
HAGUE-HOLMES Digby	Basingstoke passenger
HALE Clifford	BR Regional Signal & Telecommunications Engineer (until 12.12.88)
HARMAN Ian	BR Signal Maintenance Engineer
HARRIS Neil	Kennedy Henderson Ltd
HAYWARD Paul	BR Guard
HEALY Lynne	LAS, Ambulance Officer
HEARN Martin Lloyd	Basingstoke passenger
HEMINGWAY Brian	BR S&T Senior Technician
HILL Wing Commander Ian	RAF Pathologist
HINDS Stephen Charles	BR Trainee Guard
HINES Dr Kenneth	BASICS
HODGSON Kenneth	BR Director Signal & Telecommunications (until 31.3.89)
HOLMES Maurice	BR Director of Safety
HOWARD Michael	Basingstoke passenger
INGRAM Carol	Basingstoke passenger
JACOBSEN Michael	Basingstoke passenger
JAMIESON Crawford	Basingstoke passenger (Surgeon, St. Thomas's Hospital)
JONES Paul*	BR Booking Boy
KEATING David	BR Driver
KESSELL Clive	BR Assistant Director (Telecommunications)
KIDDLE Peter*	AA Patrolman
KNAPP James	General Secretary, NUR
LIPPETT James	BR S&T Supervisor
LOWE Terence	Kennedy Henderson Ltd
MAIDMENT David	BR Reliability Manager
MALONE Patrick	BR Driver
MANSBRIDGE Graham	BR Driver
MARSH Neil	BR S&T Health & Safety Supervisor
McCLYMONT Alexander	BR Driver
McGREGOR William	British Transport Police, Assistant Chief Constable
McMILLAN James	LFCDA, Assistant Chief Officer
MILLIGAN Neil	General Secretary, ASLEF
MILLS Glyn	LFCDA, Temporary Station Officer
MORGAN John	BR Train Crew Project Manager
MURIE Simon	Emanuel School Pupil
NOORANI John	BR Station Manager Clapham Junction
O'HARE Sean	LAS, Ambulance Officer
PATTERSON Michael	Secretary, CTCC
PEARSON William	BR Works Assistant
PENNY Roger	BR S&T Area Signal Engineer
PERRY John*	BR Depot Engineer
PETTITT Gordon	BR General Manager, Southern Region
PIKE Barry	BR Driver
PORTER Colin	BR Acting Regional Signal & Telecommunications Engineer
PRESTON John	Basingstoke passenger
PRISTON Robert	BR Driver
RAY David	Metropolitan Police, Chief Superintendent
RAYNER David	BR Joint Managing Director (Railways)
REEVES Ronald	BR Electrical Control Operator
REID Sir Robert	BR Chairman, British Railways Board
RICHARDSON Alan	BR S&T Supervisor
SAYERS Martin	BR S&T Assistant Technician

* = Statements read out in Court

SEYMOUR Robin	Chief Inspecting Officer Railways, Department of Transport
SIMPSON Allan	BR Project Assistant
SPENCER Richard*	BR Signalman
STATON Ernest	Poole passenger (ASLEF Official)
SWEETENHAM Dr John	Basingstoke passenger
TERRY Jane*	LFCDA Control Officer
THOMPSON Christopher	BR Regional Signal & Telecommunications Engineer (from 22.12.88)
TODD Peter	Bedfordshire Constabulary, Inspector
WALTON Thomas	LAS, Chief Ambulance Officer
WARBURTON Ivor	BR Director of Operations
WESLEY John	Basingstoke passenger (BR Senior Systems Assistant Track Recording)
WEST Dr Iain	Forensic Pathologist, Guy's Hospital
WHITE John	BR Driver
WHITE David	BR S&T Supervisor

This list describes witnesses' positions on 12 December 1988, unless otherwise stated.

★ = *Statements read out in Court*

ASLEF	=	Association of Locomotive Engineers & Firemen
BASICS	=	British Association for Immediate Care
BR	=	British Railways
BTP	=	British Transport Police
CTCC	=	Central Transport Users Consultative Committee
LAS	=	London Ambulance Service
LFCDA	=	London Fire & Civil Defence Authority
NUR	=	National Union of Railwaymen
S&T	=	Signal & Telecommunications Department, British Rail Southern Region

Appendix D

Video tapes presented to the Investigation

During the 57 days of the public investigation, five videos were shown to the Court. They served to increase understanding of the rest of the evidence presented, and to enable everyone to appreciate the scale of the rescue operation.

I am grateful to British Rail, British Transport Police and the London Fire and Civil Defence Authority for their care in preparing those videos and for allowing them to be used during the hearing.

1. *"A Helicopter View of the Scene"*
   A British Transport Police video shown on day 1, transcript reference page 15G.

2. *"Video of the Route and Clapham Junction "A" Signal Box"*
   A British Rail video shown on day 1, transcript reference page 38F, and day 2 page 35E.

3. *"Clapham Junction "A" Signal Box, Relay Room and Lineman's Office"*
   A British Transport Police video shown on day 57, transcript reference page 3B.

4. *"Emergency Services Control Centres on Spencer Park"*
   A London Fire Brigade video shown on day 57, transcript reference page 4B.

5. *"Emergency Services Control Centres"*
   A British Transport Police video shown on day 57, transcript reference page 4C.

Appendix E

Glossary of Terms and Abbreviations

Arcing	A passage of an electrical current across an air gap when two conductors are sufficiently close which manifests itself as sparks or a flash.
ATP	Automatic Train Protection.
Auto-brake gauge	A gauge recording the application and pressure of the automatic braking system; usually repeated in the guard's van.
AWS	Automatic warning system.
BASICS	British Association for Immediate Care.
Bell tests	A testing procedure where the wires, once in place, are made live so that by connecting a bell at one end of the circuit one can hear that the wire goes to the correct point.
Bogies	The under-carriage assembly incorporating the wheels, suspension, brakes and, in powered units, the traction motors.
Bonds	Short wires used to bridge gaps in electrical circuits, usually at track circuit joints or between rails.
Brake cylinder	A part of the braking system which converts an applied vacuum into mechanical leverage thereby operating the brake shoes.
Buckeye coupler	A particular form of coupler which will lock automatically when the two parts are pushed together.
Buzz Test	Similar to a Bell Test, but with buzzer replacing the bell
Commissioning	The bringing into use of a new or revised system usually by way of a formal hand-over
Colour-light signals	Signals whose aspects are conveyed by lights alone; they may have 2, 3 or 4 aspects.
Couplers	An arrangement where two forces, though acting in opposite directions, complement each other, as with a tommy bar.
Dead-man's handle	A safety mechanism on a train controller which automatically applies the brakes if the lever is released. Intended to stop a train if the driver becomes incapacitated.
Detonators	Small charges placed on a running rail which explode when run over; used to warn drivers in following trains of an incident ahead.
DOO	Driver only operation.

ECR	Electrical Control Room or Lamp Proving Relay (according to sense in fact).
EP gauge	Electro-pneumatic brake gauge; recording the application and pressure of the service brake, usually repeated in the guard's van.
Eyes	The end of a wire adapted to form a ring which will fit on a terminal, or a proprietary addition to the end of a wire for the same purpose.
False feed	A current/voltage unintentionally fed into a circuit.
FRAME	Fault Reporting and Monitoring Equipment.
Functional testing	Testing by means of simulating the full operation capacity of the system.
Impedance bond	A bond which can discriminate between alternating and direct current allowing the passage of D.C. only.
Insulated rail joint (IRJ) Insulated block joint (IBJ)	Rail joints incorporating insulation to isolate individual track circuits.
Location case	A trackside cabinet used to house signalling equipment such as relays/transformers.
Loudaphone	Voice powered system of communication between driver and guard.
Mechanical semaphore signals	A signal whose aspect is conveyed by moving an arm in addition to a light. These are gradually being superseded by colour-light signals (qv).
Moment	A force acting in conjunction with a lever which amplifies the effect of that force.
Multiple aspect signalling	A system of colour-light signalling in which the signals may show 3 or 4 aspects.
NRN	National Radio Network.
Overlap	A distance, normally 200 yards, beyond each signal which must be clear before the preceding signal can display a proceed aspect; allows a margin in case a train overshoots a signal before stopping.
Plastic airways	An especially shaped plastic tube for insertion in the throat to allow breathing under restricted conditions.
Point machine	A motor (or device) which operates points.
Points	A short section of line which can be moved to direct traffic onto another line.

Pump	A fire appliance specifically designed to pump water (or foam).
Relay room	A room dedicated to housing relays often as part of a signal box.
Relays	An electro-mechanical device which operates a switch under the control of an electric current. They can be wired to operate as "on" or "off" when a current is applied.
Right-side failures	A failure in a system which leaves the system in a safe condition.
Rolling stock	The wagons of a freight train or carriages of a train, but not including the powered car unless this carries passengers: i.e. all but a locomotive.
Signal aspects	The colour shown on a signal, or the position of the arm on a semaphore signal, indicating the track status: green = clear red = stop double yellow = preliminary caution single yellow = caution
Solid state interlocking (SSI)	A group of micro-processors arranged to provide the same fail-safe work as electro-magnetic relay interlocking.
SPAD	Signals Passed At Danger (red).
SPT	Signal-Post Telephone : a direct no-dial link to the relevant signal box.
Stageworks	Programme of work intended to bring a new system into operation by individual set stages.
Terminal	A point on an item of equipment (often in the form of a threaded post) to which a wire can be firmly connected.
Track circuit	An electrical circuit, part of which is carried by the running rails, used for detecting the presence of trains.
Track circuit clips	Two stout clips connected by wire which, when clipped between the lines, give the same electrical effect as a passing train thereby setting preceding signal to red.
Track circuit interrupter cable	The cable joining the track circuit interrupter to the location case. A track circuit interrupter is a device for ensuring that when trap points are run through, the track circuit remains de-energised to indicate that fact.
Traction supply	The supply for the driving motors of electric trains.

Train register	A book or loose-leaf sheets kept in a signal box and used to record the passage of trains, messages passed, and other prescribed events.
Tree	The collective description of a number of individual wires bound tightly together to form "branches" and thence branches combined into the "trunk".
Tripping of circuit breakers	Circuit breakers are electro-mechanical fuses which switch off automatically if too much current passes through. They can then be reset. Tripping is when the switching off occurs.
WARS	Waterloo Area Resignalling Scheme.
Wire counts	A checking procedure where the number of wires going into a terminal is compared with the number shown on the circuit diagram.
Wrong-side failure	A failure in the signalling system which leaves the system in a dangerous condition.

APPENDIX F

The Signalling Failure : A Technical Assessment

1. The power to light the lamps of signal WF138 is derived from a 110v AC source in location WD1, a steel cabinet situated at the trackside some 10m from the signal. Which particular lamp or lamps are lit depends on the state of 138HR, the controlling relay for the signal, which is also located in WD1 as will be seen from Appendix K.8. When the coil of 138HR is de-energised the front contacts are open and the back contacts closed. Current flows across one of the back contacts to light the red lamp. However, when the coil is energised the front contacts are made and the back ones open cutting the power to the red lamp and allowing it to pass to the green, or one or both yellow lights depending on the state of the other relays.

2. The power to feed the coil of 138HR is derived from a 110v AC source in Clapham Junction "A" relay room and passes through cables which link the relay room to location WD1. It passes through a number of other location cases where, except at location 3/4 the linking cables are merely terminated on the input and output sides of the terminal rack and joined by a movable link or jumper. However, at location 3/4, which contains the relays which operated the replaced signal WA25, the cables are terminated in such a fashion that relay WA25 HR operates in parallel with 138HR. In location WD1 the feed for 138HR is transformed and rectified to produce the 50v DC which is the operating voltage in the miniature plug-in relay. A composite circuit diagram, which incorporates the relevant parts of those circuits for the relay room and location cases, is shown in the bottom part of Appendix K.9. (The upper part of the diagram of Appendix K.9 shows what the state of the wiring should have been if Job No.104 only had been done).

3. As can be seen from the left-hand side of the lower part of Appendix K.9 the feed for the coil of 138HR passes through one of the front contacts on each of relays DM TRR and DL TRR. Therefore, unless both DM TRR and DL TRR are energised there is no power to feed 138HR. TRRs (track repeater relays) repeat the state of the actual track-circuit relays (TR) which are normally situated in location cases near the tracks themselves. The coils of the TRs can only be energised when the circuit, of which they and the running rails form a part, is complete. An axle or a piece of wire stretched from one running rail to the other provides a short-circuit path and the track-circuit relay is by-passed or de-energised. This description is an oversimplification of the actual arrangements at Clapham post 26/27 November when the relevant track circuits were altered that week-end from low frequency AC track circuits to high-audio frequency (1.5kHz to 2.6kHz) ones. The new audio-frequency track circuits NA and NB were arranged to drive directly the repeater relay DL TRR in Clapham Junction "A" relay room until such time as the latter is abolished. The old DL TR in the location case was strapped out. However, in all descriptions in the report DL track-circuit has, for convenience, been used to describe its replacements, the combined track circuits NA and NB.

4. The lower part of Appendix K.9 represents the state of the wiring on the morning of 12 December 1988. The "rogue wire" is shown connected to fuse R12-f107 and touching terminal 4-Arm (4A) of DM TRR. Thus, if DM TRR was energised power would be fed to 138 HR, energising it and enabling a proceed aspect to be shown at signal WF138, irrespective of the state of DL TRR. In other words, even though a train was occupying DL track circuit and de-energising DL TRR the signal behind would not be showing red. It should be noted here that if the "rogue" wire had been touching terminal 4-front (4-f) of

DM TRR that relay too would have been by-passed and signal WF138 would always show a proceed aspect and only turn red if there was a red lamp failure in signal WF46/47.

5. The normal sequence of signal aspects as a train passes from Earlsfield to Clapham is shown in Appendix K.13A. However, with the "rogue" wire in place on the morning of 12 December 1988, the sequence of faulty signal aspects for the passage of a single train is shown in Appendix K.13B. Appendix K.13C shows the passage of 1B06 (the 06:06 ex-Bournemouth driven by Driver Christy), of 2G06 (the 07:20 ex-Guildford driven by Driver Priston) and of 2L10 (the 07:18 ex-Basingstoke driven by Driver McClymont) and the signal aspects which they saw and which are fully explained by the fault and by the actions of Signalman Cotter. The changes in the signal aspects whilst Driver McClymont was reporting to the signalman and which would have been seen by Driver Rolls are shown at Appendix K.13D.

6. Mr Bell in evidence (2.29) stated that it was electrically impossible for Driver Christy to have seen signal WF148 showing green at exactly the same moment at signal WF142 was showing single yellow. For signal WF148 to show green relay 142 HHR requires to be energised, but for signal WF142 to show single yellow 142 HHR must be de-energised which, of course, is impossible at one and the same time. Hence, in the absence of a fault in the circuitry associated with signals WF142 and 148, Driver Christy could not have seen instantaneously, signals WF142 at single yellow and 148 at green.

APPENDIX G

The Rolling Stock: A Technical Assessment

1. With regard to human casualties and collision damage the main features which characterise the accident are as follows:

(i) A head-on impact between the rear end of the 12-coach stationary train and the front end of the 12-coach following train moving at between 35 and 45 mph under full braking conditions. Ensuing longitudinal collapse of the vestibule ends of those few coaches in both trains nearest to the plane of impact.

(ii) Impulsive vertical lifting of the two rear coaches of the initially stationary train to a maximum exceeding coach height, and impulsive translation to the left-hand or near-side by a similar distance. The rearmost coach came to rest on its left-hand side on the rising embankment of the cutting at the top of a retaining wall. The second rearmost coach took up an intermediate position but below the retaining wall.

(iii) Impulsive right-ward translation accompanied by a ploughing motion, of the first two coaches of the moving train, with separation from the heavy motor bogies of the first coach. Both coaches slid past the stationary train with an ensuing stripping separation of their left-hand sides arising from contact with contiguous coach ends of the stationary train.

(iv) Lesser contact damage, particularly at the front right-hand ends of these two coaches, arising from glancing impact with an oppositely fast-moving empty train on the adjacent line. The track separation at this position is more than the standard distance. Thus, the colliding train eventually overran the stationary train by just more than two coach lengths, and the foremost third-length of the front coach experienced total disintegration.

(v) Most of the passenger fatalities occurred within this zone, but there were others in both coaches, mostly arising from the stripping separation of the left-hand coach side.

2. A significant measurement, to which further reference will be made, was that that the stationary train in its braked condition was impelled forward about 10ft by the collision. The lighter undriven rear bogies of the stationary train were also held captive to their respective coaches, and the rearmost came to rest upon the forward luggage compartment of the third coach of the moving train, partially crushing this compartment and one passenger trapped within it.

3. The collision took place on a large (2000m) radius curve which, in combination with the nearside retaining wall of the cutting, obscured the forward view of Driver Rolls of the moving train, and in the absence of a timely signal check gave him too little time and distance to bring his train safely to rest. Otherwise, this large radius curve influenced the course of the collision events in only one respect to which further reference is made.

Mark I Coaching Stock   4. The 32 coaches of the three trains were of traditional slam-door Mark I stock, each coach having a structural composite steel backbone member just below floor level, attached through sprung drawgear to buckeye couplers at its ends. Each has two bogies secured to the backbone through transverse body bolsters near the ends, but most of the bogies are undriven. The passenger spaces are contained by (non-structural) corrugated steel flooring, and framed sides and roof, together with vestibule ends provided each with two or more transverse steel bulkheads. Most of the passenger spaces are open throughout the coach length, but the rearmost coach of the stationary train had first-class closed compartments with a side corridor in its front half, and the second coach of the colliding train comprised an open buffet with a longitudinal division along part of its length. The shutters were closed at the time of collision, which afforded some protection to many standing passengers on the right-hand side when the left-hand coach side was stripped and separated during the collision. It did not protect passengers placed at tables in the rear half.

5. Most of the coaches of Mark I stock involved in this collision at moderate speed performed as intended in a situation of last resort. The closed and locked couplers held together, with notable exceptions, and longitudinal collapse was confined in most cases to vestibule ends, as intended. It is important to acknowledge that two-thirds of the coaches in the three trains sustained no main structural damage, as here defined, and remained on the track; there were no fires. The severe damage in other cases, mainly to vehicles adjacent to the collision plane, justified detailed examination of wreckage, subsequently arranged so as to permit observation from above and below, assisted in the case of the leading coach of the moving train by a spatial reconstruction. It was revealed as a by-product of these examinations that the vehicles were not much weakened by atmospheric corrosion effects, as might possibly have been expected at lower edges of the side and end panels near the joint with the underframe.

Main structural damage

6. The front end of a train which moves in opposition to pronounced braking adopts a drooping position although the downward displacement may only be a few millimetres, and this accounts adequately for the tendency to wedge itself under the train with which it collides. This initially small effect is enhanced as impact deformation increases, for reasons which will be addressed, and if not checked may eventually develop into a full vertical override, as seen in previous collisions. It is consistent in the present case with the sudden upward jump of the rear coach of the stationary train.

7. A corresponding small initial mismatch of contact in the horizontal plane may have precipitated another pronounced effect, in that the buffer headstocks and coplanar end bulkheads of both moving and stationary trains were afterwards found to be bodily rotated in the same direction about a vertical axis by an amount in excess of 30 degrees. This certainly accounts for the observed sideways motions, of the rear of the stationary train to the left and of the front of the moving train to the right, as a slipping occurred of front end over rear end. A well-defined source of initial mismatch was not detected in this case, but these nucleating effects of disproportionate significance are also addressed in a following section.

8. The irreversible plastic deformations which not only permitted these translational and rotational collapse effects to occur, but also accommodated at least one-half metre of longitudinal collapse of the vestibule ends of both trains, were readily related to the central pair of I section members forming the composite structural backbones (underframes) of the relevant coaches. These were observed to be heavily buckled in the horizontal plane as in Appendix K.11 and also to some extent in the vertical plane, particularly between the drawgear housing (behind the relevant headstocks) and the body bolster structures of grid-like form. They are indeed designed to collapse by buckling in the collision situation of last resort, but in a symmetric mode in order to accommodate longitudinal deformations of the coach ends. Several examples of lesser buckling

deformations, but closer to the ideal, were observed within two coach lengths of the main impact plane. It is possible to see from Appendix K.11 how asymmetric buckling deformations between the coach ends and the body bolsters were eventually supplemented by pronounced, almost right-angle buckles in the backbone members between body bolsters. It was these buckles which accommodated the hinging type of bending deformation of the whole coach at the position shown in Appendix K.11 leading to disintegration of the shell enclosing the passenger spaces at this end of it. From the disposition of wreckage on the track it seems likely that first occurrence of the hinging deformation preceded contact with the oppositely moving train on adjacent track. From loading considerations it would seem most likely that the hinge-like deformation was driven by the cumulative longitudinal inertia force of the eleven coaches to its rear. It is certain that subsequent contact between the forward end of this coach and trailing coaches of the adjacent, oppositely moving train completed the destruction, since the retardation of this train through glancing contact was sufficient to separate the front coach by de-coupling, accompanied by derailment of the coaches behind it as they were hit.

9.   The extensive damage to the leading coach of the moving train contrasts markedly with the limited damage to the rear coach of the stationary train, considering that a common accumulation of longitudinal impulsive force was applied to both. This must remain enigmatic, despite the need for understanding, since the evidence from examination of wreckage is complex, and subject to uncertainty with regard to timing of sequential events. The most cogent factors appear to be as follows.

10.   Firstly, the leading coach of the moving train had two heavy motor bogies, and the vertical attachment pin of the leading bogie exhibited heavy bruising consistent with a large impulsive retarding force, applied just before separation of the bogie from the underframe. The existence of such an additional force would accentuate buckling of the backbone in the front of the body bolster, and attenuate it behind. However, this protection would be lost immediately after separation of the bogie, which was observed to occur on the moving coach, but not on the stationary coach where the bogie remained captive.

11.   Secondly, the early nucleation of override of the rear coach of the stationary train would lift its underframe, and particularly the headstock and solebars, so as to present a stiff, chisel-like structure, capable of shearing off the lighter sidewall panels of the colliding coach of the moving train. Thus weakened, the whole of the latter structure would be rendered more vulnerable to completion of buckling collapse within the forward half of its length. The rear and initially stationary coach would not be affected in this way, in accord with observation.

12.   It is noted thirdly, that the flanges of the composite backbone member of the underframe had been pared away locally to accommodate transverse displacements on short radius curves of the somewhat larger wheels of the motor bogies. This reduction of cross-section coincided with the main buckle behind the body bolster of the leading coach.

13.   Thus, all three effects positively stem from detailed observations of the wreckage, are unique to the moving, leading coach, and would have acted in summation. It was tentatively considered at an early stage of the investigation that the superior performances of the stationary trailing coach might have much depended upon the stiff transverse bulkheads of the closed first-class compartments and its front end. In the light of the three discrete factors above, this view has been relegated.

Internal damage 14. Beyond the influence of extensive main structural damage in coaches adjacent to the impact, internal damage was remarkably slight, although there were a few local penetrations through the sidewalls of dense and compact high-speed projectiles, some of which were excrescences dislodged and impelled by the high relative speed of the oppositely moving adjacent empty train. Some of these injured passengers. Coach windows mainly offered protection comparable with that of adjacent metal panels, and few were broken. External slam doors mainly remained intact, although a proportion could be opened only with difficulty after impact, because of small permanent distortions to the surrounding structure. However, at least one internal vestibule door became detached and caused injury as a projectile. Many seat cushions with light timber surrounds were dislodged, and may have caused some light injuries to passengers. Continuously longitudinal overhead luggage racks performed well, but there were numerous cases of passenger injury thought to be from dislodgement of luggage placed upon them, particularly with regard to rigid plastic attache cases.

15. Attention should particularly be drawn to transverse eye-level luggage racks, fitted in two open coaches relatively near to the plane of the impact, where there were centre gangways. These racks each comprised a tubular metal framework spanned with netting, rectangular in plan with attachments at one side to the coach wall and at the gangway side to pillars extending upwards from the seat ends. A significant proportion of these racks were wholly or partially broken off, ostensibly from passenger contact or by reason of heavy baggage retained in them. The adverse performance of these racks deserves attention; in other respects they may have given useful handholds to standing passengers before becoming detached.

Pathological effects 16. Despite immense difficulties, and with an almost superhuman effort in cross-referencing, stimulated by the severity of the accident in those faced with the painful task, a remarkable success was achieved in tracing the seated or standing positions of the human casualties. No-one survived in the forward one-third length of the leading coach of the moving train, and the injuries were mainly attributed to compression of the passenger space. Behind this zone the survival rate increased almost sharply, but there were fatalities along the near-side, mostly among those adjacent to the sidewall which had been stripped off. There was a similar experience along the near-side of the buffet car, which was also stripped off. It needs no emphasis that there can be no survival where the integrity of the passenger space is completely breached, leading to outward projection of some occupants.

17. With regard to extent of injury the pathological evidence is complex. The foregoing conforms with the evidence of Dr West, whose examinations were direct, and conducted with minimal delay. The examinations of Wing Commander Hill, who was consulted by virtue of deep experience of aircraft and road accidents, were confined to a later time, and access only to detailed medical records. They led to an additional observation that multiple internal and external injuries sustained by casualties (mainly survivors) were greater where seated near the centre aisle, and tentatively indicated collision with hard protrusions of items of internal furniture. There was general agreement that the edges of tables caused internal injuries and asphyxia in certain cases, and that loose seating and tables seriously increased the chances of injury. There was

general agreement, however, that standing passengers at the time of this accident were no more at risk of death or injury than those seated.

18. It is a recurring tribute to the safety of rail travel that it is consistently an order of magnitude greater than road travel. The casualties in this serious accident were essentially confined to two of twenty-four coaches (recognising that the third train contained no passengers), and the lesson of the event is that the integrity of passenger space should never be breached by disintegration of the main containing structure.

Analytical review of the collision

19. Although contributing no more than a framework, the science of Newtonian mechanics in terms of momentum exchanges during impact is valuable because it leads to firm and trustworthy conclusions. Thus, the observation of Driver McClymont that his train was projected forward after impact, by an amount later confirmed by measurement to have been 10ft, allows the calculation of its maximum speed at this juncture. Assuming the braked condition with locked wheels together with the largest possible friction coefficient of 1/2 between dry metallic surfaces, this speed could not have been greater than 5.5m/sec (12 mph). This is just greater than one-half of the mean speed of the trains (of approximately equal masses) at impact, and confirms that the moving train was still in possession of much of its initial kinetic energy, after the impacted ends had separated. This accords with the long travel of the moving train after impact, and the continuing trail of destruction.

20. This upper limit of forward speed of 5.5m/sec. (which may have been exceeded at the impact plane because of local collapse of the vestibule ends) may be compared with a corresponding estimate of the speed at which the rear of the stationary train lifted. Given that the lift itself was 3m or more, to clear the retaining wall, this estimate becomes approximately 8m/sec.

21. Given that the speed of the moving train was approximately 18m/sec (40 mph) at the time of impact, so that the relative speed of the trains when separating again was just less than 12.5m/sec, it follows that the vertical angle at which the stationary would override the moving train would have exceeded 30 degrees, if it could have been observed. It is instructive to compare this with the Bellgrove head-on collision at corresponding relative speeds, where this vertical angle was clearly defined at approximately this magnitude, and the train under full braking was similarly overridden. The essential difference between these collisions was that the trains were each composed of three coaches at Bellgrove, whereas the trains at Clapham Junction each had twelve coaches.

22. It should not be concluded that the longitudinal forces at similar impact speeds were greater at Clapham Junction than at Bellgrove, because of different lengths of trains. The study of deformation wave motions tends to predict otherwise, although the impact load would have tended to persist for a longer time with the train at Clapham Junction, if the two impacted ends had not prematurely disengaged.

23. The most important question concerned with this disengagement involves the collapse mechanisms operative at the impacted ends of the trains, which caused such a large measure of common rotation about a vertical axis before they separated again. This rotation was conspicuously absent at Bellgrove. A small initial horizontal mismatch of the impacted ends has previously been adduced as the nucleus of the rotation. Although uncertain, a plausible explanation of this is to be found in the super-elevation of the track at the curve.

This would cause the stationary bogies to hug the inside of the curve, and the moving bogies to hug the outside, although to a lesser extent at the relatively low speed, accounting for an eccentricity of approach of, perhaps, 10mm. The absence of the effect at Bellgrove lends confirmation, since both trains travelled at similar speeds, and would have hugged the outside of the curve.

24. Another possible source of eccentricity is to be found in the antisymmetric planform of the couplers, which could give rise to a transient force couple at the instant of engagement. Although of the correct sense, and neutralised by premature fracture of one of the impacted couplers at Bellgrove, no previous evidence of such an effect has been discovered in the literature of rail collisions.

25. Although the source of eccentricity will remain obscure, the mechanisms of amplification during impact, and of diminished resistance to headstock rotation are much more clear. The first of these is concerned with the pinned mountings of the buckeye couplers within the drawgear housings, and the circumstances in which the couplers were the first components at the headstocks to make mechanical contact, as intended. Couplers normally retain connection, even under extenuating circumstances when locked in the coupled position. When subjected to coupling at impact there is no recent evidence to raise doubt that they function correctly, although connection is not retained since locking requires human intervention which is obviously absent under such conditions.

26. It can be safely assumed that the couplers at Clapham Junction presented a solid compression connection at the instant of impact, but the nature of the pinned connections at their further ends and the sprung transverse support between is that they would permit the headstocks, with light contact between the buffers, to slide relatively and transversely with little restraint. There is clear evidence from deformations of couplers and mountings that this occurred. The effect of this would be to amplify the eccentricity in the horizontal plane (and to some extent in the vertical plane), as is the experience when a two-wheeled trailer is manoeuvred in reverse by the vehicle to which it is captive.

27. The next effect to be considered is the response of the backbone of the underframe to longitudinal forces which are now subject in this way to an increasing degree of eccentricity. It is well-known in the study of engineering plasticity of metals that a strut which reaches its maximum supportable compressive load, causing it to approach a state of total plasticity, loses all capacity to resist coincident bending moments. This influence remains, even when strut failure is by buckling, and sufficiently explains the observed large rotations of the ends. There is likewise no mystery concerning the immediately subsequent slipping off of one coach end against the other, with a resultant parting of the couplers at this stage, having reached their limit of design capacity in the unlocked state.

Lessons to be learned 28. The sequences of events are complex in all collisions, and the absolute priority is to prevent their occurrence by improving the quality of track and signalling, and the competence with which they are used. Although the history of railways demonstrates progressive improvements in safety, it also reveals that the sources of possible error are so diverse that absolute safety is approached rather than reached. The case is made in this way for minimising the risk of death and injury by improvement of collision resistance, especially in passenger stock on intensely worked routes where these risks are greatest. Improved understanding of sequences of events in collisions can contribute to this process, and the severity in terms of human cost of this accident has provided an intellectual driving force throughout the Investigation. It has shown that the first split-second events are susceptible to scientific understanding, albeit imperfect. This is sufficient to identify matters of detail from which practicable improvements can emerge, which themselves promise improved control of more cataclysmic events that would otherwise follow. There are several factors helpful to understanding thus, the collision was head-on, involving two twelve-coach trains of structurally identical stock on track with minimal curvature, and thereby conferred membership of an important class with minimal complexity and maximum future significance. A contemporaneous collision at Bellgrove at similar relative speeds between two three-coach trains of structurally similar stock permitted the same team to inspect both comparatively. This experience in itself induced a measure of agreement, both on causes and on future actions.

29. Three clear objectives emerge:

(i) the structural integrity of passenger containment should be such that its boundaries are not breached during a collision;

(ii) passenger seats should withstand collision loading and luggage containment should fulfil its function under similar conditions; and

(iii) since passengers cannot be totally confined, the design of tables and other furniture should obviate hard spots which are injurious under impact conditions.

30. Since great quantities of kinetic energies have to be absorbed in a collision of the last resort it will never be possible to resist collisions without accepting a degree of structural collapse, and the concept of using vestibule ends of coaches for this purpose is well founded and realistic, although it offers no protection for drivers. The special lesson of this accident is that collision resistance at vestibule ends should not be compromised by alternative deformation modes, such as rotation followed by slipping off, whereby kinetic energy is retained through a glancing blow which leads to override, whether lateral or vertical.

31. It has been confirmed in this respect that transverse sliding of one headstock over another during the early stages of collision, such as is facilitated by first heavy contact between buckeye couplers pinned to the drawgear housings at their remote ends, is subsequently conducive to vertical and transverse overriding, in the manner described above. One way in which to suppress this initial mode of displacement is to interpose firmly located large rectangular hard rubber blocks, which alternatively carry most of the compressive load. This feature has been employed for a similar purpose by London Underground Ltd, and corresponding blocks on Paris Metro trains appear to have treads similar to tyres on off-road vehicles.

32. On the same basis of considering crucial structural details, the bogies are retained at the bolsters of Mark 1 vehicles by washers and nuts at the heads of the pivot pins, but these were inadequately proportioned to withstand the extra weight of the motor bogies, and parted on the moving leading coach. It seems likely, subject to reasonable doubts concerning the complexity of events in the collision, that the hinge collapse of the whole coach would have been usefully restrained if the parting of coach and bogie had not occurred, and that it should be future practice to strengthen these retaining components.

33. British Rail has pondered the structural problems of rolling stock for many years, and has actively contributed to international, and more importantly, European collaboration. An important aim has been defined to provide lateral in addition to longitudinal crushing resistance – in brief, resistance to diagonal loading. This property has been provided in principle in all stock originated since Mark I, through adoption of monocoque construction whereby the floor, walls and roof comprise an integrated tubular structure, with most of the structural cross-section distributed through the floor, lower sidewalls and eaves of the roof. Mark III and later coach constructions have developed this property, without sacrifice of overall longitudinal strength compared with that of the strong backbone of Mark I stock.

34. Despite these developments, the traditional approach to proof of collision resistance in rolling stock has been through full-scale static proof testing. It is therefore encouraging to learn that British Rail has recently proposed to commence development by dynamic testing, apparently as a pioneer in the international field. Experience in the aircraft and automotive fields has hitherto demonstrated that such testing is essential to permit prediction of collision resistance and can only be undertaken at full scale. This must be so in relation to effects on the human body, but an open mind should be retained in the case of structural testing. Whereas satisfactory structural models cannot economically be made of the very thin-walled aircraft and automotive structures, the characteristic proportions of railway vehicles are such that this limitation need not apply. The use of structural models, if demonstrated to be feasible as is thought likely, would greatly increase the rate of accumulation of data, for a given budget, and permit the comparative study of structural details involved at an early stage of collision which have been shown at Clapham Junction and Bellgrove to exert a disproportionate influence on ultimate behaviour.

35. The inventory of Mark I coaching stock is large, and much of it has not reached an end of economic life, nor will do so for another decade or more. Mark I vehicles have good riding qualities, and are not intrinsically lacking in collision resistance, since the latter has emerged by a process of natural selection over forty years. The limited diagonal strength demonstrated for the first time in this accident could be adequately supplemented in various ways through attention to structural details, which would be expected to be revealed in dynamic model tests. Reinforcement of the corners between headstocks and solebars might be one such improvement. It is relevant in the best interests of BR customers to point out that a head-on collision between twelve-coach trains did not occur during the past half-century, and would be a rare probability in future. That being the case, it could be forcibly argued that there are more rewarding candidates for large capital investment in the railway than would be incurred by early replacement of these vehicles.

36. It is both instinctive and recognised good practice immediately after such an accident for all those involved with rescue to release passengers and crew and take care of those who are trapped and injured. This is endorsed as a foremost priority. Restoration of traffic is a longer term, but equally necessary priority. It has to be accepted that much evidence is lost under these conditions, by cutting and early removal of wreckage as was the case at Clapham Junction. Photography of the scene and the wreckage represents the most comprehensive and best means of securing evidence for later detailed scrutiny, and need not be unduly intrusive. Prevention and amelioration of further accidents depends upon securing such firm evidence, to which a corresponding priority should be accorded. Acknowledgement is made to BR and the emergency services for the valuable efforts that they made to secure evidential photographs, despite other

198

pressures upon them. Sharp black-white as well as colour photographs continue to have sound evidential value. Much use was made of video on this occasion, and it is well suited for panoramic reference. The need for expert close-up still photography remains, both to establish how and where casualties are trapped, and to identify significant components of wreckage in their spatial contexts; this may be regarded as a legitimate lesson of the event.

WRONG SIDE SIGNALLING FAILURES

CAUSED BY S & T STAFF/CONTRACTORS

WHERE CHECKING/TESTING WAS INADEQUATE

1985 TO 1988

DATE	LOCATION	INCIDENT	CAUSE
05-04-85	Fairwood Jct (WR)	Passenger train took wrong route and derailed when setting back (no injuries).	Points not correctly set because of wiring error during resignalling works
21-04-85	Brighton (SR)	Irregular indications noticed by Signalman	Contractor prematurely replaced fuses during resignalling works
11-09-85	Redhill (SR)	Irregular indications noticed by Signalman	Track circuit controls omitted because of installation error
23-09-85	Rugby (LMR)	Irregular aspects and train took wrong route	Wiring error during resignalling works
10-11-85	Northfleet (SR)	Irregular indications noticed by Signalman	Track circuit controls omitted because of bonding error
04-11-85	Oxted (SR)	Irregular aspects observed by Driver	Track circuit controls omitted because of installation error
05-11-85	East Croydon (SR)	Side-on collision between passenger trains (no injuries)	Interlocking error caused by design error
26-03-86	Queenstown Road (SR)	Irregular indications noticed by Signalman	Track circuit controls omitted because of wiring error
13-04-86	Portchester (SR)	Irregular aspect observed by Driver	Track circuit controls omitted because of wiring error
13-05-86	Between Tonbridge & Hastings (SR)	Defective wiring discovered by S & T staff	Wiring error by contractors in three signal heads

PG1-F9N

201

DATE	LOCATION	INCIDENT	CAUSE
04-07-86	Gloucester Road (SR)	Approach locking ineffective - noticed by Signalman	Control omitted because of wiring error
14-08-86	Hither Green (SR)	Signalman noticed interlocking irregularities	Design error in signalling control circuits
18-08-86	Gowerton (WR)	Signal passed at danger	Wiring error during signalling alterations
07-10-86	Severn Tunnel Jct (WR)	Irregular track circuit indications noticed by Signalman	Wiring error during signalling alterations
08-11-86	Shields Jct (ScR)	Derailment of Passenger train (minor injuries)	Points not correctly locked because of wiring error
18-01-87	Latchmere Jct (SR)	Irregular indications noticed by Signalman	Track circuit controls omitted because of bonding error
27-01-87	Camden Road (LMR)	Irregular indications noticed by Signalman	Incorrect aspect exhibited because of installation error
04-02-87	Fishbourne LC (SR)	Points failure	Failure of mechanical facing point locking because of installation error
08-04-87	Hunts Cross (LMR)	Irregular indications noticed by Signalman	Irregular signal aspect caused by installation error
15-04-87	Lewes (SR)	Irregular indications noticed by Signalman	Track circuit controls omitted because of wiring error eleven years previously

PG1-F9N

DATE	LOCATION	INCIDENT	CAUSE
19-10-87	Havant (SR)	Track circuit failure	Track circuit controls omitted because of wiring error
02-11-87	Copyhold Jct (SR)	Light locomotive took wrong route	Points not correctly locked because of installation error
20-02-88	Bowesfield (ER)	Track circuit failure	Irregular signal aspect caused by wiring error
14-06-88	Queenstown Rd (SR)	Train took wrong route	Irregular signal aspects caused by installation error
06-09-88	Cowlairs (ScR)	Derailment of empty stock train (No injuries)	Points not correctly locked caused by design error by contractor
10-10-88	Manchester Piccadilly (LMR)	Points run through	Points not correctly set because of design error by contractor

PG1-F9N

<u>WRONG SIDE SIGNALLING FAILURES</u>

<u>WARS AREA 1985 TO 1988</u>

PG1-F10N
10-02-89

ANALYSIS OF REPORTS OF WRONG SIDE FAILURES - WARS (JUNE 1985-DECEMBER 1988)

1. Wrong side failures where the cause is relevant to the
   investigation of the Clapham Accident   2

   Queenstown Road   26/3/86
   Queenstown Road   14/6/88

2. Wrong side failures where the potential consequences are relevant
   to the investigation of the Clapham Accident   1

   Waterloo   19/11/87

3. Other Failures reported as Wrong Side.   103

   (a) Imperfect Aspects   67

       Signal lamp failures   39
           Colour light signal   30
           Position light   8
           Buffer stop   1
       Lamp holder failures   13
           Colour light signals   12
           Position light   1
       No Light - Other causes   9
           Cable damage   3
           Other disconnection   6
       More than one aspect at once   2
       Banner signal stuck off   2
       Corrupt indication on Theatre Type RI   1
       Power failure causing blackout   1

   (b) Other incidents reported as Wrong Side not having serious
       implications and not relevant to Clapham   10

       Point affected by cable damage   1
       Trainstops   2
           Broken   1
           Obstructed by ballast   1
       AWS Incorrect installation   1
       Track Circuits   6
           Indication only   3
           Disconnection   2
           Out of adjustment   1

   (c) Other incidents wrongly allocated Wrong Side or reported as
       Wrong Side but equipment found to be functioning correctly.   20

   (d) Other incidents reported as Wrong Side but insufficient
       information available to allocate.   6

Director of S & T Engineering
10. 2. 89

205

OTHER WRONG SIDE SIGNALLING FAILURES

RELEVANT TO THE CLAPHAM INQUIRY

-1-

DATE	LOCATION	INCIDENT	CAUSE
22-06-83	Waterloo (SR)	Track circuit failure	Track circuit controls omitted because of design error
11-01-84	Waterloo (SR)	Irregular signal aspect observed by Driver	Incorrect signal aspect caused by installation error during resignalling works
19-11-87	Waterloo (SR)	Train took wrong route	Points not correctly set because of cable fault during installation work

PG2-F10N

207

BRITISH RAILWAYS BOARD

MANAGEMENT OF SAFETY SYSTEMS

Specification For The Acquisition Of Consultancy Assistance
To Define And Implement Management Of Safety Systems Throughout BR

INTRODUCTION

BR operates their management of safety using the conventional approach of safety conscious industry in the UK and Europe. The BR culture combines three elements:

*   Operational Safety through the line management of the railway on a regional basis (the ethos of striving for zero accidents).

*   Reliance on the professional conduct of the range of engineering, technological and scientific disciplines involved.

*   Adherence to best aims of health and safety at work principles in the monitoring and achievement of occupational safety.

These three elements operate, to a greater or lesser extent, in each tier of the BR management matrix.

*   Functional advisory departments coordinate and promote the elements of the safety culture.

*   A system of committees at high level facilitate the flow of information throughout the company structure.

*   Business sectors where the development of the business interests coordinate and maximise the benefits in safety which result from investment programmes.

The management of safety thus follows the matrix for the management for efficient and economical operation of the rail network.

The critical questions are:

a) What degree of effectiveness is being achieved within this approach?

b) How can greater effectiveness be achieved?

DM1-A11N

NEED FOR QUANTIFICATION

In recent years the approach to the management of safety has become more professional with increased emphasis on quantification mirroring the developments in business management. The principle of modern safety management is in achieving improved performance. This requires the measurement of performance.

To measure performance it is essential to decide:

- what is it important to measure
- how it should be measured
- what targets should be set as an indication of performance
- how these should be monitored.

Improvement within the management system will result from:

- sharper accountability
- highlighting of achievements and failings
- provision of additional assistance where the need is demonstrated
- reward mechanisms.

Good data handling and control is a requirement for the proactive use of the data in accident prevention.

AUDITING

In business management, auditing procedures are structured and designed for specific purposes. However, the audit needs must reflect the character of the area being investigated, eg: different business or technical needs. Therefore there is a need for a measure of flexibility in audit plan.

As in financial auditing there is a need to ensure the results are used constructively.

Auditing must take place at different levels within an organisation so that a typical model could well include:

- Management/supervisory inspections at the work place.

- Vertical technical audits of procedures behaviour - how they are interpreted/implemented and the results achieved.

- Overview assessment which can include the regular review of performance indicators, eg: International Safety Rating System or 5 star System.

DM1-A11N

Clearly the following points are important:

1. What is going to be subject to audit?
2. How and at what frequency?
3. By whom?
4. To whom the findings are reported and circulated?

METHODOLOGY TARGET SETTING AND PERFORMANCE REVIEW

The Main Board of Directors sets the safety policy. The programme to achieve this policy has to be built up within the company so that all levels are involved in and committed to the agreed objectives.

Ideally the safety objectives of any department should be set by that department. These should be ratified or rejected by the Board. This requires the development by each department of a safety improvement programme which should include the development of specific initiatives.

Initiatives should have directed at a range of activities such as:

- accident rates
- auditing
- training
- implementation of specific procedures
- technical improvements.

Initiatives should be a realistic target date for completion and be quantified where possible with designated accountability. Achievement against plan should be reviewed on a regular basis. The safety programme should be reviewed on an annual basis and new initiatives added.

SUMMARY

The essential primary features of safety management are:-

- analysis of routine safety statistics;
- special investigations of incidents;
- a structured audit system; and
- a comprehensive safety improvement programme.

BR require to devise and implement a programme of improvement in three areas:

1. A top down change in attitude to safety management in which the concern of top management is manifest in the need for professionalism in safety performance assessment.

DM1-A11N

2. In the engineering and middle management where latent problems lie hidden in the records (requiring qualitative and quantitative assessments).

3. A bottom up approach to complement (1) above to improve the quantification of safety performance and to provide the data for ongoing audit and control.

The system must provide sufficient information to allow the management to:

a) react quickly and positively to change; and

b) obtain the maximum benefit to safety from any development with the rail network.

PROPOSAL

Tenders are invited for specialist consultancy assistance to work alongside Senior BR Managers.

1. To assess how far existing systems on BR meet the specification for a modern professional management of safety system.

2. To identify the areas in which improvement is necessary.

3. To identify and formulate plans to carry out the necessary improvements.

4. To work with BR management in implementing changed or new systems.

5. To recommend to BR the ongoing organisational structure resources and skills necessary to maintain an effective management of safety programme.

SCOPE

The review should embrace both staff and customer safety (occupational health and operations/technical safety) in the following functions:

- Operations
- Civil Engineering
- Signal & Telecommunications Engineering
- Mechanical & Electrical Engineering
- Personnel (Environmental Health)

DM1-A11N

The review should cover all levels of the organisation, in each function above, using the West Coast Main Line (Euston-Glasgow route) and designated Area/Depot Managers on that line of route for initial study, but testing with other regions to ensure "best practise" identified, and systems capable of common implementation are recommended.

BR would provide a Project Manager, and part time Managers from each of the five functions mentioned, with contacts at the Regional/Area levels of organisation.

TIMESCALES

1. Initial assessment of existing practises and identification of improvement areas within 6-8 weeks.

2. Recommendation on proposed new and changed practises, with supporting BR organisation required within 12-16 weeks.

3. Implementation of systems on West Coast Mainline within 12 months.

4. Extension to remainder of BR, by BR Safety Management Organisation with necessary consultancy support within 2 years.

April 1989

DM1-A11N

RELE

TR/

(Note: /

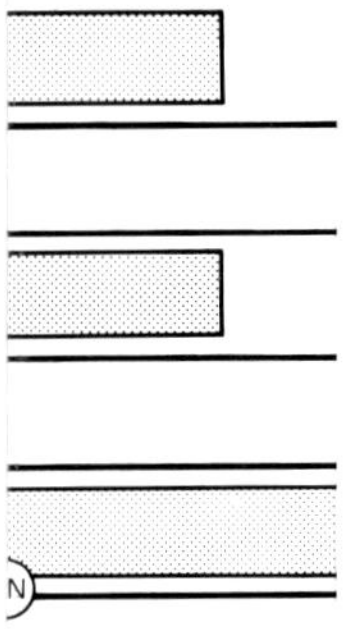

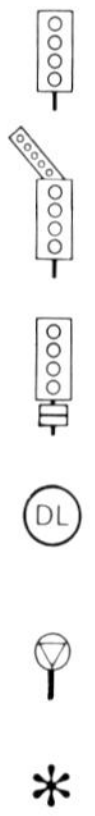

OL

Extract from Design Office Working Diagram for Jobs
104 and 201, showing Mr Hemingway's Pencil
Additions.

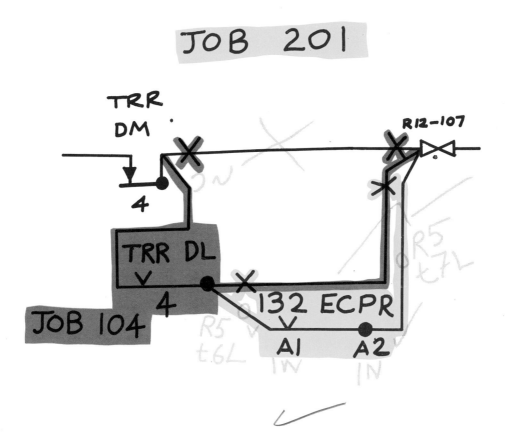

Diagram of Accident Site and Spencer Park showing Emergency Services Control Vehicles and Additional Buildings Used.

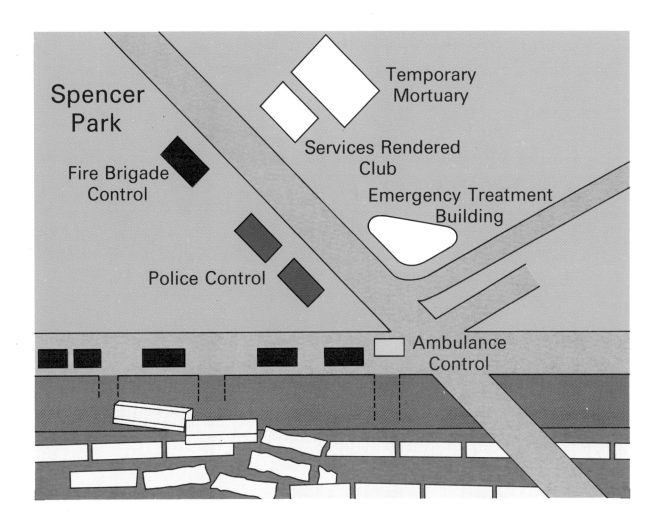

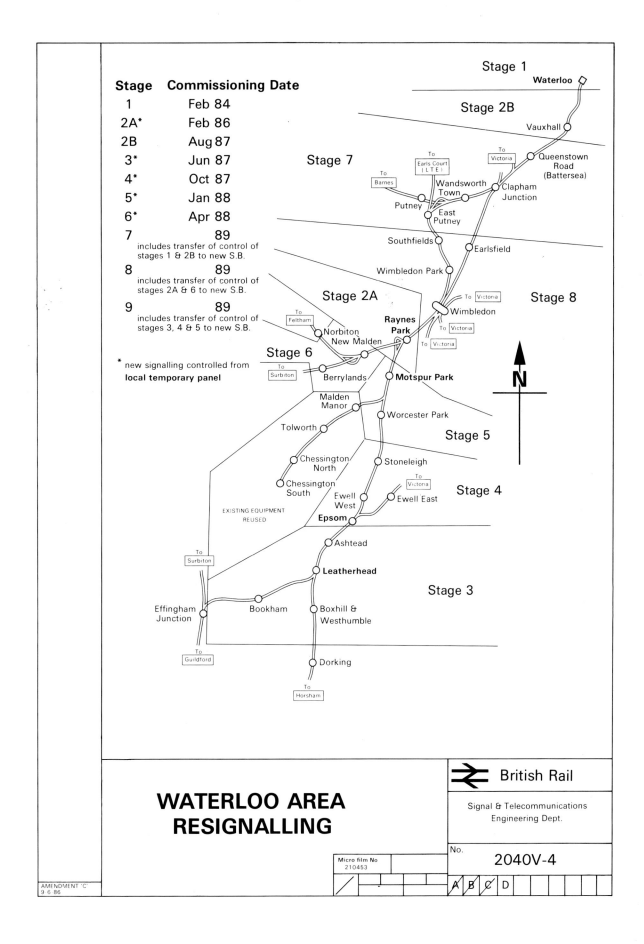

Stage	Commissioning Date
1	Feb 84
2A*	Feb 86
2B	Aug 87
3*	Jun 87
4*	Oct 87
5*	Jan 88
6*	Apr 88
7	89

includes transfer of control of stages 1 & 2B to new S.B.

| 8 | 89 |

includes transfer of control of stages 2A & 6 to new S.B.

| 9 | 89 |

includes transfer of control of stages 3, 4 & 5 to new S.B.

* new signalling controlled from **local temporary panel**

WATERLOO AREA RESIGNALLING

British Rail

Signal & Telecommunications Engineering Dept.

Micro film No 210453

No. 2040V-4

A B C D

AMENDMENT 'C' 9 6 86

EXTRACT OF ORGANISATIONAL STRUCTURE OF BR's SOUTHERN REGION S&T DEPARTMENT FROM SEPTEMBER 1986 UNTIL REORGANISATION IN MAY 1988.

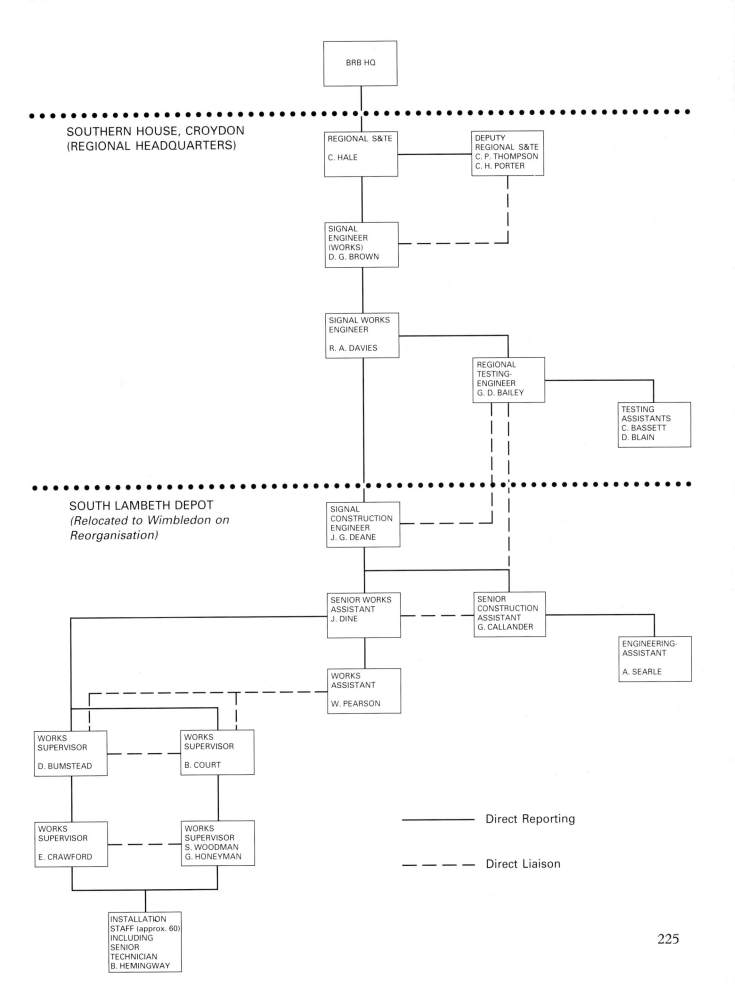

BRB HQ

SOUTHERN HOUSE, CROYDON
(REGIONAL HEADQUARTERS)

REGIONAL S&TE
C. HALE

DEPUTY
REGIONAL S&TE
C. P. THOMPSON
C. H. PORTER

SIGNAL
ENGINEER
(WORKS)
D. G. BROWN

SIGNAL WORKS
ENGINEER
R. A. DAVIES

REGIONAL
TESTING-
ENGINEER
G. D. BAILEY

TESTING
ASSISTANTS
C. BASSETT
D. BLAIN

SOUTH LAMBETH DEPOT
(Relocated to Wimbledon on Reorganisation)

SIGNAL
CONSTRUCTION
ENGINEER
J. G. DEANE

SENIOR WORKS
ASSISTANT
J. DINE

SENIOR
CONSTRUCTION
ASSISTANT
G. CALLANDER

ENGINEERING-
ASSISTANT
A. SEARLE

WORKS
ASSISTANT
W. PEARSON

WORKS
SUPERVISOR
D. BUMSTEAD

WORKS
SUPERVISOR
B. COURT

WORKS
SUPERVISOR
E. CRAWFORD

WORKS
SUPERVISOR
S. WOODMAN
G. HONEYMAN

——————— Direct Reporting

– – – – – – Direct Liaison

INSTALLATION
STAFF (approx. 60)
INCLUDING
SENIOR
TECHNICIAN
B. HEMINGWAY

225

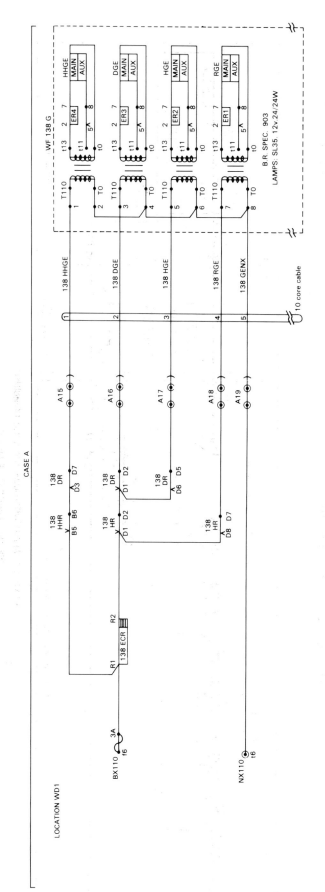

Clapham Junction 'A'
Part Detail of Control Circuits
For Automatic Signal WF 138.

Appendix K9

Wiring Symbols

Contacts closed when relay coil energised – Front or top contact

Contacts closed when relay coil de-energised – Back or bottom contact

Electro magnet (relay coil)

fuse

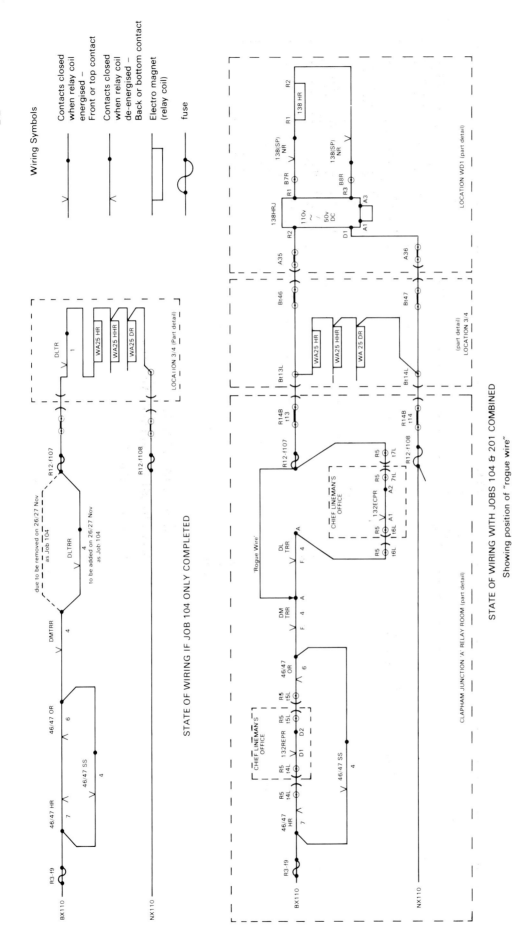

STATE OF WIRING IF JOB 104 ONLY COMPLETED

STATE OF WIRING WITH JOBS 104 & 201 COMBINED
Showing position of "rogue wire"

CONTROL CIRCUITS FOR SIGNAL WF 138

Appendix K10

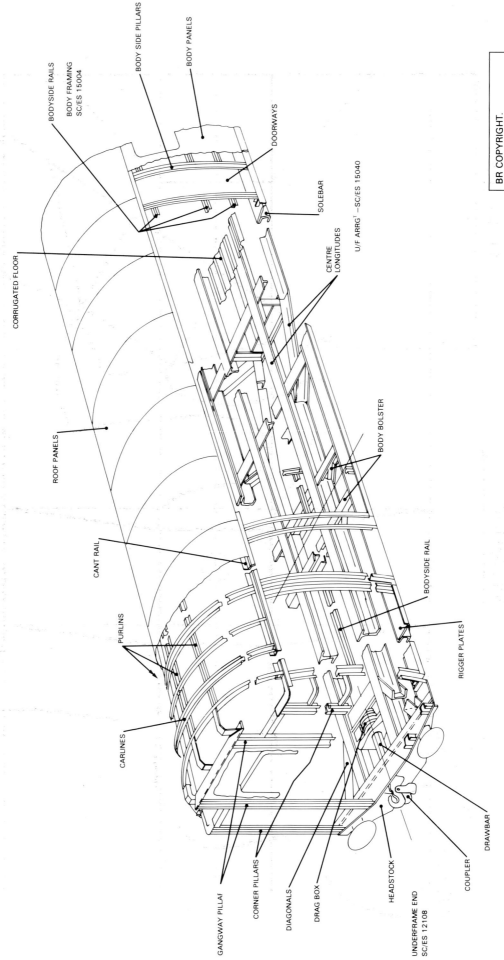

ARRG^T OF FLOOR—SC/ES 15013
SECTIONS THROUGH FLOOR – SC/ES 15215

BODYSIDE RAILS

BODY FRAMING SC/ES 15004

BODY SIDE PILLARS

BODY PANELS

DOORWAYS

SOLEBAR

U/F ARRG^T –SC/ES 15040

CENTRE LONGITUDES

CORRUGATED FLOOR

ROOF PANELS

CANT RAIL

BODY BOLSTER

BODYSIDE RAIL

RIGGER PLATES

PURLINS

CARLINES

GANGWAY PILLAR

CORNER PILLARS

DIAGONALS

DRAG BOX

HEADSTOCK

UNDERFRAME END
SC/ES 12108

COUPLER

DRAWBAR

PLAN VIEW OF PERMANENT DEFORMATION OF
DMS 62146 (Leading End)

Waterloo

left side

right side

1500 mm

300 mm

Original Outline ——————
Deformed Outline ——————

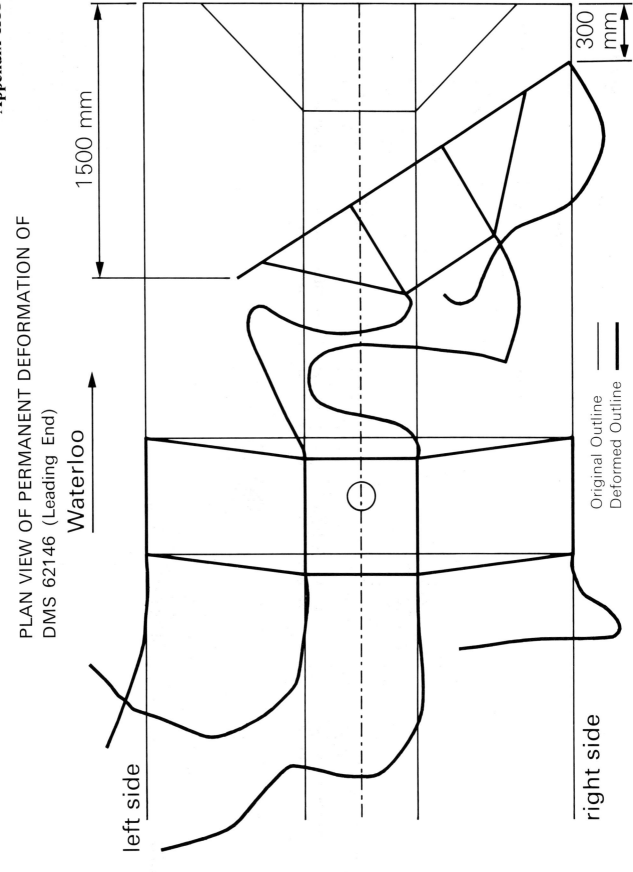

A Line Diagram of a typical Four Aspect Signal as supplied by ML Engineering (Plymouth) Limited

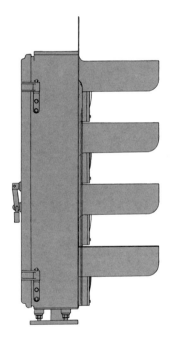
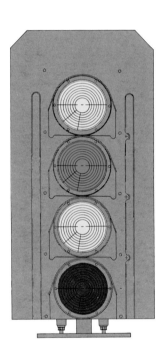